MASS MOTORIZATION
+
MASS TRANSIT

MASS MOTORIZATION
+
MASS TRANSIT

An American History and Policy Analysis

David W. Jones

Indiana
University Press
Bloomington &
Indianapolis

This book is a publication of

Indiana University Press
601 North Morton Street
Bloomington, IN 47404-3797 USA

http://iupress.indiana.edu

Telephone orders 800-842-6796
Fax orders 812-855-7931
Orders by e-mail iuporder@indiana.edu

The paper used in this publication
meets the minimum requirements of
American National Standard for Information Sciences—Permanence of Paper
for Printed Library Materials, ANSI
Z39.48-1984.

Manufactured in the United States of
America

Library of Congress Cataloging-in-
Publication Data

Jones, David W., date
Mass motorization and mass transit : an
American history and policy analysis /
David W. Jones.
p. cm.
Includes bibliographical references and
index.
ISBN 978-0-253-35152-4 (cloth : alk.
paper) 1. Transportation, Automotive—
United States—History. 2. Transporta-
tion, Automotive—Government policy—
United States—History. I. Title.
HE5623.J658 2008
388.40973—dc22
                                2007052738

1 2 3 4 5 13 12 11 10 09 08

This book is dedicated to my mentors Dick Shevell, Bill Garrison, and Marty Wachs, my students in civil engineering and city planning, and my wife, Inta, whose love and patience made possible the prolonged research effort that went into writing this book.

Part 1 ∘ 1

U.S. Motorization in
International Context

1 ∘ 3
Motorization in the United States
and Other Industrial Nations

CONTENTS

TABLES

ILLUSTRATIONS

ACKNOWLEDGMENTS

The inspiration for this book came from an oral history interview with Dick Zettel, my predecessor at the Institute of Transportation Studies at UC Berkeley. In turn, my ability to track down data and documents essential for writing a history that spans some 130 years of transportation history hinged on the transit and highway archives at the ITS Library at Berkeley. I am deeply indebted to librarians Bev Hickock, Michael Kleiber, Catherine Cortelyou, Dan Krummes, and Rita Evans, who have assembled the archives and kept them up to date. I am also deeply indebted to the highway engineers and city planners who lived this history and shared their recollections with me, especially Chuck Pivetti, who chaired Caltrans' History Committee. Thanks also go to MIT's Alan Altschuler, who encouraged my first efforts in this domain, and Howard Rosen, who invited my participation in AASHTO's oral history of the interstate highway system. For comments on early drafts, very special thanks go to Bill Garrison, Brian Taylor, and Marty Wachs. Last but certainly not least, I am thankful to George Smerk, professor emeritus at Indiana University, Linda Oblack at Indiana University Press, and my editors, Miki Bird and Elaine Otto, who helped me hone my presentation and added immeasurably to the clarity of the text. Thank you all.

MASS MOTORIZATION
+
MASS TRANSIT

PART ONE

U.S. Motorization in International Context

Mass Motorization and Mass Transit is a history of America's streetcar and freeway eras. It begins with a focus on transit in the 1880s and 1890s, when New York, Boston, and Philadelphia were the world's premiere transit markets. It ends with an appraisal of the search for new automotive technologies and fuels that can sustain personal mobility without generating an excessive volume of CO_2 emissions. In between, it explains how the United States came to rely so heavily on the automobile for mass transportation, why so many street railways were unable to sustain profitable operation after World War I, and why the automobile diffused so much earlier in the United States than in Europe.

There are two answers to the last of these questions. One is that World Wars I and II suppressed motorization in Europe; the other is that the sale of grains, foodstuffs, and dry goods to Europe in the wake of World War I provided a powerful stimulus to the U.S. economy in the 1920s. In turn, America's post-war boom produced a surge in household income and home and automobile ownership, vaulting the automobile industry to the uppermost level of America's industrial pecking order. A second surge in middle-class home and automobile ownership followed World War II, fueling suburban growth and producing what we have characterized as mass motorization. Still another wave of suburbanization accompanied the construction of the circumferential routes to the interstate highway system. It was stimulated by the growth of suburban employment in the 1970s and the increase in household incomes that accompanied women's increasing participation in the workforce.

These successive waves of economic growth, income growth, and suburban growth have made the United States the world's most thoroughly motorized nation. These same dynamics have frustrated transit's efforts to rebuild its market share, which has been stabilized by public ownership, but at a level close to its twentieth-century low. This suggests that the United States will have to rely on advances in automotive technology as the centerpiece of its national strategy for conserving petroleum and reducing the CO_2 emissions produced by motor vehicles. But the volatility of oil prices and the pace of global warming also make it imperative that we Americans have a serious discussion about higher gasoline taxes and their appropriate role in fuel conservation.

ONE

Motorization in the United States and Other Industrial Nations

More than any other nation, the United States relies on cars and trucks for mass transportation. Describing cars and trucks as "mass transportation" may sound like a contradiction in terms, but it is a functionally accurate description of the outcome of mass motorization. Personally owned vehicles have become America's primary form of mass transportation.

If we take 400 vehicles per 1,000 population to be the definitional threshold of "mass motorization," the United States and 22 other wealthy industrial nations had experienced mass motorization by the year 2000. Taken together, this 23-nation peer group accounts for only 8 percent of the world's population but fully 67 percent of its motor vehicle registrations and 53 percent of global GDP.

Although mass motorization has occurred in most of the world's advanced industrial nations, the duration and present intensity of U.S. motorization is unique. The United States had already established overwhelming leadership in motorization by the year 1925, and by the year 2000, the cumulative result of another 75 years of motorization was a level of motor vehicle ownership that is far more pervasive than that found in any other G-7 nation. In this sense, it is accurate to describe the United States as a "peer group of one" in terms of the intensity of its automobile and truck ownership and use.

Table 1.1 *Intensity of motorization in G-7 nations in 2000*

	Motor vehicles per 1,000 pop. (a)	Motor vehicles per worker (b)	Vehicle km. per capita (c)	Motor vehicle CO_2 per capita (d)
United States	784	1.58	15,618	5,202
Canada	676	1.43	10,831	3,741
Japan	651	1.30	5,976	1,762
Italy	626	1.73	6,274	1,917
Germany	576	1.29	7,126	2,067
France	574	1.44	8,778	2,153
United Kingdom	511	1.10	7,662	1,933
G-7 average	625	1.41	8,895	2,682

SOURCE: (a) Vehicle registrations: *Ward's Motor Vehicle Facts and Figures*, 2002; population date for all series: Maddison, *World Economy: Historical Statistics*; (b) *Statistical Abstract of the United States*, 2002, "Comparative Labor Force Statistics, Ten Countries, 1959–2001"; (c) *Highway Statistics 2002*, table IN-4, "Vehicle Travel for Selected Countries"; (d) International Energy Agency, CO_2 *Emissions from Fuel Combustion, 1971–2000*, country tables, II.143ff.

The work of this chapter is to compare the intensity of motorization in the United States and other advanced industrial nations and to explore why the United States experienced motorization so much earlier than any other nation in its industrial peer group.

Table 1.1 compares the intensity of motorization in the United States with that of the other six nations in the so-called Group of Seven, or G-7. Taken together, these seven advanced industrial nations accounted for 45 percent of the world's GDP and 63 percent of its motor vehicles in 2000.

The United States is both the largest and wealthiest nation in the G-7, and table 1.1 shows that it far exceeds the average for its peer group on every per capita measure of motor vehicle ownership and use. Italy, however, leads the United States in vehicles per worker. By every other measure, the United States is far more intensely motorized.

Table 1.2 presents a somewhat different picture. It shows that the intensity of U.S. motorization lies below its peer group norm when the intensity of motorization is measured in terms of motor vehicles per billion dollars of GNP. Using this metric, Italy, Germany, Japan, and France are more intensely motorized than the United States, relative to the size of their national economies. In turn, this strongly suggests that the intensity of U.S. motorization is attributable to our long-term leadership in GNP, GDP, and GDP per capita. It also suggests that the United States' peers will experience continuing catch-up in motorization as their GDPs increase and their suburbanization continues.

Table 1.3 provides further reason for pause. Read in concert with the first

Table 1.2 *Motor vehicles per $billion GNP in 2000*

Italy	33.4
Germany	31.0
Japan	30.9
France	27.3
United States	26.8
United Kingdom	25.9
Canada	25.3
Peer group average	28.6

SOURCE: *Ward's Motor Vehicle Facts and Figures*, 2002, and *National Accounts of OECD Countries*, 2002.

Table 1.3 *Contribution of trucks to motorization in the United States and other G-7 nations in 2000*

	Trucks per 1,000 pop.	Cars per 1,000 pop.	Trucks as % of all vehicles
United States	304	480	39
Canada	236	440	35
France	169	405	29
Japan	159	492	24
Italy	62	564	10
United Kingdom	56	455	11
Germany	43	533	7
Peer group average	147	481	24

SOURCE: *Ward's Motor Vehicle Facts and Figures*, 2002, and Maddison, *World Economy: Historical Statistics.*

column of table 1.1, it shows that trucks (including pickups and sport utility vehicles) account for the entire margin of U.S. leadership in motor vehicles per 1,000 population. It also shows that Italy, Germany, Japan, and the United Kingdom would have to be considered more intensely motorized than the United States if motorization were defined exclusively in terms of automobile ownership. Trucks, of course, cannot be excluded from an appraisal of the intensity of motorization, because light trucks have come to play such an important role in personal transportation in the United States where pickups, SUVs, and other light trucks accounted for 70 percent of all trucks in use in 2000.

As the intensity of U.S. motorization increased following World War II, trucks increased from 17 percent of the motor vehicles in operation in 1950 to 40 percent in 2000. Most of this increase occurred after 1970 and reflected increasing ownership of pickups, panel trucks, vans, and later SUVs. Equally important is the role that commercial trucking has come to play in the logistics

Table 1.4 *Most thoroughly motorized nations in 2000*

Nation	Motor vehicles per 1,000 pop.	GDP per capita[a]
United States	784	$28,129
New Zealand	698	$16,010
Canada	676	$22,198
Japan	651	$21,069
Luxembourg	648	$36,914
Iceland	640	$33,308
Italy	627	$18,740
Germany	575	$18,596
France	574	$20,808
Austria	547	$20,097
Spain	539	$15,892
Australia	530	$21,540
United Kingdom	511	$19,817
Switzerland	511	$22,025
Sweden	495	$20,321
Belgium	492	$20,742
Portugal	474	$14,231
Denmark	470	$23,010
Netherlands	470	$21,591
Finland	470	$20,235
Kuwait	464	$10,210
Ireland	405	$23,039
Greece	405	$13,281
World	121	$6,000

SOURCE: Vehicle registrations: *Ward's Motor Vehicle Facts and Figures*, 2002; population and GDP per capita: Maddison, *World Economy: Historical Statistics*.
[a] GDP per capita is reported in 1990 international Geary-Khamis dollars.

of metropolitan goods movement and wholesale distribution. Such roles are important in serving the dispersed constellations of residential and commercial activity that are characteristic of a society that has experienced extensive motorization and suburbanization.

Finally, table 1.4 lists the 23 nations that had experienced mass motorization by 2000, as well as motor vehicle ownership rates per 1,000 population and GDP per capita. The list of nations that have crossed the threshold of mass motorization is clearly dominated by western and westernized nations that experienced early industrialization or that command oil wealth. All can be described as wealthy nations in terms of their GDP per capita. Seventeen of the 23 are European nations, and the United States, Canada, Australia, and New Zealand are commonwealth nations. Japan and Kuwait complete the list. Together, these 23 nations account for 67 percent of the world's cars and trucks and 53 percent of its GDP, but less than 8 percent of its population.

The United States is the most thoroughly motorized member of this group of 23 and, in the aggregate, the wealthiest. In 2000, it alone accounted for 21 percent of the world's GDP and 29 percent of its motor vehicle registrations, but only 5 percent of the global population. In other words, the United States is a virtual peer group of one in the world community of motorized nations. Table 1.4 clearly shows that in 2000, mass motorization was an OECD phenomenon and not a global phenomenon. It also shows that economic development —and especially GDP per capita—has been a decisive factor in determining national membership in the small club of nations that have achieved mass motorization.

Explaining how the United States came to be a peer group of one atop a global peer group of 23 is a history that could be told in many ways. One might entail a national history focused on the exceptionalism of the U.S. experience. Another might entail a focus on public policies that were favorable to automobiles and highways and not so favorable to mass transit. Still another storyline might emphasize international differences in the timing of initial urbanization, differences in urban development patterns, and differences in metropolitan densities.[1] But none of these histories would capture the primary reasons that Americans could afford automobile ownership so much earlier than their counterparts in other G-7 nations. Nor would they do a very good job of explaining the early displacement of mass transit in the United States. It takes an American history told in international context to get the story right.

The United States in the 1880s

In 1880, it would have been hard to anticipate that the United States would become the world's leader in the ownership and use of cars and trucks. In the 1880s, walking was the primary means of urban transportation, railroads were the primary means of intercity transportation, and horse carts and pushcarts were the primary means of urban goods movement. Walking and riding on horseback or by horse and wagon were the primary means of rural and small-town transportation. Walking remained the primary means of urban transportation because the ownership of a horse and buggy was prohibitively expensive for most Americans and because horsecars served a relatively small slice of the urban population—primarily middle-income households. Most workers lived within walking distance of their place of work, whether in the city, in a smaller town, or on a farm.

By 1890, a new technology—the electric street railway—had begun to transform both the travel habits and the location options of the urban middle class.[2] The late 1880s were boom years for street railway investment, and by 1890 New York, Boston, Chicago, and Philadelphia had become the world's leading transit markets in terms of rides per capita by streetcar. In 1902, an international study conducted by the U.S. Bureau of the Census showed that the United States also ranked first among the world's nations in terms of streetcar and subway ridership and the diffusion of streetcar service in cities with a population of 4,000 or more.[3] During this period, General Electric and Westinghouse were the world's leading vendors of the power station equipment needed to electrify street railways and subways.

Initial U.S. leadership in streetcar and subway development may come as a surprise to many readers, but it is part of a larger pattern. One part of that larger pattern was world leadership in aggregate GDP, which the United States took from Great Britain in the 1880s.[4] Another part of the larger pattern was leadership in the commercialization of new technologies, in which the United States had overtaken Britain by 1875.[5] Britain's leadership in global GDP had been based on its primacy in those "new technology" industries associated with coal, the steam engine, and its use in powering looms and railroads. The United States' successor leadership was based on a next generation of new technologies, those associated with heating and motive power derived from electricity and oil. This next generation of new technologies included streetcars and subways and later automobiles, trucks, tractors, farm combines, and earth-moving equipment.[6]

The domain in which the United States seems to have been uniquely proficient has been the commercialization of new transportation technologies. First evidence of this proficiency came with the rapid catch-up in the development of steam railroads. Next came U.S. leadership in the commercialization of elevators used in high-rise buildings, the development of electric generating plants, and the deployment of electric street railways and subways. Then came world leadership in the mass production of automobiles and trucks. Only one of these technologies—the elevator—was invented by an American.[7] With all the rest, initial innovation occurred elsewhere: the steam locomotive and subway in the United Kingdom and the electric streetcar and the automobile in Germany. With many technologies, the U.S. contribution was the ability to convert prototypes into street-worthy technologies—and then to get from technology through financing to commercialization and rapid diffusion. In other words, the commercialization and capitalization of new technology have been American strengths. But diffusion and commercialization were also easier to accomplish in the United States, because it was a newer society with a more open weave and fewer entrenched interests to throw up roadblocks to the introduction of new

Table 1.5 *Per capita ridership of streetcars and subways in the United States and Europe, 1890, 1901, and 1909*

Cities	1890 (a)	1901 (a)	1909 (b)
New York	233	266	330
Chicago	164	232	285
Boston	225	246	285
Philadelphia	158	256	275
London	74	75	245
Glasgow	61	222	275
Manchester	38	129	200
Liverpool	51	155	187
Paris	56	120	345
Berlin	91	130	226
Dresden	53	187	205
Frankfurt	43	175	200
Leipzig	48	143	188

SOURCE: (a) U.S. Bureau of the Census, *Street and Electric Railways*, 1902, 153; (b) Doolittle, "Load Curve for a Typical Day," 254.

technologies. As a result, the commercialization of new transport technologies became an American strong suit in the late nineteenth and early twentieth centuries.

This was certainly the case for mass transit, as is evident from table 1.5. It shows that New York, Chicago, Boston, and Philadelphia were the world's premiere streetcar and subway markets of 1890 and 1901. By 1909, Paris had edged ahead of New York, and Glasgow had topped Philadelphia in streetcar and subway rides per capita, but the United States remained the nation with the largest number of cities with world-class transit systems. In fact, Paris and London both turned to the United States for the proprietary technology needed for the initial electrification of their subway systems.[8]

U.S. leadership in streetcar use was attributable to its early success in developing a practical method for delivering electricity from overhead wires to a streetcar's on-board electric motors. It was also attributable to a franchise system that guaranteed streetcar companies monopoly operating rights and a fixed five-cent fare. U.S. investors were eager to lock up monopoly operating rights because a fixed fare was perceived as a virtual guarantee of long-term profitability in the deflationary economy of the 1880s and early 1890s. Thus initial streetcar investment was much more aggressive in the United States than in Europe.[9]

In Europe, cities were more likely to insist on relatively short-term franchises and an option for public buyout at the expiration of the initial franchise, which discouraged aggressive private investment of the sort that occurred in the United States. European cities were also more likely to insist on public

Table 1.6 *Per capita ridership of mass transit in the United States and Europe,*
1909 and 1990

Cities	1909 (a)	1990 (b)
New York	330	155
Boston	280	114
Chicago	285	96
London	245	325
Paris	345	295
Frankfurt	200	436

SOURCE: (a) Doolittle, *Studies in the Cost of Urban Transportation Service*, 216; (b) Kenworthy and Laube, *International Sourcebook of Automobile Dependence*, 537, table 5.3. Each column uses a consistent metric for comparing ridership, but the counts for 1909 and 1990 are not based on fully comparable methodologies.

ownership of their electric power systems, an ownership pattern that inclined many of the same cities to capitalize and operate their own streetcar service as a synergistic local investment. In turn, public ownership typically led to conservative capitalization and relatively cautious expansion of service.

In the United States, on the other hand, private ownership led to a rush to capture additional franchise rights and a period of speculative overinvestment that ultimately damaged the streetcar industry's credit. In turn, damaged credit and soured relations with local governments made it difficult for the streetcar companies to secure municipal cooperation when the streetcar companies came face to face with automotive competition. In the United States, the disinvestment that gradually eroded streetcar service began before World War I and accelerated during the war, leading to wholesale abandonment of streetcar service during the Depression and after World War II.[10] In Europe, delayed motorization combined with public ownership and the rationalization of transit service to build and then sustain transit ridership. The result was a sharp divergence in U.S. and European patronage trends.

As table 1.6 shows, transit experienced a significant decline in rides per capita in U.S. cities between 1909 and 1990, while gains were made in two of Europe's most prominent transit markets. Asked to explain these strikingly different metropolitan outcomes, the reflex reaction of many U.S. planners and urbanists is to point to the interstate highway program and attribute transit's loss of U.S. market share to the combined effect of "unbalanced transportation policy" and "suburban sprawl." But this often proffered "explanation" tells only a selective and recent part of the story. The historical record indicates that U.S. transit's decline was a dynamic of much longer duration. It began with financial difficulties that predated World War I and became acute in the context of virulent wartime inflation. These financial difficulties were further exacerbated by the early and explosive growth of U.S. auto ownership that followed World War I.[11] Conversely, the diffusion of the automobile was delayed in Europe because of the destructive social and economic impacts of the two world wars. We will now focus on the acceleration of motorization that occurred in the United States and the destruction of buying power and industrial potential that occurred in Europe due to the two world wars.

Early Motorization in America

U.S. leadership in motorization was not a by-product of the interstate highway program or the explosive growth of suburban population that followed World War II. It dates instead to the first decade of the twentieth century, when the United States established world leadership in GDP per capita and global primacy in automobile manufacturing. Table 1.7 shows that the United States had already established a small lead in GDP per capita by 1905, nine years before World War I began. A year later, Henry Ford introduced assembly-line production to motor vehicle manufacturing and manufactured his first Model T in 1908. American buying power and the size of the U.S. population validated Ford's risky experiment in mass production. This, in turn, laid the groundwork for initial U.S. dominance of global automobile production. Early dominance was possible because the United States was already the world leader in industrial output, petroleum production, and per capita GDP.[12]

The United States' twentieth-century dominance in automobile production was sealed by World War I, which badly damaged European economies while stimulating across-the-board gains in the U.S. share of world manufacturing output. From 1913 to 1928, the combined share of world manufacturing output generated in France, Germany, and the United Kingdom declined 20 percent, while the U.S. share of world output increased 24 percent. During the same period, the combined GDPs of France, Germany, and the United Kingdom increased only 14 percent, while aggregate U.S. GDP increased a stunning 63 percent. U.S. per capita GDP increased 24 percent from 1913 to 1928 alone, creating the middle-class buying power to support rapid motorization in the 1920s.[13]

Table 1.8 shows that the United States had established a dominant position in world manufacturing and overwhelming dominance in world oil and auto production by the mid-1920s. Taken together, tables 1.7 and 1.8 indicate that it was no coincidence that the United States was the only G-7 nation to achieve initial motorization before World War II. Table 1.9 shows that the United States did so in 1925. No other nation except Canada did so before 1950.[14]

Table 1.9 shows that initial motorization proceeded much more rapidly in

Table 1.7 *U.S. leadership in GDP per capita, 1905*

United States	4,642
United Kingdom	4,520
Canada	3,562
Germany	3,104
France	2,847
Italy	1,984
Japan	1,157
G-7 average	3,117

SOURCE: Maddison, *World Economy: Historical Statistics.*

Table 1.8 *U.S. dominance in the world economy of the 1920s*

Share of world population in 1927 (a)	6%
Share of world industrial output in 1928 (b)	39%
Share of world GDP in 1928 (c)	26–28%
Share of motor vehicle production in 1927 (d)	85%
Share of motor vehicle registrations in 1925 (e)	81%
Share of world oil production in 1926 (f)	70%
Share of world oil-refining capacity in 1926 (f)	>80%

SOURCE: (a) Maddison, *World Economy: Historical Statistics*; (b) Bairoch, "International Industrialization Levels from 1750 to 1980," 304; (c) author's estimate based on partial data in Maddison; (d) MVMA, *Motor Vehicle Facts and Figures*, 1927, 52; (e) MVMA, *Motor Vehicle Facts and Figures*, 1925, 62; (f) Fanning, *Foreign Oil and the Free World*, 7, 350.

Table 1.9 *G-7 motorization levels in 1925 and 1950*

	Vehicles per 1,000 pop. in 1925	Vehicles per 1,000 pop. in 1950
United States	172	314
Canada	75	186
Great Britain	20	70
France	18	59
Germany	4	22
Italy	3	16
Japan	<1	4

SOURCE: Automobile Manufacturers Association, *Motor Vehicle Facts and Trends*, 1926 and 1952.

the United States and Canada than in Europe or Japan. Indeed, it shows that the combined effect of World War I, the Great Depression, and World War II was to suppress economic growth in Europe and to accelerate both economic growth and motorization in the United States and Canada.

The Development of U.S. Highway Policy

The United States was the first nation to experience substantial motorization and thus the first to develop a coherent policy for financing modern highway development on a nationwide basis. The highway policy that emerged in the 1920s was assembled piece by piece, but it produced an orderly division of responsibilities between the federal government, the states, and the counties. More important, it provided a framework for reconciling the frictions between states—large and small, industrial and agricultural. According to Richard M. Zettel, economic consultant for the California State Senate Committee on Streets and Highways, the precepts that enabled and informed the legislative consensus that prevailed during the early years of U.S. motorization can be summarized as follows:

A *hierarchy of responsibilities:* Local governments should be primarily responsible for building and maintaining local streets and roads. Counties should be primarily responsible for building roads between local communities. The states should be primarily responsible for building those major trunk-line highways that connect major cities.

A *national partnership rather than a federal system:* The federal government should not build and maintain highways of its own. Rather, it should share the expense of building a continuous network of state and county roads which has the connectivity needed to serve as a national highway system.

Shared financial responsibility: The federal government should provide matching funds for road improvement. Its proportionate contribution should reflect the national interest in each class of roads—local, intercounty, and interstate.

A *limited system:* Federal aid should be restricted to a select network of limited mileage—a continuous network that consists of the most heavily traveled interstate and intercounty highways.

Formula apportionment: Federal aid for highways should be apportioned in accord with a formula which ensures that both populous and sparsely settled states have revenues sufficient to build highways of safe and serviceable design.[15]

In the early years, federal funding for state highway improvement was limited to rural construction and was financed with general funds, not fuel taxes. Over time, U.S. highway policy was balanced and rebalanced so as to create an investment program that was focused on priority needs both urban and rural and could be considered reasonably fair because its users paid the fuel taxes used to build American highways.

The initial impetus for federal funding of highway improvement came from the sorry condition of rural roads, many of which were graveled but not paved until the 1920s. Before World War I, most rural roads were maintained by the owners of abutting property rather than by trained road crews. The war gave additional impetus to state and federal involvement in road construction. That impetus came from the inability of the railroads to efficiently deliver and unload armaments at urban ports for transshipment to Europe. This breakdown in military logistics led to a collaborative effort of the Department of the Army and the Bureau of Public Roads to develop a sketchy first plan for a national system of defense highways—the first iteration in the development of what would eventually become the interstate highway system. This plan for the development of "national highways" was superimposed on the Bureau's map of the state highways connecting the nation's most important cities.

The eventual assignment of the states to perform urban duties occurred during another national emergency, the Great Depression. In 1934, the new Democratic majority in Congress authorized the funding needed to take on the additional responsibility for upgrading and maintaining urban arterials that served as "the urban extensions of the state highway systems." Counterpart state legislation assigned state highway departments principal responsibility for developing those urban arterials that connected with state highway systems. Beginning during the Depression and again after World War II, this authority was used by the leading states to finance and build a first generation of divided highways within cities—an investment program that was applauded by most cities because it enabled them to enjoy the benefits of safer highways without raising local taxes or preempting other local expenditures. Under the auspices of the interstate program, which was not fully funded until 1956, the state highway departments built a second generation of divided highways in American cities. These were built as freeways and expressways with full access control. But that is getting ahead of our story.[16]

Differences between U.S. and European Highway Policy

Extensive development of urban freeways is the defining supply-side difference between the metropolitan transportation policies of the United States and the other nations in its G-7 peer group. Different arrangements emerged in Europe—in part because most European nations lacked the domestic oil supplies to support motorization without creating balance-of-payments problems and because of the age and corresponding density of European cities.[17] As in the United States, key decisions were made during the Great Depression.

In Germany, for example, the engineers of the national Autobahn concluded that superhighways should skirt rather than enter large cities.[18] In the United Kingdom, several plans for a national motorway system were developed in the 1930s but could not resolve "the London question." A ring road has been largely completed, but the construction of London radials has been stalled for decades.[19] Likewise, expressways have been built in the metropolitan suburbs of Paris but not in the Isle de Paris.[20]

Clearly, American cities have a shorter developmental history than that of their European peers: they are less densely settled, and a larger share are industrially and commercially based than their European counterparts. Just as important, American cities experienced initial motorization after World War I, two generations earlier than their European counterparts. For all of these reasons, the early expressway plans developed by the state highway departments for American cities were more ambitious and less deferential than those executed in Europe.

In Europe's major cities, both engineers and planners warned that the road space and parking requirements of the automobile could not be met without massive displacement of other land uses. Space for parking was a principal constraint. There simply wasn't room in the weave of the oldest and largest European cities to provide it. This had further implications: it meant that express highways should skirt central cities rather than penetrating to their urban core—to avoid heavy volumes of pass-through traffic and excessive demands on the limited parking supply of the urban core. And, contrary to the view that evolved in the United States, commuter traffic was not seen as having a priority claim on the capacity of major boulevards and arterials in European cities. Instead, European engineers argued that it was more essential that arterials be able to move trucks and the goods they carry as efficiently as possible.[21] In turn, urban expressway development was focused in industrial and commercial corridors. Not coincidentally, an expressway that links the Thames dockyard with the National Motorway network was one of the few built in London.

In heavily traveled commute corridors, European engineers proposed replacing street railways with subways designed to accommodate travel to the urban core.[22] They also argued for the reorientation of street railways and bus lines to provide connecting service to rapid transit. Limiting the parking supply of the urban core was seen as the essential control that would balance road use and road space while ensuring the intensive use of rapid transit. Such measures were not expected to deter motorization per se, but were expected to discourage automobile commuting in cities and prevent the urban dislocation associated with expressway construction. The fulcrum of this characteristically European approach to traffic management was strict regulation of the central area's parking supply, with subways the essential investment in commuter service and expressways the essential investment for goods movement in industrial corridors with heavy truck traffic.

Europe could still pursue this option in the 1950s because motorization had been suppressed by the impacts of the world wars and the Great Depression and because transit ridership was still robust. In the United States, on the other hand, per capita ridership of mass transit had peaked in 1926 and collapsed after World War II.[23] Thus the United States and Europe traveled different pathways between 1913 and 1950. In Europe, motorization—especially urban motorization—was just getting under way in 1950. In America, urban motorization was already well advanced by 1950, and so was the decline of mass transit—six years before construction of the interstate highway system was fully funded in 1956.

War, Wealth, and Postwar Motorization Differentials

The buying power underlying U.S. leadership in motorization is distilled and summarized in table 1.10. It shows the increase in GDP per capita for each of the G-7 nations from 1913 to 1950. It also shows the percentage increase in motor vehicles per 1,000 persons for the same nations over the same period. The U.S. and Canadian economies dramatically outperformed those of the battlefield nations of World War II—Japan, Italy, the United Kingdom, France, and Germany—in terms of their increase in per capita GDP. Just as clearly, the United States and Canada far outdistanced their industrial peers in terms of their increase in motor vehicles. The table also shows that the victorious battlefield nations—France and the United Kingdom—registered larger increases in motor vehicle ownership per 1,000 population than their defeated peers. Clearly, the world wars had impacts on both personal income and the pace of national motorization that were both sizeable and differentiated in predictable ways.

Table 1.11 shows the motorization level of the G-7 nations for 1950 and the size of the motorization gap separating the battleground nations from the United States and Canada. It shows that Canada gained ground on the United States in terms of motor vehicles per 1,000 population between 1913 and 1950. This is the kind of convergence that is often seen in economic and social data as second-adopters make up ground on first-adopters. But no similar convergence occurred between the United States and any of the battleground nations— another clear indicator of the economic and social trauma experienced by the battleground nations. In other words, wartime destruction and dislocation and

Table 1.10 *GDP and motorization trends in the G-7 nations, 1913–50*

	Increase in GDP per capita (a)	Increase in vehicles per 1,000 pop. (b)
United States	80.4%	314
Canada	67.2%	179
France	51.2%	57
United Kingdom	40.4%	65
Germany	6.4%	21
Italy	36.5%	15
Japan	38.7%	4

SOURCE: (a) Maddison, *World Economy: Historical Statistics*, 60–64, 88, 184; (b) AMA, *Motor Vehicle Facts and Trends*, 1926 and 1952.

Table 1.11 *G-7 motorization levels and differentials in 1950*

	Motor vehicles per 1,000 pop. (a)	Gap vis-à-vis United States	Gap vis-à-vis Canada
United States	327	—	—
Canada	186	141	—
United Kingdom	70	257	116
France	59	268	127
Germany	22	305	164
Italy	16	311	170
Japan	4	323	182

SOURCE: AMA, *Motor Vehicle Facts and Trends*, 1951; Maddison, *World Economy: Historical Statistics*.

the resulting dissipation of GDP explain much of the motorization gap that separated the United States and Canada from the other five G-7 nations in 1950.

Table 1.12 shows the incremental motorization that occurred during the postwar years that Maddison has called "the golden age" of the advanced industrial nations. The increase in motor vehicles per 1,000 population is strikingly uniform from nation to nation, with only France and the United Kingdom lagging behind. Thus the table does not show the pattern that a diffusion-of-innovation model would predict—late adopters gradually catching up with early adopters. The gap between the United States, Canada, and the rest of the G-7 was not reduced. Instead, the United States and Canada added motor vehicles at the same per capita rate as Germany—and at a faster rate than France, Italy, Japan, and the United Kingdom.

Based on table 1.12, it would be tempting to attribute sustained motorization in the United States to the interstate highway program and public policies

Table 1.12 *Incremental motorization in the G-7 nations, 1950–75*

	MV per 1,000 pop. in 1950	MV per 1,000 pop. in 1975	Increase per 1,000 pop.
United States	327	620	293
Canada	186	479	293
United Kingdom	70	286	216
France	59	340	281
Germany	22	315	293
Italy	16	295	279
Japan	4	253	249

SOURCE: AMA, *Motor Vehicle Facts and Trends*, 1950 and 1975, and Maddison, *World Economy: Historical Statistics*, 38, 85.

Table 1.13 *Mass motorization in the G-7 nations: Threshold years and time lags vs. the United States and Canada*

	Year crossed	Lag vs. U.S.	Lag vs. Canada
United States	1958	—	—
Canada	1971	13 years	—
France	1980	22 years	9
Germany	1980	22 years	9
Italy	1984	26 years	13
United Kingdom	1987	29 years	16
Japan	1987	29 years	16

SOURCE: Derived from previous tables.

favorable to home ownership and suburbanization. But caution is in order because Canada sustained motorization at exactly the same pace as the United States with no comparable national commitment to metropolitan freeway development or tax advantage for home ownership. By 1975, Canada also had crossed the threshold of mass motorization. All that can be surely concluded at this point is that highway capacity did not constrain mass motorization in either the United States or Canada, a subject to which we will return in chapter 5.

Table 1.13 shows the year in which each of the G-7 nations finally crossed the threshold of mass motorization, defined as 400 motor vehicles per 1,000 population: the United States in 1958, Canada in 1972, France and Germany in 1980, Italy in 1984, and Japan and the United Kingdom in 1987. The time lag between mass motorization in the United States and the world's other advanced industrial nations ranged from roughly half a generation for Canada to a full generation for Italy, the United Kingdom, and Japan.

If we use Canada as our yardstick for gauging the impacts of the world wars on these time lags, it suggests that they could have accounted for a lag of roughly 10 years—the lag between Canada and Germany, the most devastated of the battleground nations. Buying and borrowing power differentials, with their impacts on both auto and home ownership rates and indirect impacts on the growth of suburban population and employment, could well account for another 5–10 years. That would leave U.S. leadership in the mass production of motor vehicles, in domestic oil production and in highway development—plus the decline of transit use to account for another 5–10 years. This is structured guesswork, but we are comfortable with the structuring—and thus reasonably comfortable with the "guesstimates" that it has produced. As this itemization suggests, highway policy contributed to the intensity of U.S. motorization, but was probably not the prime mover intimated in many journalistic accounts.

First Doubts about the Merits of Intensive Motorization

In the 1950s, motorization was a source of pride in the advanced industrial nations, especially the United States. But by 1960, intensive motorization was already beginning to be seen as a double-edged sword. The reasons for this shift in valence and perception were economic, environmental, and geopolitical. In 1950, intensive motorization was a commonwealth phenomenon. It was found only in the United States, Canada, New Zealand, and Australia. But by the late 1960s, increased motorization was generating heavy traffic, congestion, and visible air pollution in Western Europe. During this same period, pioneering Swedish and British research linked motorization and industrialization to both acid rain and increasing atmospheric concentrations of CO_2—suggesting that they could be a primary cause of a small but worrisome increase in global temperatures.[24]

By 1970, these issues were being linked under the rubric of environmental sustainability. The question was being posed: Is global motorization sustainable? This issue was salient because intensive motorization had become an international phenomenon that had created a truly multinational automobile industry and increasingly strenuous demands on world oil supplies. In 1980, the United States alone paid $78.6 billion for oil imports and $24.1 billion for more fuel-efficient import cars.[25]

The oil shocks of 1973–74 and 1980 precipitated brief global recessions and contributed to a sharp downturn in the salability of the full-sized family cars that were the bread and butter of the U.S. automobile industry.[26] From 1970 to 1980, automobile production in the United States declined by 28 percent, while Japanese production increased 109 percent, primarily to meet U.S. demand for subcompact cars.[27] During the same period, imported oil increased from

23 percent of U.S. oil consumption to fully half. The same epoch marked the beginning of deficits in the U.S. balance of trade as consumers looked to Japan and Europe for fuel-efficient vehicles.[28] In other words, there has been good reason to view intensive motorization as a mixed blessing for the United States since the 1970s.

Gradual Convergence in G-7 Motorization Levels, 1975–2000

Table 1.14 shows motorization slowing in the United States and Canada after 1975, but surging in Japan and Italy while continuing at a strong pace in Germany, France, and the United Kingdom. It also shows Canada gaining ground on the United States. In 1975, the differential between the most and the least motorized nations in the G-7 was 367 motor vehicles per 1,000 population. By 2000, the differential between the most and least motorized of the G-7 nations had fallen to 273 per 1,000. Clearly, motorization had increased in every G-7 nation, but just as clearly, convergence was also under way.

What explains the shrinking motorization differential between the United States and the six other G-7 nations after 1975? Part of the answer lies in the increasing saturation of the American market in terms of both vehicles per capita and vehicles per dollar of household borrowing power. But four other factors served to sustain continuing U.S. motorization during this period: the size of the postwar baby boom generation, increasing workforce participation among the married women of the boomer generation, and the associated increase in households with two workers, two incomes, and the borrowing power to afford two cars. Shifts in intrametropolitan and interregional population shares also contributed. These included the emergence of suburban population majorities within U.S. metropolitan areas, population decline in many of the nation's old-line manufacturing centers, the growth of suburban employment, and dramatic increases in sunbelt population and employment. These demographic and geographic dynamics sustained motorization and led to the emergence of suburban majorities in most U.S. metropolitan areas, propelling the United States over the threshold of pervasive motorization in 1980.

At the same time, accelerating motorization in Europe and Japan continued to narrow the United States' lead in motorization vis-à-vis its peer group nations. In 1950, the United States accounted for fully 70 percent of global vehicles registrations. By 1980, that share had shrunk to 38 percent. The U.S. share of production volumes declined even more rapidly—from 76 percent in 1950 to 21 percent in 1980. This decline in the United States share of global vehicle production was largely attributable to the growth of Japanese and European income and the resulting increase in domestic vehicle production. At the same time, the U.S. automakers surrendered domestic sales share due to the

Table 1.14 *Incremental motorization in the G-7 nations, 1975–2000*

	MV per 1,000 pop. in 1975	MV per 1,000 pop. in 2000	Increase per 1,000 pop.
United States	620	784	164
Canada	479	676	197
Japan	253	651	398
Italy	295	627	332
France	340	575	235
Germany	315	574	259
United Kingdom	286	511	225

SOURCE: MVMA, *Motor Vehicle Facts and Figures*, 1976; *Ward's Motor Vehicle Facts and Figures*, 2002; and Maddison, *World Economy: Historical Statistics.*

shift to smaller, more fuel-efficient imports that occurred in the United States following both the OPEC embargo and the Iranian oil crisis. The oil shocks reduced the sales volumes of the U.S. domestic automakers and increased U.S. demand for fuel-efficient Japanese and European imports. During this same period, the United States and Canadian share of world registrations was shrinking, due primarily to the growth in automobile ownership that was occurring in Japan, Italy, Germany, France, Great Britain, and other advanced industrial nations. Clearly, mass motorization had evolved from a Commonwealth phenomenon in 1950 to an OECD phenomenon by 1980.

Motorization could finally increase rapidly in Europe and Japan because the work of rebuilding both cities and savings after World War II was complete, which freed governmental revenues, bank capital, and personal savings for other purposes. Home and auto ownership could now assert themselves as personal priorities, and automobile manufacturing could emerge as a domestic economic priority. In Europe, especially, the result was a long-deferred increase in both home ownership and suburbanization—and a subsequent increase in suburban commerce and employment. In turn, increasing suburbanization of population and employment was paired with further increases in auto and truck ownership, as it had been in the United States during the 1950s, 1960s, and 1970s. By 2000, Canada and Japan still lagged behind the United States (and New Zealand) in motor vehicles per capita, but both were approaching the threshold of pervasive motorization.

Along with the rapid catch-up in motorization that occurred in Europe during the 1970s and 1980s came unexpectedly rapid growth in suburban population and employment and further increases in motor vehicle ownership. It has become increasingly obvious to European observers that many of the same dynamics that have propelled pervasive motorization in the United States are now at work in Europe, too.

These dynamics were well described in a 1995 ECMT/OECD report:

[Metropolitan] settlement patterns [in Europe] are becoming more complex and the continuing suburbanization of population and jobs is one of their major features. Travel by car has increased in almost all countries and at a rate which, 50 years ago, would not have been thought possible. This has been due to long-term annual increases of two to three percent in national wealth, a general lowering in the real costs of using a car and the emergence of more car-dependent lifestyles.

Trip length by both car and public transport has been increasing as activities have become more dispersed. Suburb-to-suburb journeys have shown the fastest growth. At the same time there has been a shift from walking and cycling to mechanized modes.

Car ownership has conferred a . . . freedom to travel anywhere at any time and enabled jobs, shops, and services to relocate to peripheral areas. It has also allowed more people to enjoy living in spacious surroundings.

Industry has not been slow to take advantage of the freedom offered by road movement. The ease with which goods can [now] be transported from anywhere to anywhere has allowed innovations such as just-in-time production and a reduction in warehousing facilities. Firms of all kinds have, at the same time, tended to move to edge-of-town sites to exploit the increased personal mobility of their car-owning customers and employees.

As this report indicates, Europe is now experiencing motorization much like that which the United States experienced in the 1960s and 1970s, even in the absence of an aggressive program of urban expressway development like that in the United States. "Lagged convergence" seems an appropriate description of the catching-up process that has occurred in Europe. At the same time, we should emphasize that it remains unlikely that convergence will ultimately culminate in vehicle ownership rates as intensive as those found in the United States—or VMT as lengthy. This is unlikely for seven reasons: (1) restrained development of urban motorways; (2) higher taxes on gasoline and diesel fuel; (3) the snowbelt location of many of Europe's primary transit cities that has contained urban sprawl; (4) urban densities that will continue to deflect motorization more readily than those of U.S. cities; (5) the absence of fast-growing new cities likely to become the European equivalent of Houston, Phoenix, or Tampa Bay; (6) the seeming stability of the European habit of automobile use for social and recreational purposes and the use of public transportation for urban commuting—a pattern of automobile use that has suppressed the need for second vehicles in urban households and third vehicles in suburban households; and (7) populations with a much larger age cohort over 70.

A cultural difference is also significant: No European nation comes close to equivalency with the United States in terms of the personal ownership of pickup trucks or SUVs, and no European nation seems likely to catch up. Trucks accounted for 72 percent of the total increase in U.S. motor vehicle registrations between 1973 and 2000. Before the OPEC embargo, trucks accounted for 19 percent of the vehicles in operation in the United States; by 2000 they accounted for 41 percent. Most of this increment in truck ownership was attributable to trucks used as passenger vehicles or work-and-recreation vehicles. By 2000, pickups, SUVs, and other light trucks accounted for 74 percent of all trucks registered in the United States and almost 29 percent of all registered motor vehicles.[29]

Pop sociology used to make frequent reference to "America's love affair with the automobile." Now these references are to suburban cowboys and their pickup trucks and soccer moms and their SUVs. There does remain a bit of cowboy in many American males, but the more telling reason for U.S.-European differences in truck ownership are differences in the age composition of the U.S. population, differences in family size, and differences in the share of the workforce engaged in housing construction—relevant considerations because pickup trucks and SUVs are very useful for hauling tools and shuttling children. Differentials in the ownership of SUVs also reflect the lower fuel taxes that have long prevailed in the United States and the historic low in real-dollar gasoline prices that the United States plumbed in 1998.

Nor is it likely that U.S. and Canadian motorization levels will fully converge. The United States' lead in GDP per capita has declined vis-à-vis Canada, but not enough to erase the residual differential in motorization levels, because much of the remaining residual can be attributed to differences in fuel-tax rates and urban transportation and land-use policies. Canada and its cities embraced public ownership of mass transit earlier than the United States and have pursued land-use policies that have sustained ridership more effectively—Toronto being a prime example.[30] Perhaps more important, Canadian gasoline prices are almost 1.4 times higher than those in the United States.[31] Canadians made more than twice as many transit trips as their U.S. counterparts in 1992—88 transit trips per capita, compared with 33 per capita in the United States.[32] Canada has also taken a more restrained approach to metropolitan expressway development than the United States, thus the vehicle miles traveled per capita in Canada's prime transit markets are only 60 percent of the per capita VMT in a roughly equivalent set of U.S. cities.[33]

If present trends persist, we would expect to see continuing growth of motor vehicle registrations per capita in Canada, Europe, and Japan, but we would also expect less-than-complete convergence with present motorization levels in the United States and thus substantial residual differentials in VMT.

Looking beyond the G-7, every current trend except the present volatility of petroleum prices and the uncertainties posed by global warming suggest that the future will bring widening membership in the club of nations that have experienced mass motorization. In fact, if present trends hold, the 23 nations that have already experienced mass motorization will be joined by another

15 nations that can be expected to cross the threshold of mass motorization within a generation. Despite increasing concern over global warming, we think this outcome likely because both the wealth and mobility of the G-7 nations are envied and being emulated in developing nations around the world.

Motorization in the Next Tier of World Nations

Table 1.15 identifies the 46 nations that made up the first and second tiers of global motorization in 2000. Second-tier nations are those that have attained or are approaching initial motorization but have not yet crossed the threshold of mass motorization. The nations that make up this second tier of global motorization include many of the industrialized nations of Eastern Europe, the recently industrialized Four Asian Tigers, a few oil-rich nations in the Middle East and North Africa, the next tier of wealthy nations in the Americas, and the Union of South Africa.

The nations listed in the second column of table 1.15 have per-capita income levels that are much higher than the global norm but lower than those of first-tier nations. More important in terms of the future pace of motorization in these nations, less of these nation's aggregate income belongs to middle-income households with buying power sufficient to afford personal ownership of a car or truck. Consumer-oriented commercialism is also less prominent, and the development of commercial trucking and delivery services is correspondingly limited. Both outcomes reflect the fact that middle-income households with the buying power to afford motor vehicle ownership account for a smaller share of the national population in nations that occupy the second tier of global motorization.

In Eastern Europe, present motorization levels reflect middle-class incomes that were stunted by Soviet era economic policies and managed economies that were shocked by abrupt transition to market capitalism. In the tiger nations of Asia, motorization levels reflect the growing wealth and buying power generated by recent industrialization, but also the relatively small share of middle-income households. In the oil emirates, motorization levels reflect both the huge wealth generated by oil and the relatively narrow base of the middle class. The story in the Spanish-speaking nations of the Americas is much the same: the middle class is growing but is still not as broad-based as in the 23 nations that have already crossed the threshold of mass motorization.

Two nations with large and fast-growing economies—China and India—are not among the 23 nations we have characterized as belonging to the next tier of global motorization. Nor is Russia. That is because their year-2000 motorization levels remained much lower—on a per capita basis—than those of the nations

Table 1.15 *First and second tiers of global motorization in 2000*

First tier nations	Motor vehicles per 1,000 pop.	Second tier nations	Motor vehicles per 1,000 pop.
United States	784	Czech Republic	363
New Zealand	698	Estonia	319
Canada	676	Bahrain	310
Japan	651	Poland	305
Luxembourg	648	Lithuania	295
Iceland	640	Latvia	285
Italy	627	Israel	281
Germany	575	Bulgaria	280
France	574	Hungary	274
Austria	547	Slovak Republic	266
Spain	539	South Korea	255
Australia	530	Brunei	251
United Kingdom	511	Taiwan	243
Switzerland	511	Puerto Rico	230
Sweden	495	Malaysia	225
Belgium	492	Bahrain	205
Portugal	474	Uruguay	197
Denmark	470	Mexico	189
Netherlands	470	Argentina	179
Finland	470	Brazil	170
Kuwait	464	Romania	160
Ireland	405	South Africa	157
Greece	405	Libya	154

SOURCE: *Ward's Motor Vehicle Facts and Figures*, 2002, and Maddison, *World Economy: Historical Statistics.*

listed in table 1.15. India stood at 7 motor vehicles per 1,000 population in 2000, China at 11 per 1,000, and Russia at 83 per 1,000.[34] Chinese buyers bought almost 16 million passenger cars from 2000 through 2004, which more than doubled China's motorization level to 23 per 1,000 population in 2004. But China does not have the household buying power to sustain motorization at this recent pace. In fact, Japan's experience suggests that it could take India and China another 25 to 30 years to reach the threshold of mass motorization. Nonetheless, because of the size of their populations and the rapidity of their economic growth, both China and India will be making a significant contribution to the intensity of global motorization by 2025—a concern in the context of global warming, the world's finite oil supplies, and U.S. dependency on the automobile for mass transportation.

In the United States, the breadth and buying power of the middle class produced mass motorization in 1958 and pervasive motorization by 1980. In

Europe, mass motorization lagged by more than 20 years, but development of suburban character and the growth of suburban employment are now laying the groundwork for European motorization just short of U.S. intensity. Table 1.15 shows that another dozen nations are fast approaching mass motorization. This is most imminent in those Eastern European nations where the development of a broad-based middle class is also under way. If it can shed its residual affinity for a Stalinist view of economic development, Russia could join them, but not by 2025. In other nations of the second tier, the timing of mass motorization will likewise hinge on the growth of the middle class and per capita GDP, producing a lag that could exceed a generation or more.

The common thread is clear: motorization is now prized around the world, and initial motorization is under way in every nation with a substantial GDP and a robust middle class. But global motorization also indicates a quickening and broadening of demands on the world's known petroleum reserves and an increase in CO_2 emissions. The ability of the automobile and energy industries —both American and international—to meet these new challenges will determine whether motorization on a near-global scale can produce outcomes that are socially and environmentally acceptable. This seems likely to hinge on the successful development of economical alternatives to both the internal combustion engine and carbon-based fuels, supplemented by efforts to increase transit's market share in those settings where it can provide service both effectively and efficiently.

This book is about the American piece of this puzzle—past, present, and future. It is set in an international context because much is to be learned from international comparisons and because ultimately the constraints on U.S. motorization as we now know it will be global constraints—most notably, global warming and the gradual depletion of world oil supplies.

In the analysis that follows, we start with history because any sound analysis of future prospects must begin not with rosy expectations but with a full understanding of both the momentum and the inertia that the past brings to the future.

Summing Up

1. Motorization occurred earliest in the world's most advanced industrial nations. It is presently most intense in those nations with high per capita GDPs and a domestic automobile industry.

2. Mass motorization has only occurred in 23 nations that are much wealthier than the global norm. The United States is one of only three that have also crossed the threshold of pervasive motorization. The others are Luxembourg and New Zealand. Canada and Japan are close behind.

3. Motorization lagged in Europe because of the destructive impact of the world wars. It occurred earliest in the United States because of the wealth of the U.S. population, the size of the U.S. market, the size of its middle class, and the economies of scale created by the mass production of cars and trucks and the low cost of producing gasoline from then-unused fractions of a barrel of oil.

4. Assembly-line production was an innovation of the U.S. automobile industry. The timing of its introduction and the size and buying power of the U.S. population—plus the two world wars—ensured that the United States would dominate world automobile manufacturing for most of the twentieth century.

5. In Europe, the density of larger cities and the continuing serviceability and financial stability of public transportation slowed the diffusion of the automobile. In the United States, the financial difficulties of mass transit produced disinvestment after 1916. As a result, transit was unable to deflect motorization in U.S. cities as it did in Europe.

6. More than any other nation in its international peer group, the United States has proactively accommodated urban motorization by building metropolitan freeways and expressways.

7. In Europe's older cities, the use of cars for the journey to work has been constrained by the scarcity of parking—which, in turn, was conducive to continuing transit use. Extensive subway development and the rationalization of streetcar service also sustained transit market shares that are substantially higher than in U.S. cities. On the other hand, the growth of suburban population and employment is now producing European circumstances conducive to more intensive motorization and more extensive automobile use.

8. Historically, mass motorization was confined to a handful of advanced industrial nations, most of them large enough to support a domestic automobile manufacturer. By 2000, 23 nations had experienced mass motorization and another cluster of nations was approaching mass motorization. In other words, the world is trending toward motorization that is increasingly global in scope and scale.

9. The volatility built into the geopolitics of oil demonstrates that intensive motorization is a double-edged sword. Global warming also raises serious questions about the sustainability of intensive motorization on a worldwide scale. What is known to date suggests that the sustainability of global motorization will hinge on developing economical alternatives to the internal combustion engine and to petroleum-based fuels, while sustaining and increasing transit use in settings where it can provide service both effectively and efficiently.

PART TWO

U.S. Motorization in
Historical Context

Part 1 closed with the observation that the future sustainability of global motorization is likely to hinge on the development of economical alternatives to the internal combustion engine and petroleum-based fuels, supplemented by efforts to increase transit's market share in those settings where it can provide service both effectively and efficiently. Part 2 will focus on how much the United States can realistically expect from mass transit, given the intensity of its motorization and how long and how deeply motorization has been ingrained in American lifestyles and the settlement patterns of U.S. metropolitan areas. What follows is a broadly comprehensive overview of the intertwined histories of mass transit, motorization, highway development, and suburbanization in the United States.

TWO

Transit's American History, 1880–1929

To understand the decline of the U.S. transit industry, we must describe the circumstances that made streetcar development a promising private investment in the 1880s and 1890s. We must also convey the deterioration in the streetcar industry's financial position that had occurred before World War I and how seriously the industry's earning power was then compromised by wartime inflation and initial motorization. This analysis will situate the beginnings of transit's decline in the early twentieth century, laying the groundwork for a factually accurate interpretation of the collapse of transit ridership that followed World War II. We will begin with a description of the transit industry in the streetcar era.

Transit during America's Streetcar Era

The primary form of transit in the late nineteenth and early twentieth centuries was the electric street railway. The typical street railway of 1890 was a privately owned, investor-financed transit property that operated under franchise rights granted by its home city. In some cities, the electrification of streetcar service was carried out by the same companies that had operated horsecars. In other cities, electrification was financed by new companies that operated under new franchise agreements. The best capitalized of these new streetcar companies were affiliated with electric power companies that sought to carve out territories in which to provide street lighting and household electricity as well as streetcar service. In other cases, the introduction of streetcar service was financed by real estate syndicates, which financed streetcar lines in order to facilitate the development of suburban real estate.[1]

The technology used by electric street railways was a significant advance over that of the horsecars that they quickly displaced in the mid-1880s. Electric street railways could traverse much longer distances more quickly than horsecars, and each coach was larger and could carry more passengers. Because productivity was higher, fares could be lower. And for all of these reasons, the ridership of electric street railways was much greater than that of the horsecars. Streetcar rides per capita of the urban population rose from 98 in 1890 to 168 in 1902, and finally peaked in 1917, during the war.[2]

In most ways, electric street railways were not much different from horsecars. They operated on tracks located in the center of city streets. They were initially run by two-man crews, one to collect fares and the other to operate the streetcar. And they were operated under the terms of franchise agreements negotiated between municipal governments and would-be streetcar companies. These agreements spelled out the company's obligations to its home city and its riding public. The typical franchise of 1890 granted the right to install and operate service on a specific route or a few routes. Franchises were granted route by route, and many franchises were necessary for an operator to assemble a network that could provide citywide service and convenient connections in a large city. Fares were fixed at five cents in most franchise agreements. More problematic, franchises issued during the boom years of street railway development made no provision for subsequent increases in fares based on inflation. Nor was specific provision made for the renegotiation of fares to reflect the extension of service as the city grew and service was extended. There was, nonetheless, intense competition to secure franchises beginning in the 1880s. This reflected the perception that a fixed fare offered a virtual guarantee of future profitability given the deflation that was characteristic of the U.S. economy in the 1880s and early 1890s.[3]

Streetcar magnates made great fortunes in the early years by locking up franchise rights in major markets such as Philadelphia, New York, Boston, and Chicago.[4] In turn, the public's perception that streetcar companies were "making a killing" led to adversarial relations between streetcar companies and local governments, and many later franchise agreements were encumbered with new provisions that required street railways to provide discount fares during peak commuting hours, pave the streets on which they operated, and provide late night service. In most large cities, street railways were obliged to operate 16, 18, or even 24 hours a day.[5]

The U.S. economy shifted from a deflationary bias to an inflationary bias in the late 1890s.[6] But street railway development continued as rival electric utilities vied with each other to create territorial monopolies where they could market not only electric service but also transportation and street lighting. In real dollar terms, net capital investment in street railways peaked in 1905. In the years following, investors looking for a safer investment shifted out of street railway securities and into electric utilities. At the same time, utility holding companies shifted their investment emphasis from street railways to electric power plants and the distribution systems needed to support household electrification. As a result, gross capital expenditure for street railway development peaked in 1907. During this same period, relations between street railways and local governments deteriorated in increasingly bitter disputes over the frequency of existing service, crowding during commute hours, and the operators' obligations to extend service to accommodate suburban growth. Investor confidence in street railway securities had been thoroughly undermined by 1912, and a pattern of net disinvestment was evident after 1916. The mileage of streetcar track peaked in 1917.[7]

The Causes of Initial Disinvestment

The profitability of street railways hinged on low wages and long workdays for operators and conductors.[8] Profitability also hinged on a low inflation rate, which was needed to sustain the value of the revenues generated by a fixed five-cent fare and to ensure low interest payments on the industry's mountain of debt. Stated another way, profitability sufficient to retire the industry's heavy debt load could only be sustained as long as inflation remained mild, street railway workers remained unorganized, and immigration replenished the pool of workers willing to work for a relatively low wage. These foundations of street railway profitability were eroded by the shift in the U.S. economy from a deflationary bias to an inflationary bias, by the intense inflation associated with World War I, and by the unionization of 50 percent of all street railway workers by war's end.[9]

Before World War I, streetcar workers were paid wages that were roughly equivalent to 95 percent of the annual wage of moderately skilled workers in manufacturing. But street railway motormen worked considerably longer hours: on average, 14 hours a day, six days a week. Thus their true rate of hourly compensation floated at only 70–75 percent of the manufacturing wage. World

War I abruptly changed the circumstances that had sustained low wages for streetcar workers, low interest payments for streetcar companies, and the revenue value of the nickel fare. This was because the war years, 1914–18, and their immediate aftermath were a period of virulent inflation. If we assign an index value of 100 to consumer prices in 1914, we can report that the price level had risen to 192 by 1918 and then to 226 by 1920. Consumer prices settled back in the 1920s, but by then, the financial position of the streetcar industry had been badly damaged, streetcar labor had been unionized, wages had been increased dramatically as a result of mandatory wartime arbitration, and the industry's operating ratio had deteriorated from .60 in 1912 to .78 in 1920. With an industry-average operating ratio of .78, many weaker street railways were unable to meet debt payments or pay dividends, and many were forced into receivership.[10]

The Decisions of the War Labor Board

The immediate cause of the industry's economic distress was the financial vice created by a fixed fare and the wage increases mandated by the War Labor Board, a federal arbitration panel established by President Woodrow Wilson to arbitrate wartime wage settlements that reflected the impact of inflation on the buying power of workers. Chairman William Howard Taft explained the logic of the board's rulings as follows:

> We have found the streetcar men underpaid everywhere . . . and the general range of our rulings has been to bring them up [to wage parity with workers in other industries that were comparably skilled]. In the past, the financial conditions of the companies had actually kept down wages of the men quite below the wages paid in fields of labor of a kindred nature. We had no hesitation in reaching the conclusion that labor was as much entitled to an independent consideration of what its wages should be as a coal man who furnished coal or a material man who furnished iron. [In each case] the question must be determined by what was being paid in similar fields of labor. Therefore, we refused flatly from the first to consider the financial condition of any company in determining the rate of wages.[11]

The War Labor Board's wage increase decisions produced a financial crisis for street railways because most fares remained fixed by franchise agreement. Table 2.1 uses index values to show the relative trends between 1916 and 1920. These indices show that consumer prices increased 83 percent while streetcar wages increased 94 percent. During the same period, streetcar fares increased only 37 percent. The result was that operating expenses increased 123 percent while net revenues declined 10 percent. For hundreds of streetcar companies, the result was a ruinous financial squeeze that prevented most small

Table 2.1 *Indexing of consumer prices vs. streetcar expenses and revenues, 1916–20*

	Consumer prices	Streetcar wages	Operating expenses	Streetcar fares	Net revenues
1916	100	100	100	100	100
1920	183	194	223	137	90

SOURCE: *Historical Statistics of the United States*, Series E 135–166; Mason, *Street Railway in Massachusetts.*

and midsized operators from borrowing to finance modernization or to capitalize future improvements. It also produced a wave of consolidations in which better financed companies absorbed weaker ones.

Investors had hoped for recovery in the postwar years, but the onset of initial motorization frustrated those expectations. Public investment would have been necessary at this juncture to modernize streetcar fleets and upgrade track and rolling stock. It was not forthcoming. Instead, streetcar companies were placed under the regulatory purview of state public utility or public service commissions. State fare and service regulation enabled fare increases but did not produce financial recovery sufficient to motivate the reinvestment that would have been necessary for modernization and ridership growth.

The financial results shown in table 2.1 explain why most streetcar companies were unable to secure financing for reinvestment after World War I. Table 2.2 completes this line of analysis. It reports the peak year for eight performance indicators critical to the profitability of street railways. It shows that every significant measure of street railway performance had peaked by 1923, six years before the onset of the Great Depression. It also shows the overall trend of transit ridership, including rapid transit and bus ridership, which peaked in 1926.

As table 2.2 shows, 1902 was the streetcar industry's peak year in terms of the financial results of operation (as measured by the ratio of operating revenues to operating expenses), and 1916 marked the onset of sustained disinvestment. The mileage of streetcar track peaked in 1917, as did streetcar rides per capita of the urban population. The number of miles operated and paying customers carried by street railways peaked in 1923. The transit industry as a whole, including rapid transit and bus operations, sustained patronage growth somewhat longer. The peak for total bus, streetcar, and rapid transit ridership per capita in a peacetime year occurred in 1926, if the wartime peak that resulted from gas rationing during World War II is treated—appropriately, we think—as a wartime anomaly.[12]

Taken together, tables 2.1 and 2.2 clearly indicate that the initial cause of the streetcar industry's decline was financial. Many street railways were unable to attract significant capital investment after the stock market panic of 1906, and most were unable to restore a healthy balance sheet in the wake of the wartime

Table 2.2 *Indicators of U.S. streetcar industry performance*

Key indicators	Peak year
Revenue/expense ratio	1902[a]
Net capital expenditures	1905[b]
Gross capital expenditures	1907[b]
Value of plant and equipment	1916[b]
Streetcar rides per capita of the urban population	1917[c]
Mileage of streetcar track	1917[a]
Total passenger trips by streetcar and subway	1920[d]
Revenue passengers carried	1923[e]
Coach-miles operated by streetcar	1923[f]
Total public transportation rides per capita of the U.S. population, including bus and rapid transit	1926[g]

[a] Historical Statistics of the United States, Series Q 264-273, 721.
[b] Ulmer, *Capital in Transportation.*
[c] U.S. Bureau of the Census, *Census of Street and Electric Railways*, 1917.
[d] *Historical Statistics of the United States*, Series Q 235-250, 721.
[e] APTA, "Passenger Trips by Mode," *Transit Fact Book*, 1997.
[f] Moody's Investors Service, *Moody's Transportation Manual*, 1982.
[g] Excludes World War II and the 1946–47 demobilization period when transit ridership was inflated by gas rationing and billeted travel by servicemen.

wage rulings of the War Labor Board. As a result, few properties were able to sustain the investment necessary to replace aging equipment or expand service. And despite postwar fare increases, the streetcar industry's operating ratio continued to deteriorate after World War I, seriously damaging its credit and borrowing power.[13] Thus we concur with the conclusion reached by Brian Cudahy: "It can be stated unambiguously that the American mass transit industry was a casualty of the war and never fully recovered from its impact."[14]

Postwar Suburbanization

World War I and the suburban development boom that followed it marked the beginning of the end of the streetcar's influence over the patterns of urban development and metropolitan land use, 38 years before Congress authorized full funding for the interstate highway program. In the housing domain, the critical events were the Sixteenth Amendment, which enabled the imposition of federal income taxes, and subsequent congressional action authorizing countervailing income tax deductions. Both took force in 1913, the year that a sufficient number of state legislatures ratified an amendment to the Constitution enabling the imposition of the income tax. The same year, Congress authorized itemized deductions for interest paid by federal income tax payers, including but not limited to mortgage interest.[15]

The tax deductibility of interest fueled the growth and development of the commercial lending industry in the 1920s, which provided the financing necessary to underwrite the growth of home and automobile ownership. Both contributed to the housing boom and the suburban growth that followed World War I. And with accelerating suburbanization, the automobile became a more essential feature of day-to-day life, displacing transit from its historical role as the primary provider of the transportation needed to support suburban development.

With the advantage of historical hindsight, we can see that it would have been necessary to convert urban bus and streetcar operations to public ownership in the 1920s, if ridership were to be sustained at a robust level.[16] Only a few American cities did so, and transit ridership growth was not and could not be sustained on a nationwide per capita basis after 1926.

A Closer Look at the Financial Problems of the Streetcar Industry

In 1926, most streetcar companies remained in private ownership, and the key measure of their financial performance was the net operating revenue left over for reinvestment and dividend payments after all operating expenses were paid. These were the financial results that lenders and investors examined to determine credit and investment worthiness. These, of course, were precisely the financial results that went sour after World War I, precluding reinvestment and renewal without conversion to public ownership. Neither public investment nor conversion to public ownership occurred on any substantial scale during the 1920s with the exception of public investment in subway development in New York City. The result is that streetcar companies were unable to finance reinvestment before the Depression and unable to avoid wholesale abandonment of service during the Depression.

Using the year 1912 as an indicator of the streetcar revenues generated before World War I, table 2.3 shows the downward trend of both net operating revenue and revenue per rider that occurred during the 1920s, both in constant dollars terms. The table offers overwhelming evidence that disinvestment began after World War I, that the dynamic underlying the industry's decline was a financial one, and that the fare increases could not produce financial recovery. Table 2.3 is based on aggregate data for the streetcar industry as a whole. Thus it substantially understates the financial problems that the trolley companies were encountering in cities with a population of less than 250,000 and overstates the problems of the largest operations in markets such as New York, Chicago, and Philadelphia.

Table 2.3 *Streetcar industry's net operating revenues, 1912–28*

Year	Net revenues in millions of 1967 constant $	Net revenues per ride
1912	7,494	.0061
1917	5,961	.0041
1918	4,191	.0029
1919	3,629	.0024
1920	3,275	.0021
1921	4,179	.0029
1922	4,918	.0031
1923	4,710	.0029
1924	4,486	.0028
1925	4,487	.0026
1926	4,360	.0025
1927	4,386	.0026
1928	4,397	.0026

SOURCE: Author's computations based on data in AERA, *Urban Transportation Problem.*

Table 2.4 *Transit's ridership gains and losses by size of city, 1921–28*

Population	Ridership change
50,000–100,000	−18.9%
100,000–250,000	−20.2%
250,000–500,000	−11.4%
500,000–1 million	−15.2%
1 million+	+8.9%

SOURCE: American Transit Association, *Transit Fact Book,* 1947.

Table 2.4 shows the punishing loss of ridership that was experienced in smaller cities during the 1920s. In the smallest cities, streetcar companies also experienced net operating deficits on an on-and-off basis. Indeed, table 2.4 indicates that ridership losses were epidemic in all but the largest markets and that the streetcar industry's economics were already marginal before the Depression. It also shows that the few largest cities with population densities sufficient to support rapid transit were the most successful in deflecting motorization—the pattern shown in Kenworthy and Laube's studies of the correlates of transit use and automobile dependence.

That motorization lagged in the very largest U.S cities during the 1920s should not be surprising. They had the lion's share of the nation's boardinghouses, tenements, and other forms of rental housing, and they had the lion's share of the nation's nonagricultural low-income population. They also had the highest densities, the least parking, and the most frequent transit service. Among American cities, only that handful of major financial centers with the very largest populations and the highest population densities was able to deflect the diffusion of the automobile and sustain the growth of transit ridership during the 1920s. These same cities were where street railways had the most robust balance sheets and carried the most riders per capita of the local population. In American cities of every other size class, the decline of transit ridership had already begun before the Depression. In fact, street railway "earnings were only slightly more than enough to pay fixed charges, leaving little or no return for stockholders."[17]

Transit in Milwaukee: A 1920s Case Study

In 1920, Milwaukee was the United States' thirteenth largest city and its fifteenth largest metropolitan area. With a metropolitan area population of 539,400 in 1920 and a robust industrial base, Milwaukee was a prime transit market, and the Milwaukee Electric Railway and Light Company was widely seen as one of the transit industry's most progressive operators. Measured in terms of the share of CBD trips made by transit, Milwaukee with its 50 percent transit share was in the same league as Louisville with its 54 percent share, but behind St. Louis with its 65 percent share. In other words, it was one of the top 20 street railway cities in terms of transit's market share to downtown.

The Milwaukee Electric enjoyed synergies with its parent electric utility, and the streetcar company's managers were highly regarded by their peers in the American Electric Railway Association. In fact, the Milwaukee Electric's general manager, R. H. Pinkley, was president of the AERA in 1927. The financial and operating problems that Pinkley described in Milwaukee were characteristic of the problems that streetcar companies experienced in most U.S. metropolitan areas during the late 1920s:

> The Milwaukee Electric Railway and Light Company operates a transportation system which thoroughly covers the city of Milwaukee and its suburban communities, besides reaching out to other cities to distances upwards of 100 miles.
>
> The communities served are all in a district where the number of automobiles has grown as rapidly as in any section of the United States. Moreover, the communities are all of that size in which there are no compelling reasons for effective restrictive measures concerning parking. Hence, owners of auto—

mobiles are free to use them for business and pleasure without substantial restraint.

The organized local transportation system serving this group of communities has, therefore, suffered its full share of positive loss in traffic [the terminology then used to denote ridership], together with loss of opportunities for increased traffic with the growth of the population.

As in many other communities similarly situated, the local public transportation problem has been further complicated by impaired load factor. It has required, for several years, more streetcars, more facilities, more power and more men, and of course greater investment to handle a stationary volume of traffic because the patronage has become more concentrated during the rush hour periods.

Furthermore, the city of Milwaukee and its suburbs have experienced considerable expansion in area and building in the past few years. This has brought the problem of how to provide public transportation service to new and populous subdivisions growing up in the outskirts in all directions. Notwithstanding these disadvantages, the company has maintained a high standard of service to all of these communities during and since [World War I].

- Power costs have been substantially reduced through radical and original developments in power plant design and operation.
- The number of cars operated in Milwaukee city and suburban service has been increased by . . . 27.7 percent.
- By reconstruction of old equipment and reassembling into two-man trains and through liberal introduction of one-man operated cars, the company has increased maximum seats operated daily by . . . 31.1 percent.
- Antique interurban railway equipment has been reconstructed into the highest speed and most luxurious type of rolling stock, supplemented by feeder lines of motor coaches, likewise of the speediest and most luxurious type.
- The business of the interurban lines has been increased by rendering a high-speed regular and efficient express service for the carriage of freight.
- By means of the motor coach, the territory tributary to the interurban lines has been greatly expanded wherever there was a prospect that persistent operation of high-class equipment on schedule would attract passenger business.
- City and suburban local lines have been extended with rails where justified or as ordered by regulatory authorities, such extensions being further supplemented by crosstown motor bus lines and radial motor bus lines operating as part of the railway system, and
- The local field has been thoroughly occupied by the company through early installation of motor buses.

The Milwaukee Electric also experimented with the operation of a premium bus service with guaranteed seat availability offered at a premium price. Despite these progressive efforts to enhance service, build ridership, and reduce costs, Pinckney reported, "The constantly increasing disadvantages of load factor and traffic conditions generally [are] increasing the cost of service more rapidly than [can] be offset by improvements in devices or methods."[18]

These, of course, were precisely the market dynamics, operational difficulties, and ridership trends that were exacerbating the financial difficulties of other streetcar companies and producing the operating results that were shown in table 2.1.

In 1927, when Pinckney made this cogent report, the diffusion of the automobile was well in progress, but the development of so-called superhighways—a first generation of highways with dual carriageways and a median strip—was just getting under way. In Wisconsin, as in other states, the construction of highways connecting major cities was a state responsibility. Wisconsin's state highway department and its county road departments looked to Michigan and Wayne County, where Detroit is located, for a progressive model of highway building practice.

By 1927, state, county, and city engineers in Milwaukee were following Michigan's example and making plans for the development of a first generation of divided highways that would enable traffic to enter, leave, or circle the city of Milwaukee and the surrounding area at the greatest possible speed with a minimum of confusion and congestion. The development of such superhighways was already in progress in Wisconsin's Waukesha County, and state and county authorities proposed to follow suit in Milwaukee in 1927. Proposed were divided highways with two-lane carriageways to be built within county rights-of-way "ranging from 90 feet to 160 feet to take care of future highway requirements."[19] Highways proposed for redevelopment as superhighways were the northward extension of U.S. Route 12 from Chicago to Milwaukee and then northwest to Madison—highways that would eventually become routes I-43 and I-94 under the auspices of the interstate program. In turn, planning for such superhighways reinforced the concerns that transit veterans like Pinckney voiced at AERA's national convention in 1927—the spreading of settlement and the speed and convenience of automobile use.

Two observations are pertinent. By 1927, state and local authorities in leading industrial states such as California, New York, Massachusetts, New Jersey, Pennsylvania, Michigan, Illinois, and Wisconsin were already planning for a first generation of highways that anticipated the dual carriageway concept underlying the interstate. And in Milwaukee and other cities of less than a million people, street railways had already begun to experience serious financial and competitive difficulties, 30 years before the interstate highway program was funded.

The implication is that public ownership of mass transit and subsidies for transit operation would have been necessary by the mid-1920s in order to restore transit's financial stability and enable it to sustain ridership growth. Instead, a half step was taken: state legislatures intervened to void transit's municipal charters, exempt transit properties from most forms of municipal regulation, and subject them to state regulation by public utility or public service commissions, often at the properties' own request. This created a legal venue in which transit properties could seek and receive legal authorization to increase fares or reduce service. It also provided an alternative to bankruptcy court and judicially supervised reorganization and receivership.

State regulation prolonged transit's ability to operate under private ownership, but did not produce industrial recovery and renewal. In part, this was because utility commissions typically granted fare increases sufficient to sustain operation but insufficient to finance thorough modernization and reorganization. The resulting loss of ridership was significant in small towns and midsized cities and in larger cities less progressive than Milwaukee. But even the Milwaukee Electric was unable to sustain ridership growth in the face of increasing automobile use, the loss of off-peak ridership, and the automobile's evolution into an all-weather utility vehicle that could be used for daily commuting. In other words, transit management that was both seasoned and entrepreneurial was insufficient to generate renewed ridership growth in a midsized metropolitan area experiencing rapid motorization. Public investment was needed but was not forthcoming. Instead, the Depression followed, and under the auspices of the New Deal, Congress authorized federal highway investment in American cities. No symmetric long-term commitment was made to federal investment in transit until the 1960s.

Early Experiments with Public Investment in Transit

Public investment in public transportation first occurred in San Francisco, Boston, New York, Philadelphia, and Chicago, but outright public ownership and operation of transit service had been established in only four major U.S. transit markets before World War II: New York, San Francisco, Seattle, and Detroit.[20] In most other U.S. cities, transit was unable to secure public investment. More often, investor-owned properties fought off local plans for municipalization. Reciprocally, voters rejected proposals for public financing of rapid transit in both Cleveland and Los Angeles. In most cities, state regulation prolonged private ownership, but it also led to recurrent fare increases and contributed to consequent loss of ridership. Some cities—Milwaukee, for example— pursued notable service innovation but still experienced ridership losses due to the decline of off-peak and weekend ridership that accompanied ongoing motorization.

The financial difficulties of the streetcar companies discouraged private investment and stymied innovation of the scope and scale that would have been necessary to reverse the streetcar industry's decline. The exception was New York. It adopted a pioneering approach to subway investment and taxation that entailed public ownership of the subway system and leaseback for private operation. It was financed with a two-tiered tax system that imposed a modest property tax citywide and a higher tax in the vicinity of subway stations. Cool and sometimes adversarial relations between streetcar companies and local governments stymied such cooperative efforts in other cities.

New York, an Atypical American City

Alone among U.S. cities, New York has been able to sustain levels of transit ridership that are closely equivalent to those found in Europe's capital cities and major financial centers. New York's continuing dominance in commuter transit use is obvious from the 2000 census, which shows that the New York metropolitan area still accounts for more than 38 percent of all commuter transit use in the United States. No other U.S. metropolitan area accounts for more than 8 percent.

What explains the gap between New York and every other American metropolis? The density of New York's population is one reason. Another is New York's early commitment to public ownership. But the most telling explanation lies in New York's developmental history. Its dominance in transit commuting has been continuous since the late nineteenth century, when it was the world's leading transit market. In those years, New York's transit systems carried more riders than their counterparts in London, Paris, Berlin, or any other imperial city on a per capita basis.

In 1890, New York's population already exceeded 2.5 million and its leadership in transit use reflected its roles as the United States' financial capital and as a dominant railroad terminus and port city. In turn, these roles reflected New York's national dominance in banking and finance and its historic role as the primary port and transshipment center for beef and grains making their way to European markets, a role made possible by the Erie Canal and the Hudson River. Built in 1825, the Erie Canal made New York the primary transfer point for grain shipments from the north central states to Europe. According to the *Encyclopedia Britannica*, the canal "guaranteed the city's preeminence as a seaport and world entrepreneur in commerce."

It was New York's early advantage in freight movement and ocean shipping that explains the city's later dominance in counting house functions and financial services which, in turn, laid the foundations for its present global dominance in banking, stock market transactions, financial services, and corporate administration. Investment in rapid transit enabled New York to accommodate an unrivaled concentration of financial and administrative functions in Manhattan. Reciprocally, the continuing growth of the financial sector has sustained New York's lead in transit ridership. Transit was able to keep up with the demands of this role because New York made an aggressive commitment to subway development based on benefit-district financing. It was the only U.S. city to achieve such a consensus in the 1920s and the only major metropolitan area to expand its rapid transit system during the decade of initial motorization. Los Angeles and Detroit tried in the 1920s, but they did not succeed because their downtowns were unwilling to pay a fair share of subway construction costs.

Economists would say that "agglomeration economies" enabled New York to establish leadership in financial services and commuter transit. We would add that New York's leadership reflected its geographic advantages, the willingness of local authorities to "think big," and their ability to reach political consensus on local infrastructure and financing commitments that were critically important.

New York proceeded with another subway project during the 1930s, using funds from the New Deal, as did Chicago and San Francisco. No other city was able to agree on how to pay for rapid transit until federal funding became available in the 1960s.

Street Railways, the Automobile, Suburbanization, and Home Ownership

From the beginning, street railways were intimately involved in the growth of the suburbs and in creating the potential for middle-class families to purchase a home of their own. Indeed, the initial investment in street railways was intimately connected to both real estate speculation and the development of suburban housing in the 1890s and early 1900s.[21]

Before World War I, it was a streetcar ride and the relatively affordable land at the end of the line that made home ownership affordable for the urban middle class. In 1920, 41 percent of the United States nonfarm population that lived in cities or towns of more than 4,000 people owned a home of their own. By 1930, this share had climbed to 46 percent, an increase of 12.5 percent. Most of this development occurred in streetcar suburbs and a next ring of suburbs dependent on the automobile.

Before World War I, suburban development occurred at a pace that can be described as one house at a time. In this era, contractors typically built new homes under contract with individual buyers; a successful contractor might build five or six houses in the course of a year. Larger-scale development was precluded by the limited availability of credit and the limited-scale economies that could be achieved in the development of homes one buyer at a time. With the creation of the income tax deduction on mortgage interest in 1914 and the rapid diffusion of both the automobile and installment credit after World War I, home ownership became affordable for a larger slice of the middle class. From 1920 to 1930, the automobile, the tax deductibility of mortgage interest, and a wider array of location options combined with the prosperity of the Roaring Twenties to produce a 12.5 percent increase in nonfarm home ownership.

Although it is getting ahead of our story, we will note that the percentage of increase in home ownership that followed World War I was substantially larger than that which accompanied the development of the interstates. From 1956 to 1980, the share of Americans owning a home of their own increased only 8.6 percent, compared with the 12.5 percent increase between 1920 and 1930.[22]

Thus it would appear that the automobile, income growth, installment credit, and the income tax deduction for mortgages were sufficient to fuel the rapid growth of home ownership. What the interstate and the GI Bill did after World War II was make home ownership affordable to a broader slice of the middle and working classes. But just as clearly, these dynamics were already at work in the 1920s, long before the interstate highway system was proposed or financed.

Summarizing Transit's Initial Difficulties

As the history above suggests, transit's initial difficulties were financial, which produced subsequent competitive weaknesses. Transit's financial difficulties were rooted in the speculative excesses of the streetcar industry's initial investment boom and in the later mismatch between a fixed fare and the inflation-biased economy of the twentieth century. Both damaged the industry's credit standing and borrowing power, producing gradual disinvestment after 1906. World War I intensified inflation and led to federally mandated wage increases for streetcar workers, a body blow that permanently compromised the ability of street railways to secure the loans they would have needed to finance modernization or service extensions. In turn, the growth of operating costs outpaced the growth of operating revenues, damaging the industry's credit rating and borrowing power.[23]

After World War I, the focus of street railway planning necessarily shifted from expansion to cost control and, in many cases, managed contraction. Contraction seems to have been relatively orderly and entailed the rationalization of networks, the elimination of redundant service, and the conservation of capital for fleet replacement. Although their balance sheets deteriorated during and after World War I and the quality of service declined, most streetcar companies were able to remain in business because state legislatures intervened to reclassify street railways and other transit companies as public utilities or public service corporations subject to state fare and service regulation. In turn, state courts voided the fixed-fare provisions of local franchise agreements on the basis of public necessity.[24] This enabled fare increases and partial restoration of the industry's earning power. But as table 2.1 indicates, the fare increases of the 1920s did not restore most companies' operating ratios to a level that would reassure bankers or the bond market that street railways were a good credit risk. Quite the contrary, streetcar company operating ratios deteriorated further during the 1920s, denying the companies access to the capital they would have needed for sustained modernization and renewal. The unavoidable conclusion is that with the exception of the premiere operations in the very largest cities, the streetcar industry was already a distressed industry a full decade before the onset of the Great Depression and three decades before Congress funded the interstate highway program.

After World War I, many transit properties no longer had the profit margins or the balance sheets to secure credit on favorable terms. The more complete answer is that the industry could not recover from the battering of wartime inflation and the loss of investor confidence because of the onset of motorization and other challenges, both old and new. These included (1) the impacts of initial motorization, including the loss of weekend and off-peak ridership and the increasing conflict between auto traffic and streetcar operations, (2) transit's inability to price service based on cost due to regulatory constraints, (3) the millstone of suburban service obligations, (4) a legacy of adversarial relations between local governments and local streetcar companies, (5) downtown's unwillingness to shoulder a fair share of the cost of transit investment, and (6) the onset of the Depression.

The Onset of Initial Motorization

The automobile's initial use was as a touring and recreation vehicle, and its initial buyers were likely to be wealthy sportsmen and self-styled adventurers. Nonetheless, the automobile's evolution into a means of day-to-day transportation occurred quickly in the United States—much more quickly than in Europe or even Canada. James Flink reports that Americans were already predicting that "a cheap, reliable car for the masses would soon be built" and that the automobile was commonly described as "a necessity" as early as 1907.[25] Henry Ford initiated mass production of the Model T in 1908, having tested the market with the Model N in 1906. The Model T soon became "an item of incredible mass consumption" and "automobility quickly became a mass movement."[26] Thanks to mass production of the Model T and its eventual imitators, the aggregate sales of the U.S. automobile industry routinely exceeded 100,000 after 1909 and 1 million after 1916. Annual sales exceeded 3 million by 1924. A year later, the United States attained initial motorization, 150 motor vehicles per 1,000 population.

During this period, the automobile evolved from a touring machine to an all-weather utility vehicle. Only 10 percent of the automobiles manufactured in 1920 were closed vehicles, but by 1927, 83 percent of all newly cars were closed-body models. Other features that marked the automobile's coming of age as a means of day-to-day transportation included electric starters (1911), shock absorbers (1920), balloon tires (1922), the all-steel closed body (1923), power-operated windshield wipers (1923), bumpers as standard equipment (1925), and car heating (1926). Clearly, the automobile had been domesticated by the mid-1920s.[27]

Ford dominated the U.S. market from 1906 to 1926, while General Motors dominated most years after 1926. GM's successor leadership was built on a marketing strategy that was radically different from Ford's. Ford's strategy was to use mass production to market one reliable model at a price as affordable as possible. GM's strategy was to manufacture "a car for every purse and purpose."[28] GM's approach entailed manufacturing cars under five nameplates: Chevrolet, Pontiac, Oldsmobile, Buick, and Cadillac, each with a stable of their own models, styling, colors, and price tags. In other words, GM invented the modern marketing strategies of product and price differentiation, which, in turn, allowed GM to sell affordability, prestige, and everything in between. GM's strategy also entailed providing credit that enabled its dealers to open shop and acquire inventory at wholesale. It was the first automaker to offer its customers installment credit through its own credit subsidiary, known as GMAC.

From 1927 to 1940, Chevrolet outsold Ford all but three years, and General Motors emerged as the nation's dominant automaker. Writing in 1963, GM president Alfred P. Sloan attributed mass motorization to advances that GM pioneered in the 1920s: "installment selling, the used-car trade-in, the closed body, and the annual model."[29] The other critical factor was improved roads.

The Geography of the Automobile's Initial Diffusion

In the early days of the automobile industry, when Ford was the dominant manufacturer, the diffusion of the automobile was centered in small towns of 1,000 to 5,000 and in the truck-farming counties of New Jersey, New York, Massachusetts, Pennsylvania, Connecticut, Rhode Island, and California. Rapid diffusion of the automobile also occurred on farms and in the farm towns of Iowa's corn belt, California's Central Valley and citrus belt, Washington apple country, and the wheat belts of Kansas, Nebraska, and the Dakotas.[30]

During these early years, motorization lagged conspicuously in the tobacco states and in the cotton belt where farm income was much lower. Motorization also lagged in 15 cities with a population of 500,000 or more that were the nation's primary transit markets. These cities with extensive transit service accounted for 16 percent of the U.S. population in 1920 but only 9 percent of U.S. auto registrations. On the other hand, towns of 1,000 to 5,000 were home to only 9 percent of the U.S population but accounted for 22 percent of the nation's auto registrations. Farm families still accounted for almost half of the U.S. population in 1920 and another 38 percent of motor vehicle registrations. Thus the diffusion path of U.S. motorization was from farms and small towns to small cities and metropolitan suburbs.[31] The largest cities—for all their financial clout and aggregate wealth—were the laggards of American motorization. In other words, the pattern of ridership losses for mass transit was the obverse of registration gains for the automobile.

Only in the very largest U.S. cities were street railways able to stage any substantial recovery from the financial distress associated with World War I. In most other cities, street railway "earnings were only slightly more than enough to pay fixed charges, leaving little or no return for stockholders."[32] These streetcar companies could not finance modernization because the diffusion of cars and trucks had profoundly changed their competitive environment.

Crossing the Threshold of "Initial Motorization"

The United States crossed the threshold of initial motorization—150 cars and trucks per 1,000 population—in 1925. No other advanced industrial nation did so until after World War II. The full ensemble of automakers that made up the Big Three was in place by 1925, and car and truck sales volumes exceeding 3 million per year were already the norm. The United States also crossed another threshold in 1925—more than 20 million motor vehicles registered nationwide. At this juncture, some 90 percent of U.S. households were thought to own at least one car.[33] That year the United States accounted for roughly 5.7 percent of the world's population, a little more than 24 percent of global GDP, but a stunning 81 percent of global motor vehicle registrations and 88 percent of motor vehicle production. In this era, the United States was also the global leader in auto exports. Mexico, Central America, and South America were the U.S. auto industry's prime export markets.

In 1925, Ford sold 1.25 million cars and almost 270,000 trucks. GM name-plates sold 617,000 cars and trucks the same year, and GM nameplates exceeded Ford sales the year following. Clearly, the economic and industrial precondi-tions for high-volume automobile sales and eventual mass motorization were already in place in the United States by 1925. One of these prerequisites was the maturation of the automobile into an all-weather utility vehicle. Another was the steady growth of GDP that had begun in 1914 and the consumer credit expansion that accompanied it. All of these contributed to the decline of street-car ridership and compounded the preexisting financial problems of the U.S. streetcar industry.

Transit's Difficulties after Initial Motorization

The diffusion path of the automobile led from farms and small towns to mid-sized cities. But in 1927, motorization still lagged in the nation's prime transit markets—cities with a population exceeding 1 million. In these largest cities, motorization was rapidly gaining ground among urban elites and the suburban middle class, but not the urban middle or working classes.

The first use of the automobile by urban and suburban households was not for day-to-day commuting but for social and recreational travel—going to town, going to church, taking a spin in the country, or going shopping. Most cars sold in the early 1920s did not have hard tops, and none had heaters or defrosters.[34] Closed-body models were the norm by 1928, but not in 1920. Most households that bought a car in the early 1920s were buying a recreational vehicle designed for weekend use, not an all-weather utility vehicle suited to icy roads or rainy weather. This fact explains the initial impact of motorization on mass transit. Transit generally retained riders who traveled during commute hours, but be-gan to lose riders on weekends and during off-peak hours. Transit also experi-enced increasingly difficult operating conditions as urban traffic increased.

The Loss of Weekend and Off-Peak Ridership

During the 1920s, many street railways experienced simultaneous increases in peak hour weekday ridership and declines in weekend, midday, evening, and off-peak ridership. Weekend riders were the first to abandon transit because the initial use of automobiles by city and suburban households was for weekend recreational travel. Indeed, the diffusion of the automobile catalyzed a huge change in leisure possibilities, and with new destinations accessible, "touring" became all the rage for middle- and upper-income households with automobiles. Saturday and Sunday touring displaced weekend transit use. After families bought cars, they drove to shops and to church.[35]

The effects on transit were more significant than one might expect. Most street railways relied on the revenues generated by weekend and midday ridership to balance the financial losses they suffered providing the extra coaches and paying the extra motormen needed to serve the commuter peak during the evening rush hour. The extra motormen and streetcars had no profitable use during off-peak weekday hours.[36] Thus when streetcars lost weekend and midday ridership, they were losing revenues that were absolutely essential to the overall profitability of their operation.

Significant financial consequences were also involved when streetcar companies lost late-evening ridership or riders traveling in the counter-commute direction. These riders could be carried without adding or extending service, and the street railways of the 1920s relied on them for the revenue surplus needed to offset the high marginal cost of serving the weekday peak.[37] Unfortunately, these riders were quick to abandon transit after purchasing an automobile.

Seasonal ridership was still another off-peak market segment that streetcar companies could ill afford to lose. In fact, it was an old saw among the veterans of the streetcar industry that the net revenues of a streetcar company hinged on the weather at Christmas, the holiday crowds in downtown department stores, and the difficulty of getting a table at a downtown restaurant. Good weather at Christmas, busy department stores, and crowded restaurants signaled a good year for downtown, for night and weekend ridership, and thus for the streetcar company's bottom line. But seasonal, weekend, and night riders were quick to abandon streetcar use after buying a hardtop car. The same occurred when chain stores and banks began opening suburban branches. Suburban customers who had previously used the streetcar to travel downtown on Saturday or in the middle of the day now drove to the store or the branch office near home. Profitable streetcar operation hinged on retaining these off-peak riders, but the diffusion of the automobile and the dispersion of retailing, services, and doctors' offices made it increasingly difficult to do so. Such was the nature of oblique competition.

The Inability to Price Service Based on Cost

Streetcar companies were able to secure fare increases from state public utility and public service commissions after state legislatures and state courts intervened to relieve street railways of their original franchise obligations. These rulings increased streetcar fares during the 1920s, but did not substantially revise the industry's fare structure. Transit companies were still obliged to provide commuter discounts and expected to charge more for single-ride tickets. Thus the industry's fare structure continued to provide discounts for the riders most likely to ride during the peak when it was most costly to provide service, while charging more for patrons to ride at times of day that additional riders could have been served without additional cost. The industry's fare structure was popular with commuters, employers, and regulators, but it was counterproductive from a financial point of view. It encouraged ridership by those peak-hour riders that were most costly to serve and discouraged ridership by those off-peak riders that would have made the most productive contribution to the industry's bottom line. Regulation further compounded this problem: under regulatory order, streetcar companies had to extend suburban commute service during the 1920s to accommodate suburban growth, and their profit margins suffered accordingly.[38]

The Millstone of Suburban Service Obligations

From the beginning, the provision of suburban service was viewed as a burden by most street railways because flat fares virtually guaranteed that attenuating a route would reduce both productivity and the company's operating ratio. Many transit companies took on suburban service because it was the unavoidable quid pro quo that went along with urban operating rights that were highly profitable. Street railways owned by suburban developers were a different story: Their investment calculus was driven by their parent companies. Once on their own, many of these former developer-held companies had weak balance sheets that destined them for financial failure.

Predictably the diffusion of the automobile and the onset of automobile commuting increased suburban operating losses. At the same time, increasing traffic and congestion made suburban service more difficult to operate. When the track and streetcars in suburban service eventually wore out, trolleys were typically replaced with buses. Bus service was no less costly to operate, but it enabled streetcar companies to shed their regulatory obligation to pave the streets next to their tracks. It was also attractive because some bus manufacturers, such as GM Coach, were willing to extend credit to cash-starved transit companies.[39]

Increasing Conflict between Auto Traffic and Streetcar Operations

Streetcars operated on tracks that were located in the median of city streets where passengers boarded from raised islands adjacent to the tracks. This arrangement was both safe and serviceable until the advent of the automobile, fast-moving vehicles, and heavy traffic. With motorization, fast-moving vehicles became a safety hazard for transit riders accustomed to dashing across the street to catch the streetcar that was first in line. Increasingly heavy traffic also slowed streetcar operations, made streetcar turning movements more difficult, and increased the likelihood of accidents between cars and streetcars that could cause injury, damage, delay, or streetcar bunching. These were key factors in the eventual decision to convert from streetcars to bus service and curb loading.

For streetcar patrons, one result of increasing congestion was that service was slower and increasingly unreliable. Another result was increasing dissatisfaction with the streetcars that provided it. Eventually these many factors—and the industry's credit problems—forced the replacement of streetcars with buses. This was a hard decision, because without traffic congestion and traffic accidents, streetcars were more cost-effective on a life-cycle basis than the first generation of buses. But as bus technology evolved and motor vehicle traffic increased, the balance shifted in favor of bus substitution.[40] Both operating and financial factors were central to the eventual decision to convert from streetcar to bus operation. The factor that finally proved most decisive in tipping the balance in favor of buses was the need to replace aging streetcars. Replacement in kind was simply impossible in the many cities where streetcar companies were now strapped for cash and no longer able to qualify for commercial credit. Financing arrangements offered by bus manufacturers during the Depression proved decisive for many streetcar companies with damaged credit.

A Common Thread

The world that street railways served was changing much faster than their capacity for adaptation and adjustment. This was true of their financial circumstances, which were transformed by the onset of inflation. This was true of their wage scales, which had been transformed by wartime mediation. This was true of their competitive environment, which was transformed by installment credit, the tax deductibility of interest payments, and the rapid diffusion of the automobile and home ownership in the 1920s. This was true of their routes, which were attenuated by the development of successive generations of new suburbs. This was true of their passenger mix, which was transformed by the gradual loss of weekend, midday, and evening ridership, which began in the 1920s. This was true of their operating environment, which was transformed by the increasing congestion on the boulevards and thoroughfares that streetcars served. And this was also true of their work rules, which were codified in labor contracts that made service innovation and cost control more difficult. Each of these dynamics was already at work in the 1920s, and their cumulative impact explains why street railways could not make sufficient adjustments in service or methods to improve their balance sheets.

Taken together, these same factors explain why transit could no longer attract the investment necessary to compete more successfully—and why so many transit companies failed during the Depression and in the years immediately following World War II. It also explains why many streetcar companies accepted the inevitable and converted to bus operation. The transition to buses bought financial breathing room, but did not slow the pace of motorization or fully alleviate the operating problems associated with increasing traffic congestion.

Transit at the End of the 1920s

Despite the onset of disinvestment and the industry's persistent financial difficulties, transit continued to play an important role in urban transportation and an absolutely essential role in providing transportation to and from the downtowns of America's largest cities. Table 2.5 shows the share of trips still made by transit to and from the central business districts of 10 of the largest cities in the 1920s. As the table suggests, transit service remained absolutely essential, and this raises a significant question: If transit was vital to downtown, why were street railways largely unable to secure the public investment that would have been necessary to convert their most heavily patronized surface lines to subway or elevated operation?

The answer lies in downtown's ambivalence to public investment in mass transit, especially the kind of large-scale investment that would have been necessary to convert from streetcar to subway operation. In most cities, especially cities with populations of less than a million, the downtown commercial leadership viewed such taxes as unaffordable and opposed any form of property tax subsidy for mass transit. Many of the cities in table 2.5 considered building subways in the 1920s, but shied away from the proposition after assessing the cost. In some of these cases, downtown employers and merchants were agreeable to a property tax for subway development, but only if it were imposed citywide.

Only in New York were downtown property owners prepared to support a tripartite arrangement in which a citywide property tax and special taxes on properties proximate to subway stations were combined with lease payments by transit operators to finance subway construction. New York's revenue mix for subway development was explicitly based on tax equity and was seen as fair and square by operators and taxpayers, both citywide and those who were asked to pay for the benefits of proximity to a subway stop. No other city was able to reach consensus on the equities of a tripartite investment partnership. Of course, no

Table 2.5 *Share of downtown trips made by mass transit*

	Share	Year
New York	85.4%	1924
Philadelphia	79.2%	1928
Chicago	78.1%	1929
Boston	75.0%	1927
Pittsburgh	74.6%	1927
San Francisco	74.5%	1926
Detroit	66.2%	1930
St. Louis	65.4%	1930
Los Angeles	65.3%	1924
Baltimore	60.8%	1929

SOURCE: Transit share for New York reported in Regional Plan Association of New York, *Traffic and Parking Study*, 9; transit share for New York includes railroad commuters and pedestrians. All other transit shares reported in AERA, *Urban Transportation Problem*, 19.

other American city approached New York's population density or its importance as a corporate, banking, and finance center.

In most other cities, downtown property owners seem to have sought singular advantage without regard to the equities of cost and benefit. In these cities, transit tax measures that were supported by downtown typically failed because they were opposed by merchants and employers located elsewhere in the city. In this sense, the failure of early efforts to modernize transit and restore its competitiveness were a by-product of downtown's sense of entitlement—its belief that it was the epicenter of the city and that it deserved fast, frequent, and convenient transit service without having to contribute its fair share of the tax revenues needed to pay for it. Over the next 50 years, many of these downtowns would pay dearly for these outdated feelings of special entitlement.

In the next chapter, we shall see that Congress was better attuned to the politics of tax and service equity and thus successful in crafting a federal highway policy that would lead to the development of a highway system with the hierarchy of routes needed to serve local, metropolitan, intercity, and interstate traffic. Congress could do so because it was well attuned to the politics of interregional and interjurisdictional fairness. Big City downtowns were not. They were accustomed to the politics of metropolitan dominance and not yet attuned to the politics of interjurisdictional cooperation. Thus it was downtown's sense of importance and rightful entitlement, as much as any other factor, that explains why public financing for mass transit could not be secured before financial losses forced the abandonment of streetcar service, first during the late 1920s and the Depression and then on an accelerated basis after World War II.

Summing Up

1. The wave of initial private investment that launched the streetcar era was concentrated in the period 1887–1907. After 1907, capital investment in streetcar companies was discouraged by rising inflation and the conflict between a fixed fare and a fair return on invested capital in an inflationary economy.
2. The streetcar industry's financial position deteriorated sharply during World War I, due to wartime inflation and federally mandated wage increases for streetcar workers. Thereafter, street railways were considered an unattractive option for private investment. The industry's initial decline was attributable to financial rather than competitive difficulties.
3. The federal income tax and tax deductibility of interest income were both authorized in 1913. These spurred the development of the commercial credit industry—and with it, increases in the affordability of home and automobile ownership. These compounded the difficulty of transit's competitive position.
4. Further competitive problems arose with the rapid diffusion of the automobile in the 1920s. These included the loss of weekend and off-peak ridership, increasing imbalances between peak and off-peak load factors, conflict with local government over municipal demands for suburban service extension, and the increasing difficulty of operation on city streets that were clogged with motor vehicle traffic.
5. The peak year of streetcar ridership was 1923. By that year, every measure of the financial condition of street railways was downward trending. Bus companies and rapid transit lines continued to experience patronage growth, but the transit industry's aggregate ridership fell after 1926, three years before the Great Depression.
6. The decline in transit ridership was concentrated in smaller cities—those with a population of less than a million. The largest decline occurred in cities of 100,000 to 200,000. Even large cities of 500,000 to 1 million residents lost transit ridership during the 1920s. Transit ridership continued to grow in cities with a population of 1 million or more and relatively high densities. The largest cities in this class—New York, Chicago, Philadelphia, and Boston—remain today's predominant transit markets.
7. Streetcars continued to play a significant role in providing city transportation, but with the cessation of investment, transit was no longer able to play a pivotal role in the development of most cities. Our Milwaukee case study showed that role already being preempted by the automobile and highway development in the 1920s.
8. Public transportation continued, nonetheless, to play an essential and

sustaining role in serving the downtowns of the nation's largest cities. At the end of the 1920s, mass transit still accounted for at least 60 percent of all trips bound for downtown in the 10 largest cities. Cities with a population of 1 million or more were the only ones that deflected motorization and realized gains in transit ridership during the 1920s.

9. Despite transit's continuing dominance of transportation to and from downtown, the momentum of U.S. motorization had become irreversible by the end of the 1920s. In fact, most of the building blocks of mass motorization were already in place: the world's highest per capita GDP, established consumer demand for automobile ownership, mass production of cars and trucks, credit arrangements that enabled middle-class Americans to afford both a car and a home on the installment plan, the mortgage income tax deduction, suburban population growth, world leadership in oil refining and gasoline production, affordable fuels, well-paved roads in most cities, and the articulation of ambitious plans for future highway development.

THREE

The Great Depression and the New Deal: A Pivotal Epoch in U.S. Transportation History

The Great Depression was the most damaging recession in the world's modern economic history. The stock market crash of 1929 signaled the onset of the Depression in the United States, but its underlying causes were rooted in the impact of World War I on the global economy. Unemployment and economic hardships were the Depression's most significant initial effects. Its most significant long-term impact was the vastly larger role that the federal government came to play in American life. In the case of transportation, the Depression accelerated street railway disinvestment and abandonment. The Depression also engaged the states and the federal government in spending for urban highway construction. Perhaps most important, the New Deal's interest in toll roads emboldened the Bureau of Public Roads to advance its own first plan for what would become the interstate highway system.

Causes of the Great Depression

Most economic historians now agree that the Depression was an international event that was rooted in the economic stress and dislocation produced by World War I. Indeed, GDP in Australia, Canada, and Germany all peaked in 1928, a year before the U.S. stock market crash. U.S. GDP peaked the year of the 1929 crash, as did that of France, Italy, and the United Kingdom. Canada and the United States experienced the largest declines in GDP from peak to bottom, followed by Australia, Germany, and France. Recovery also took longer in Canada, the United States, and France. This suggests that the economic booms that occurred in the United States and Canada after World War I involved excesses that were unsustainable. This view is consistent with the current historical consensus, which interprets the Great Depression as a world event and World War I as "the shock that destabilized the world economy."[1]

Along with the postwar boom came significant increases in private debt. These included borrowing by farmers to finance the land acquisition and the cropland expansion necessary to satisfy export demand during and immediately after the war. Household borrowing to finance home and automobile ownership also surged in the 1920s, as did margin buying associated with the overheated stock market of the late 1920s. In turn, consumer spending and business investment slowed dramatically in the wake of the stock market crash, depriving the economy of the stimulus it needed to sustain growth. The overhang of excessive debt may also explain why recovery took longer in the United States and Canada. Heavy debt loads were punishing for farmers who added acreage. They were also punishing for investors who bought on margin late in the stock market's bull run, producing losses that inevitably destroyed confidence and curtailed buying power and personal expenditures after stocks crashed. Economist Martha Olney argues that debt incurred for automobile ownership was also important in prolonging the Depression because the auto loans of the 1920s entailed repossession in the event of default, an incentive for curtailing other household spending that could otherwise have buoyed the economy. Needless to say, the collapse of the stock market and later bank failures battered both national income and confidence, producing a sharp reduction in discretionary expenditures and in the velocity with which money circulated.[2]

In 1929 and 1930, the Hoover administration and the Federal Reserve Board seem to have misjudged the developing intensity of the Depression, and many economic historians agree that Herbert Hoover was unable to orchestrate recovery because the Federal Reserve Board continued to pursue tight-money policies.[3] In the 1932 election, Hoover was defeated by Franklin D. Roosevelt, whose New Deal pursued an expansionary monetary policy and a stimulative fiscal policy most often described as "priming the pump."

Public works expenditures were among the New Deal's chosen methods for pump priming. Most important for our story, highway projects within cities became a focus of the New Deal's efforts to create employment and stimulate the economy. Federal funding for state highway investment within cities was a transformational change in the financial context of urban transportation. It displaced local efforts to secure tax support for rapid transit and engaged the states in building urban highways and metropolitan expressways.[4]

The Social Activism of the New Deal

The extraordinary activism and interventionism that Congress was prepared to support during the New Deal can only be understood in the context of the economic and social impacts of the Great Depression. Economist Peter Temin has summarized the Depression's economic impacts as follows:

> Industrial production declined by 37 percent, prices by 33 percent, and real GNP by 30 percent. Nominal GNP therefore fell by over half. Unemployment rose to a peak of 25 percent and stayed above 15 percent for the rest of the 1930s. There were many idle economic resources in America for a full decade. Only with the advent of the Second World War did employment rise enough to absorb the full labor force.[5]

The broader social and political implications of the Great Depression have been well described by Robert Samuelson:

> The Great Depression of the thirties remains the most important economic event in American history. It caused enormous hardship for tens of millions of people and the failure of a large fraction of the nation's banks, businesses, and farms. It transformed national politics by vastly expanding [the federal] government, which was expected to stabilize the economy and prevent suffering. Democrats became the majority party. In 1929, the Republicans controlled the White House and Congress. By 1933, the Democrats had the presidency and, with huge margins, Congress. President Franklin Roosevelt's New Deal gave birth to the American version of the welfare state. Social Security, unemployment insurance, and federal family assistance all began in the thirties.[6]

In its first year, the New Deal relied on urban public works to provide temporary employment, generating criticism that the employment being generated was only make-work. In the years that followed, the New Deal systematized its public works expenditures, working with cities to build waterworks and with the states to build highways, both urban and rural. The New Deal also stimulated the development of single-family housing by providing government insurance for home mortgages. In effect, the New Deal's plan for economic recovery bet on an expansionary monetary policy, Social Security, highways, housing, and the growth of the automobile industry to restore confidence in the economy and pull the nation out of the Depression. Partial recovery had been achieved by 1940, but full recovery did not come until the United States entered World War II.

The Depression and Urban Transportation Investment

The Depression had a significant impact on American cities and their transit systems. Unemployment reduced transit ridership and compounded the financial problems of street railways, accelerating both their abandonment and their conversion to bus operation. The New Deal's antitrust policies had the same impact, accelerating the abandonment of streetcar lines by electric utility companies and hastening the conversion from streetcar to bus service. On the other hand, the New Deal provided federal funds to a handful of cities for transit capital improvements that were expected to generate jobs and stimulate the local economy. Most notable were the subway projects funded in Chicago, New York, and San Francisco.[7] Cincinnati also received New Deal funds to finance subway tunneling, but did not proceed with subway installation.

Of greater long-term significance, the Depression produced a permanent federal commitment to financing urban highway construction. This expansion of the federal role in highway development occurred in two stages—first through unemployment-relief projects and then through congressional authorization of federal funding for state highway improvements within cities.[8] By 1940, the Bureau of Public Roads and the state highway departments had also collaborated in the development of the first plan for the nationwide network of express highways that eventually became known as the interstate highway system.

Transit's Trends during the Great Depression

The peak of transit ridership for the years between the two world wars occurred in 1926. Thus the decline of transit ridership began three years before the stock market crash. This decline was largely attributable to the decline in streetcar ridership, which began in 1923. It also reflected the loss of weekend and evening ridership and the financial failure of marginal operations unable to recover from World War I and the onset of automotive competition. The ridership decline from 1926 to 1929 was small; the decline after 1929 was not. Ridership fell sharply in 1930 and then collapsed from 1931 through 1933. Ridership bottomed in 1933, the same year that the national unemployment rate peaked at 24.9 percent.[9] The financial shock and the prolonged decline in ridership that were produced by the Depression led to the extinction of streetcar service in some 250 cities. It also accelerated the substitution of buses for streetcars. Forced substitution became increasingly common during the Depression because physical obsolescence already plagued street railways. By 1932, contemporary appraisals indicated that the financial condition of most properties was "unstable . . . and becoming increasingly acute."[10]

Ironically, one of the New Deal's efforts to increase the number of jobs contributed to further declines in transit ridership. This was the Fair Labor Standards Act, which established the 40-hour workweek as the norm for workers paid on an hourly basis. Until the Depression, the six-day workweek had been the norm for industrial workers. The act's intention was to increase employment by spreading the hours of work among a larger number of workers. But its side effect was a further decline in transit's Saturday ridership and revenues.[11]

Through the Depression, most transit properties were unable to secure the commercial loans they would have needed to replace worn-out track and equipment because of preexisting credit problems. In fact, many had already been forced to invade depreciation reserves to pay current expenses. Under these extreme circumstances, some streetcar companies were only successful in replacing worn-out rolling stock thanks to "loans provided by stockholders endeavoring to avoid entire loss of their holdings through receivership or foreclosure."[12] Others replaced their streetcars with buses because streetcars were no longer a financially viable option. This was most typical in smaller cities and for larger operators with credit problems. Still others continued to operate worn-out equipment because they had no financially realistic alternatives. These operations, if they survived, reported extreme deterioration of both tracks and rolling stock by the end of World War II.

For streetcar companies in the largest markets, replacement with new streetcars would have been the investment alternative most likely to minimize life cycle costs.[13] But this option was ruled out for most properties because the Depression had forced them to invade depreciation reserves to pay current expenses. It was also ruled out for the many companies unable to secure credit. Thus most of the companies with aging streetcars and credit problems had no choice but to replace streetcars with buses, an option that was financially feasible because bus manufacturer General Motors was prepared to extend credit to secure sales.[14]

Table 3.1 shows the loss of transit ridership and the change in its modal composition between 1926 and 1940. Ridership—both bus and rail—peaked in 1926. Bus ridership continued to rise through 1929, but rail ridership declined marginally from 1926 to 1929. Major ridership losses were sustained by both

Table 3.1 *Changing modal mix of transit ridership, 1926–40*

	Total in billions	Rail* in billions	Bus in billions
1926 peak	17.2	15.2	2.0
1929 base	17.0	14.4	2.6
1933 trough	11.3	9.2	2.1
1940 close	13.1	8.3	4.8
% of change, base to close	−22.9	−42.4	+58.3

Source: *Historical Statistics of the United States,* "Public Transit Mileage, Equipment, and Passengers," Series Q 235–250, 721.
*Rail includes both streetcar and rapid transit.

bus and rail between 1929 and 1933, the depths of the Depression in terms of national unemployment. Streetcar and subway operations sustained larger proportional losses than buses, 36 percent versus 19 percent from peak to trough. Rail ridership declined another 10 percent from 1933 to 1940 due to abandonments and conversion from streetcar to bus operation. Bus ridership increased 129 percent during the same period, due to economic recovery and the ongoing conversion of streetcar lines to bus operation. As table 3.1 also shows, bus ridership increased 58.3 percent, while streetcar ridership declined 42.4 percent between 1929 and 1940.

As the divergent trends of bus and rail ridership confirm, the displacement and abandonment of streetcar service accelerated dramatically during the Great Depression. Transit's aggregate patronage declined from 17.0 million in 1929 to 13.1 million in 1940, a decline of 22.9 percent. This entire decline was attributable to the ridership losses of the streetcar industry. During the same period, buses increased their patronage 58 percent. The decline of streetcar ridership, the increase in bus ridership, and General Motors' increasing dominance in the realm of bus manufacturing attracted the attention of the Justice Department in the 1930s, raising questions about GM's market power and its impact on competition in the transit industry.

Transit and the New Deal's Antitrust Policies

The New Deal pursued aggressive antitrust policies that impinged on transit in two ways. One was to force electric utilities to divest themselves of their electric railway subsidiaries. The other was to pursue antitrust action against General Motors and other automotive industry companies for ownership linkages that were established with street railways that were subsequently converted to bus operation. In some cases, these were the same small-town transit properties that the Justice Department had forced electric utilities to divest. No contemporary attorney general would pursue such prosecutions, an indicator of the present political consensus on the social merit of joint economies of scale.

After the round of litigation against power companies that operated street-car lines, many of the now independent streetcar companies proved financially incapable of stand-alone operation. Some failed, and others were absorbed by transit holding companies or by holding companies financed by GM, Standard Oil, and Firestone Tire. The Justice Department began investigating the GM holding companies during the Depression, but did not seek an injunction against NCL until 1947. Arthur Saltzman has described the circumstances surrounding the antitrust action as follows:

> Moving into the vacuum created by the divestment of the power trusts, General Motors Corporation and several other motor bus, parts, and gasoline suppliers entered the transit business. They acquired stock in operating companies in exchange for capital and management services. This was similar to the techniques the power companies had used to electrify, and eventually control, the street railway companies. [Auto industry investment followed the same pattern.] For example, Yellow Bus and Coach, the bus-building subsidiary of GMC, had been the leader in sales since buses came on the scene in the 1920s. Its primary customers were the fleets controlled by its own subsidiary, the Hertz Omnibus Company.
>
> Hertz, originally in the taxi business, extended its control of operations to many different cities and converted all of them from streetcars to buses. Hertz also was linked to National City Lines (NCL), which, by 1946, had acquired some 46 transit systems. The acquisitions were financed almost entirely by stock shares sold to GMC and Firestone Tire and Rubber and, through [other NCL subsidiaries] to Phillips Petroleum, Standard Oil of California, and Mack Manufacturing Corporation. In 1947, the Department of Justice sought an injunction against NCL and its suppliers, accusing them of being in violation of antitrust laws. The case was ultimately settled 19 years later when GMC signed a consent decree that severely curtailed its involvement in transit operations. . . . At a time when large injections of capital were needed to replace the worn-out fleet of transit vehicles that had limped through the peak ridership of World War II, an application of federal statutes had once again deprived transit of a source of funds.[15]

We concur with Saltzman's characterization of GM's antitrust violation, but believe it also appropriate to present and critique the more controversial view advanced by Bradford C. Snell in *American Ground Transport*, a report prepared for the Senate Judiciary Committee. Snell's passionate indictment of General Motors has become something of an urban legend promulgated by filmmaker Michael Moore, among others.

Snell's Industrial Conspiracy Theory

In 1974, Snell, a staff member of the Senate Subcommittee on Antitrust and Monopoly, wrote a controversial report which argued that GM purchased street railways with the dual intention of converting them to diesel bus operation and eliminating a modal rival. Snell made his case as follows:

> [In 1932,] General Motors entered into bus production by acquiring Yellow Coach. One year later, it integrated forward into intercity bus operation by assisting in the formation of the Greyhound Corporation. Beginning in 1932, it undertook the direct operation and conversion of interurban electric railways and trolleybus systems into city bus operations. By the mid-1950s, it could lay claim to having played a prominent role in the complete replacement of electric street transportation with diesel buses. Due to their high cost of operation and slow speed on congested streets, however, these buses ultimately contributed to the collapse of several hundred public transit systems and to the diversion of hundreds of thousands of patrons to automobiles. In sum, the effect of General Motor's diversification program was threefold: substitution of buses for passenger trains, streetcars and trolley buses; monopolization of bus production; and diversion of [transit] riders to automobiles.[16]

This was the essence of Snell's indictment of General Motors. His most detailed "evidence" was presented in a case history of General Motor's acquisitions in Los Angeles. These included the Los Angeles Railway and the Pacific Electric's interurban streetcar lines connecting downtown Los Angeles with Glendale, Burbank, Pasadena, and San Bernardino.

> In 1938, General Motors and Standard Oil of California organized Pacific City Lines as an affiliate of NCL to motorize west coast electric railways. . . . In 1940, GM, Standard Oil, and Firestone assumed the active management of Pacific City Lines in order to supervise its California operations more directly. That year, PCL began to acquire and scrap portions of the $100 million Pacific Electric System including rail lines from Los Angeles to Glendale, Burbank, Pasadena, and San Bernardino. Subsequently, another GM affiliate [American City Lines] was financed by GM and Standard Oil to motorize downtown Los Angeles. American City Lines purchased the local system [Los Angeles Railways], scrapped its power transmission lines, ripped up the tracks, and placed GM diesel buses fueled by Standard Oil on the Los Angeles' crowded streets. In sum, GM and its auto-industrial allies severed Los Angeles' regional rail links and then motorized its downtown heart.[17]

Parts of Snell's case history are accurate: a City Lines subsidiary (Metropolitan Coach Lines) acquired part of the Pacific Electric in 1940, and PCL acquired the Los Angeles Railway, which provided streetcar service in central Los Angeles.[18] Both the interurban and urban lines were financially distressed at the time of their acquisition.

The Pacific Electric was an interurban electric railroad that was initially financed and built by Henry Huntington, whose family had played a key role in the development of the Southern Pacific Railroad. Huntington's investment was largely premised on the promotion of suburban development, and his interest in the interurban lines flagged after their initial deployment was accomplished. The Pacific Electric was eventually acquired by the Southern Pacific, a steam railroad engaged in freight operation. The SP converted most of the Pacific Electric's track to freight service and integrated it with its own freight operations. The remaining passenger service was allowed to degrade. Its ridership began to decline in 1924, and from 1924 to 1939 the SP curtailed the Pacific Electric's service by almost 50 percent. Local authorities in Los Angeles considered public acquisition of the PE's remaining passenger services in 1925, but public reaction to the idea was vehement and antagonistic because the cost of public acquisition was viewed as a "giveaway" to the SP, which had allowed the condition of the Pacific Electric to deteriorate. Problems reported to the California Railroad Commission included "noisy operation, jerky operation, uncomfortable seats, rough roadbed, leaking roofs, dirty windows, unclean car interiors, slow speeds, uneven acceleration, poor interior lighting, dilapidated station facilities, and unsatisfactory fares."[19]

The PE's passenger services—those which were eventually acquired by Metropolitan Coach—teetered on the edge of bankruptcy during the 1930s. SP eventually sold these services to City Lines because they were a financially ailing operation that no longer enjoyed synergies with the rest of the Pacific Electric after its conversion to freight operation. Indeed, the sales agreement enabled the SP to retain the PE's rights-of-way for freight operation after the acquired lines were converted to bus operation. City Lines' acquisition of the Pacific Electric in 1940 and its subsequent conversion to bus operation were improvements over the status quo of declining ridership and deteriorating service that was occurring under SP ownership and management. In fact, commentary in the trade press and in local magazines suggests that City Lines' bus operation was a significant improvement.[20]

The second Los Angeles acquisition made by a GM affiliate was the Los Angeles Railway, which operated streetcar lines located in central and downtown Los Angeles. Like the Pacific Electric, its ridership had already peaked in 1924, and its rolling stock was in an advanced state of disrepair by the end of the Depression.[21] Thus the L.A. Railway can also be described as a failing property at the time of its acquisition by PCL/Metropolitan Coach. In these circumstances, it is unlikely that any other investment group would have made a better offer or proposed a substantially different revitalization strategy. Public ownership and operation would have offered a better option, but no such option was in prospect, much less on the table.

Contrary to Snell's assertion, there were substantial advantages for Los Angeles and its transit riders that accrued from conversion to bus service. Bus operation permitted curb loading, a significant safety improvement for passengers who had previously been required to board streetcars from a raised island in the median of Los Angeles' congested streets. Conversion to trolleybus operation would have been preferable as a way to reduce street noise and fumes, but it also would have been more costly than conversion to diesel. GM vendored both diesel and electric-trolley buses, so it cannot be assumed, a priori, as Snell did, that GM's intention was "dieselization." GM credit was clearly salutary for both of the failing rail operations, and the infusion of GM capital stabilized these investment-starved operations, at least temporarily. In other words, it appears that Snell did not dig deeply enough to reach an informed appraisal of the economic condition of the streetcar industry as a whole or the physical and financial condition of the properties in Los Angeles at the time they were acquired by City Lines. Nor was Snell prepared to give City Lines credit for the improvements in service that resulted from the change in ownership and consequent reinvestment.

The point of this analysis is not the absolution of General Motors but rather a matter of historical accuracy: transit's decline was not the result of an industrial conspiracy or anticompetitive behavior; it was the result of a prolonged process of financial failure under private ownership. The substitution of buses did not damage the companies that GM acquired. Quite the contrary, the line of credit provided by National City Lines enabled them to purchase new buses and thus prolonged their ability to provide public transportation under private ownership. In fact, City Lines earned a reputation as a turnaround specialist that was successful in maintaining service and sustaining the profitability of transit properties that had been headed for bankruptcy or abandonment. For example, the editors of *Mass Transportation*, a trade journal for transit operators, gave National City Lines frequent kudos for its role in reinvigorating failing properties in the early 1950s.

But new equipment alone was insufficient to resolve transit's underlying financial problems: Most transit properties could no longer sustain service of high quality under private ownership without public subsidy because it now had to share congested street space with the automobile and because it had already lost so many of its most valuable customers. Those, of course, were the riders who paid a standard fare to ride in midday hours or on the weekends. New buses helped, but they alone were insufficient to restore transit companies to a stable competitive footing on a long-term basis. Stabilization would have required public subsidy, the renegotiation of work hours and work rules, a new fare structure, and more transit-friendly traffic engineering. With the exception of reinvestment and operating subsidy, these prerequisites of a robust recovery have not been forthcoming in most cities, not even under public ownership.

So Why Did Streetcar, Bus, and Rapid Transit Ridership Decline?

Since the publication of *American Ground Transport* in 1974, Snell's accusations have merged and fused with the vocal conviction of many urbanists that the decline of public transportation was a by-product of the interstate highway program. Together, these assertions have contributed to the often-repeated conviction that mass transit was a healthy industry until it was victimized by predatory competition and undermined by unbalanced public policy. A historically accurate account would emphasize that street railways had been a distressed industry since World War I—in part because of fixed fares, wartime inflation, and the rulings of the War Labor Board, in part because they could no longer secure credit for reinvestment on favorable terms. Fare increases were eventually authorized in the 1920s, but did not produce financial stability for streetcar companies due to the rapid diffusion of the automobile and transit's resulting loss of weekend and off-peak patronage. Aggregate U.S. streetcar ridership declined steadily after 1923, and the industry's financial position was further damaged by the rigors of the Depression.

The Depression forced streetcar companies into survival-mode decision making that entailed replacing streetcars with buses. Early on, such replacement occurred in smaller cities where bus operation was the only financially feasible option for ensuring the survival of transit service. In larger cities, conversion to bus operation occurred somewhat later, but had the same character: it was a survival strategy to which streetcar companies turned after wearing out their streetcars and exhausting their financial options. Unable to secure credit, many smaller streetcar companies simply went out of business or sold their operating rights to bus companies. Others turned to City Lines for credit and new equipment. This was the role that City Lines played in Los Angeles: it stepped in with the credit necessary to finance modernization. General Motors and City Lines benefited, and so did their riders and host cities.

GM, City Lines, and the streetcar companies established a sole-source supplier relationship, and a court eventually determined that this was a technical violation of U.S. antitrust law. The remedy was a nominal fine and forced divestiture. But divestiture did not improve the financial position of the transit companies. Quite the contrary, affiliation with City Lines had offered private operators with damaged credit a last chance at reinvestment. Indeed, NCL/PCL properties had developed a reputation for offering better service than comparable operations elsewhere. In other words, affiliation with GM/PCL was a financially pragmatic arrangement that enabled financially troubled transit properties to stay in business—to their advantage and to the advantage of their riders and host cities.

Following World War II, many big city mayors faced a similarly thorny problem. They would have welcomed a balanced highway and transit program that could provide federal funding for both express highways and rapid transit, but the interstate offered a substantial part of the investment program that the cities needed—and a substantial part was better than none. In 1956, the mayors fought for their fair share of the highway program and came back for the lion's share of federal transit funding in 1964.

The New Deal and Urban Highway Investment

Like the Depression that birthed it, the New Deal was a transformational event in urban transportation history. It engaged the federal government in financing metropolitan highways and engaged the state highway departments in building them. The New Deal also incubated the first plans for construction of the interstate highway system. Full financing for the interstate was not authorized until 1956, but federal financing for urban highway construction was a permanent legacy of the New Deal. No similarly lasting arrangements were made for financing public transportation, largely because most transit service was, at that time, still operated by private companies on a for-profit basis. The New Deal did provide a few cities with onetime grants for urban subway construction, but at the time Congress made no long-term arrangements for funding urban transit and urban highways on a symmetric basis, because most transit systems were expected to remain investor-owned and commercially financed. This proved an unrealistic assumption but one that was not revised until the 1960s.

Street and Highway Finance before the Great Depression

The expansion of the federal government that came with the New Deal does not seem extraordinary from the perspective of the twenty-first century, but it was a major departure from the institutional roles and fiscal relationships that had prevailed before the Depression. The first federal funding for urban highway improvement was authorized by the National Industrial Recovery Act of 1933, an omnibus spending bill. Until 1933, federal highway funds had been reserved for rural road construction.[22] The same held for state highway programs: their sphere of activity had been exclusively rural. Cities and even small towns were left to design and build their own streets and thoroughfares because they could generate the property tax revenues to do so. Rural counties could generate sufficient property tax revenues to gravel their roads, but building modern paved roads capable of accommodating the speed and volume of traffic characteristic of the 1920s and 1930s was a very different matter. Equipped with state fuel taxes and subventions from the federal highway program, the state highway departments filled this void. After 1916, the most heavily traveled rural roads were graded, graveled, and maintained by the state highway departments. Over the years, these roads were paved and widened as traffic increased.

The evolution of responsibility for highway improvement was a gradual one. In the early 1900s, cities were the "haves" of both good roads and the revenues needed for road improvement, and rural areas were the "have-nots." Federal funding for rural highway improvement was first authorized by Congress in 1912. In these earliest years, the federal road program was lodged in the post office, and its expenditures were focused on improving those roads that were used for rural mail delivery.[23] That arrangement was modified in 1916, and the newly named Bureau of Public Roads [now the Federal Highway Administration] was next lodged in the Department of Agriculture. Federal funds continued to be reserved for the exclusive purpose of rural construction. After 1916, the federal program placed increasing emphasis on orderly investment and the professionalization of highway engineering and highway administration.

The 1916 act required the states to create highway departments and designate the specific routes of a state highway system (not more than 7 percent of a state's total road mileage) as a precondition for receiving federal funds. It also required that three-sevenths of each state's road mileage consist of routes of "interstate character."[24] This requirement concentrated state investment and, in doing so, produced longer lasting improvement in the quality of the nation's primary highways.

The 1921 act required each of the then 48 states to identify the constituent routes of a state highway system that accounted for no more than 7 percent of a state's highway mileage. It also limited federal expenditure to routes important enough to be incorporated in the 7 percent system—an important efficiency measure that contributed to the development of a connected network of highways under the jurisdiction of strong highway departments.[25] With this addition, most of the essential elements of a national road building policy had been crafted and voted into law by 1921. No further modifications of any great significance occurred until the Great Depression.

The administrative precepts of federal highway policy as they had evolved up to the Great Depression can be described as follows:

- The federal government should not build and maintain highways of its own, but should assist the states and their highway departments in financing the development of a connected network of roads that can serve the 48 states.
- Cities have a sufficient tax base to finance street and road construction within their borders, but rural areas do not. Federal aid for highways should therefore be reserved for the construction of those primary high-

ways that connect major cities and those secondary highways that connect county seats. More specifically, federal funding should be reserved for the construction of the rural segments of intercity highways and intercounty roads.

- Federal funds should be provided only to those states that establish a state highway department with the full authority necessary to administer federal funds efficiently and to maintain state highways effectively.
- To ensure highway improvement of lasting value, federal aid should be concentrated on a limited mileage of principal highways. This limited system should offer the continuity to serve as a national highway system, but should not exceed 7 percent of the nation's rural highway mileage.
- The federal government and the states should share the expense of improving those roads that constitute the federal-aid highway system, with the federal government paying a larger share of the expense for those highways that serve interregional and interstate traffic. The federal match rate should be 70 percent for primary highways and 50 percent for secondary highways.
- Federal aid should be apportioned to the states by a formula that reflects each state's share of the nation's population, area and highway mileage.[26]

As this itemization suggests, federal highway policy before the Depression was premised on the development of a long-term partnership between the states and the federal government, a partnership based on shared ownership of the highway program and shared responsibility for its success. The policies that resulted reflected both the felt urgency of trunk-line highway improvement and the dominance of rural legislators in Congress and most state legislatures. The federal highway program's initial emphasis on rural construction is clearly evident in the explicit restriction on the use of federal funds within urban areas. Both the states and Congress bought into this rural partnership, and both contributed funds to finance the highways that were built. But with the onset of the Great Depression, the restriction on the use of federal funds in urban areas began to rub hard.

The Evolution of Highway Policy during the Depression

By the 1920s, funding for state highway programs was typically derived from fuel taxes, motor vehicle registration fees, and state bonds. Through 1931, federal funding for highways was derived from general revenues sources, not from fuel taxes.[27] The clear implication is that urban taxpayers and urban motorists were cross-subsidizing the construction of rural highways in two ways—through the income and excise taxes they paid to the federal government and through the income taxes, gasoline taxes, and vehicle registration fees they paid to state governments. These fiscal details of the highway program became salient issues as the cities struggled to cope with high levels of unemployment and property tax delinquency during the Depression. In this new context, it now mattered a great deal that the cities were not receiving federal funding for highway construction and that city taxpayers were cross-subsidizing the construction of rural highways with the income and gasoline taxes they paid. In turn, the 1932 election of Democrat Franklin Roosevelt to the presidency and a Democratic majority in Congress led to a significant shift in federal highway policy.

Under New Deal auspices, federal highway policy evolved in five significant ways. First, the New Deal majority in Congress endorsed the basic proposition that the federal government should finance urban road projects and authorized funding for them in the National Industrial Recovery Act of 1933. In turn, the Hayden Cartwright Act of 1934 made urban funding a permanent feature of the federal highway program. Second, the Bureau of Public Roads and the State Highway Departments steered substantial funding into the construction of divided highways within cities. Third, the provisional agencies of the New Deal brokered the funding of toll roads and toll bridges and a number of urban parkways and expressways. And fourth, but ultimately most important, the New Deal incubated and endorsed a first generation of plans for the highway network that eventually became known as the interstate highway system. This did not lead to urban expressway development on any large scale during the Depression, but it did lead to the construction of a first generation of divided highways in American cities—highways that can be accurately described as an intermediate step between urban thoroughfares and urban expressways.

Urban Highway Development before the New Deal

Property taxes provided the primary source of revenue for urban road construction before the Depression. Larger cities with a robust property tax base were able to develop paved street networks that included both major thoroughfares and neighborhood streets. Counties typically shared state gas tax collections and used these subventions in combination with property taxes to pay for the construction and maintenance of local roads in unincorporated areas. The local streets necessary to serve outlying subdivisions were typically installed by developers and sometimes financed by special assessment districts with permanent responsibility for street maintenance.

The urban roads that most planners viewed as the pinnacle of excellence in urban road design included Chicago's Lake Shore Drive and the parkways that had opened New York's Westchester County for development as a commuter suburb. Most heralded of these parkways was the Bronx River Parkway: It established a de facto aesthetic standard for the design and development of suburban parkways.

The ultimate expression of this school of suburban roadway planning was the parkway plan prepared by the privately funded Regional Plan Association of New York. This 1928 plan proposed a regional network of parkways for the New York metropolitan area that included radial commuter routes to Manhattan and beltline parkways that would allow motorists to circumnavigate New York City.

New York's national leadership in parkway development and its long-standing leadership in subway development had significant national implications because New York's governor, Franklin D. Roosevelt, defeated incumbent president Herbert Hoover in the 1932 race for the presidency. In turn, Roosevelt recruited engineers and planners who had been actively involved in metropolitan parkway planning to serve in Washington during the New Deal. They, in turn, helped diffuse New York's concept of park and parkway development to other metropolitan areas under the auspices of the New Deal. Los Angeles, for example, was an early and aggressive imitator. In the process of this diffusion, comprehensive plans for the development of both parks and parkways evolved into utilitarian plans for expressways that were eventually built by the state highway departments in the nation's largest metropolitan areas. But that is getting ahead of our story.

Next Steps in the Evolution of Federal Highway Policy

The first federal funding for urban highway construction was made available under the National Industrial Recovery Act of 1933.[28] This New Deal legislation authorized the expenditure of federal funds on urban thoroughfares that provided the connecting urban extensions of state highways within city limits. Additional rural projects were also made eligible for federal funds, even if the projects were not on a designated primary or secondary route. Some of these funds were spent to create temporary employment on an emergency basis—expenditures that the New Deal's critics labeled "make-work."

The most important outcome of the 1933 act was that it engaged the federal government and the state highway departments in the financing and construction of urban thoroughfares. This created the framework for eventual federal funding of metropolitan freeway development. The Hayden-Cartwright Act of 1934 reconciled the 1933 legislation with the traditions of the federal-aid highway program by guaranteeing that rural secondary roads would continue to receive 25 percent of federal subventions for highways. Another 25 percent was set aside for comparable urban projects, and 50 percent was reserved for projects on the primary system.[29] These parities established a new and durable congressional consensus in favor of federal funding on a formula basis for both urban and rural highway improvement. Such consensus could be achieved because Congress authorized the first federal gas tax in 1932 and increased that tax to 1.3 cents in 1933. The resulting gasoline tax collections were the highest in U.S. history in terms of constant dollars and produced a revenue stream sufficient to finance urban projects without reneging on rural commitments or preempting other domestic priorities.[30]

The New Deal also created a suite of provisional agencies to finance and manage its emergency public works programs. These included the Civil Works Administration, the Public Works Administration, and the Works Progress Administration. All provided localities with direct federal funding for public works. Notable projects that were eventually funded by these temporary agencies included the Pennsylvania Turnpike, the Golden Gate Bridge, new bridges that connected Manhattan with New Jersey and the Bronx, the Arroyo Seco Parkway in Los Angeles, the Merritt Parkway from New York to Connecticut, and many of the expressways that Robert Moses built in New York City and its surrounding suburbs. Clearly, the New Deal's provisional agencies were willing and able to finance projects that were more ambitious than the roads that had been built under the auspices of the federal aid highway program.

The New Deal agencies that financed these showcase projects functioned like a provisional government, parallel and adjunctive to the established Washington bureaucracy. They were staffed by planners and administrators recruited from New York, New England, and Chicago—veterans of parkway planning in New York and Massachusetts, regionalists who had cut their teeth with the Regional Plan Association of New York, alumni of the Regional Planning Department of Harvard, engineers from the New York Port Authority, and investment bankers recruited from Wall Street. Many of these new hands had served Roosevelt when he was governor of New York, and they had come to Washington with Roosevelt when he was elected president. With this infusion of planning and finance experts, the New Deal proved open to planning on a grand scale, and its temporary agencies gave national impetus to the development of suburban parkways, urban expressways, toll roads, and toll bridges. Additional impetus came from the cities themselves, especially New York and Los Angeles, and from select urban states, especially California, New York, New Jersey, and Illinois.

As this discussion suggests, Washington housed two governments during the New Deal—one composed of permanent departments, the other composed of temporary agencies. The temporary agencies dominated the field of public works expenditure during the early years of the New Deal that gave initial impetus to federal funding of turnpikes, toll bridges, metropolitan parkways, and urban subways. The Bureau of Public Roads returned to the fore with its plan for the development of an interregional highway system, the name first given to the future interstate system.

The Bureau of Public Roads' Initial Role in Urban Highway Development

The Bureau's early involvement in urban highway development was understandably cautious and tentative. Many of its engineers lacked urban experience, and the bureau initially lacked urban data and a clear sense of urban mission. Many of the projects built within cities under the auspices of the National Industrial Recovery Act were make-work projects conceived with an emphasis on employment rather than transportation. After a round of intense consultations with their counterparts in the highway departments of the leading urban-industrial states, the Bureau launched a major effort to define an urban highway program that could produce improvements that were more useful and permanent. Guided by the Hayden-Cartwright Act, the Bureau focused on upgrading those urban arterials that provided the connecting extension of the state highway system within towns, cities, and metropolitan areas. One goal was to replace make-work with systematic highway improvement. Another was to increase the speed and safety with which traffic could move within and through metropolitan areas.

Thus the focus of the federal program within cities evolved quickly from make-work to a systematic and focused effort to build a next generation of arterial highways that could serve as the trans-city connections of the state highway systems, an urban application of the "limited system" doctrine that had been the centerpiece of the federal government's rural highway policy. Over the next 60 years, building a new tier of urban highways—first as divided highways, then as divided highways with partial access control, and then as full freeways— became the federal highway program's appointed mission within cities.

What was accomplished during the New Deal was the construction of a relatively small initial mileage of divided highways in the metropolitan areas of New York, California, New Jersey, Illinois, Michigan, Massachusetts, Ohio, Louisiana, Minnesota, and Pennsylvania. This work continued during World War II with an emphasis on routes essential to the war effort. After World War II, the Bureau encouraged the states to build divided highways with at least partial access control. The divided highways of the first generation had been built at grade, and none had full access control. After World War II, expressway development in New York and California began to showcase the advantages of grade separation and access control, and this built a congressional constituency for the interstate highway system and for the construction of urban freeways and expressways.[31] Seen in a metropolitan context, this same progression entailed the evolution from boulevards and thoroughfares to parkways and then expressways and freeways.

From Parkways to Expressways

The first generation of American parkways was designed by landscape architects, whereas the second generation was designed by engineers. These second-generation facilities marked an important middle stage in the evolution of parkways into expressways. Parkways of this transitional genre included the Merritt Parkway in Connecticut and the connecting Bronx River Parkway in Westchester County just outside New York City. These parkways are widely viewed as the heyday of the genre for their preservation of natural vegetation and their respect for the contours of the landscape they traversed.

The Arroyo Seco Parkway, which linked Pasadena and Los Angeles, was a parkway of the transitional generation that followed. It was proposed by the Los Angeles County Planning Commission, financed by the New Deal and the California Highway Commission, and built by the California Division of Highways. It can accurately be described as the last parkway built in Los Angeles or as the first expressway. It had characteristics of both. Heinz Heckeroth, an engineer who served with both the City of Los Angeles and the state, was involved in both the design of the Arroyo Seco and its later evaluation. He remembers the experience vividly:

> You started with the arterial mentality, with curbs and cross-traffic and all of the other features of an arterial, and converted it to a free-flowing freeway concept with access control and on-and-off ramps. In the early freeways [such as the Arroyo Seco], you only deal with it as a super-arterial, grade-separated. You didn't have the experience in the traffic engineering sense of how it would operate with the curvature you put in, and the profile you put in, and super-elevation you used. You had to have experience in operation before you could visualize the improvements you could make in its operational characteristics. The Arroyo Seco provided that kind of experience.
>
> During [World War II], the construction program was on hold, and we gained experience seeing how cars operated on the Arroyo Seco and asking drivers what their reaction was. . . . The concept grew as we experienced how people drove on freeways. Acceleration, deceleration, lane configuration, length of storage, width of ramps—those things all grew.[32]

The most important result of this scaling up from parkway to expressway to freeway was safer operation. Another result was the ability to carry more traffic at higher speeds. But expressways were larger facilities that had a more industrial look and feel and were harder to weave into the fabric of a city. The transition in design orientation from boulevard to parkway to expressway to freeway accompanied the transition in planning and design responsibility from cities to county planning commissions to state highway departments. The transition from parkway to expressway began during the New Deal and, with New York and California serving as proving grounds, was essentially complete by the time Congress fully authorized the interstate highway program in 1956.

After 1956, expressway planning was driven by the geometric design standards of the interstate system and reflected little residual influence of the parkway tradition. Instead, the world's most advanced industrial nation set about building express highways that were geometric rather than architectural in design inspiration. Less verdant but far more geometrically sophisticated, freeways were substantially safer to drive than the parkways they displaced and could carry much more traffic over longer distances more quickly.

The New Deal and Interregional Highways

Despite early motorization, the United States was a relative latecomer to the construction of a national network of express highways—highways built with the wide lanes, geometrically designed curves, and the full access control needed to accommodate the high-speed movement of motor vehicles over long distances between cities. International leadership in this domain of highway development belonged to Germany. Italy's Autostrada was the world's first express highway, but for many reasons it was not the success that was expected. Germany's Autobahn was the second, and it embodied a major advance in the art and science of geometric design.[33]

The Bureau of Public Road's first focus on express highway planning came in the context of German rearmament in the mid-1930s. In 1935, the Bureau of Public Roads and the War Department initiated a joint study of the highway requirements of the national defense, while the Bureau and the state highway departments joined forces to identify highways essential for moving armaments and food supplies in case of war.[34] The issue was important because both trucking and the railroads had performed poorly under the logistical stresses of World War I. It was an urgent issue because German rearmament was occurring rapidly and the U.S. intelligence services were concerned that the construction of the Autobahn and German rearmament might be linked to a plan for blitzkrieg warfare. The first months of World War II suggest that this intelligence was accurate.

In any event, the U.S. military command asked the Bureau of Public Roads to assess the logistical implications of the German system as it was being built.

Subsequently, a delegation of engineers from the Bureau and the state highway departments visited Germany and toured the German road system. They found a highway network that had been engineered to accommodate very high speed travel between cities. All of its component geometric features were designed for safe travel at speeds well in excess of 75 mph.[35] The tour of the Autobahn was an eye-opener for the Bureau's leadership and for the state highway engineers who accompanied them to Germany. Most important, the Autobahn helped crystallize their thinking about express highways in the United States. In the process, the Autobahn became part model, part countermodel for the development of express highways in America.

The Autobahn was an interregional highways system designed to skirt German metropolitan areas and provide very high speed service between them; they relied on conventional highways for their urban connections. This is readily understandable when placed in historical context: Germany had achieved a motorization level of only 25 motor vehicles per 1,000 population by 1936. Thus its cities remained the domain of streetcars, buses, and walking. Urban traffic would have been nowhere near sufficient to justify urban expressway construction. In the United States, on the other hand, with its 1936 motorization level of 220 per 1,000 population, initial motorization was well advanced and urban traffic congestion had already become problematic during the boom years of the 1920s.

Focusing on the engineering of the Autobahn, the Bureau's engineers admired the German achievement. But focusing on the differences between the United States and Germany, the Bureau's engineers and the highway departments agreed that what the United States needed was a less aggressively engineered highway network that could seamlessly provide express service both within and between U.S. metropolitan areas.[36] This, of course, was the planning concept that had begun to inform metropolitan highway planning in New York and Los Angeles in the 1930s, and it became the design concept endorsed by the Bureau of Public Roads in *Toll Roads and Free Roads*, which concluded that "construction of the trans-city connections of the main rural highways and other express routes into the center of the cities ranks first on the list of highway projects worthy of consideration by the Congress."[37]

By the time *Toll Roads and Free Roads* was published in 1939, the construction of a first-generation toll road was nearly complete in Pennsylvania, and parkways with expressway characteristics were being built in California and New York. In fact, the initial impetus for the construction of express highways in the United States came from the toll road movement and was incubated by the provisional agencies of the New Deal. The Pennsylvania Turnpike was the first example of a modern express highway to be built in the United States and also the first modern example of a toll road. To facilitate its construction, the New

Deal bought its bonds and brokered them in the bond market. U.S. leadership in the construction of toll bridges was, likewise, advanced by the New Deal's involvement in purchasing and brokering their bonds. In turn, these bridges were built with sufficient lane capacity to match up with a next generation of express highways. Similar funding arrangements enabled construction of the first units of the toll-financed thruways that eventually extended from Chicago to Philadelphia and New York and then north to Boston.[38]

Toll Roads or Free Roads?

The public's favorable response to the Pennsylvania Turnpike stimulated White House interest in the feasibility of a national program of toll road development. In 1937, President Roosevelt personally requested a study of a national network of transcontinental toll roads, three east/west, three north/south. Congress requested a similar toll road study in 1938. Thus, with the cooperation of the states, the Bureau conducted a nationwide planning survey designed to assess the feasibility of toll roads in the United States. Simultaneously, the Bureau articulated and evaluated its own preferred alternative: accelerated development of the nation's most heavily traveled primary highways into a comprehensive network of interregional highways that included connecting expressways within metropolitan areas. This was the first iteration in the development of a plan for a national system of interregional highways—the network of express highways that would eventually become the interstate system. This first iteration plan was published in 1939 as a part of *Toll Roads and Free Roads*. It described the future interstates as "Interregional Highways" and concluded that their urban extensions should be designed to provide express service within metropolitan areas, a conclusion specifically endorsed by Roosevelt himself.[39]

Addressing the question of toll financing, the Bureau's 1939 report concluded that it would not be feasible to develop a financially "sound federal policy for the construction of a system of transcontinental superhighways, traversing the entire extent of the United States from east to west and from north to south . . . on the expectation that the costs of constructing and operating such a system would be recoverable . . . from direct tolls collected from the users."[40] *Toll Roads and Free Roads* proceeded to specify a financially feasible alternative more consistent with its traditional mission: a cooperative state-federal effort to build a nationwide network of divided highways designed to connect the nation's major cities and provide express service within them.

On first inspection, the Bureau's 1939 plan seemed straightforward. It declared that the states should design and build highways that can provide express service for both passenger cars and commercial vehicles both within and between metropolitan areas. But such a policy was proposed well in advance of the then-prevailing state of the art in most states. At the time it was proposed, state highway departments had built less than 100 miles of divided highway within cities, and only a handful of states had secured the legal authority necessary to build urban highways of limited-access design, beginning with Rhode Island in 1937; by 1943, only 17 had done so.[41] Thus the 1939 plan marked a significant departure from business as usual for the federal-aid highway program. As the Bureau's chief engineer put it just a year before the Bureau's new plan was released, "The pressure has constantly been for more miles of usable road, rather than a very limited mileage of super-service highways."[42]

Before *Toll Roads and Free Roads* was published, the states had determined which highways should be included in the federal aid system. In 1939, the Bureau made its own appraisal of which routes would be appropriate for inclusion in the new "interregional highway system." This study was based on traffic data collected by the states for the toll roads study. This data provided a profile of the traffic moving on state highways across the nation. It showed which routes carried the heaviest traffic, and it showed that traffic volumes swelled as state highways approached cities, demonstrating that most "rural" traffic was, in fact, traffic moving between cities or from the countryside to a metropolitan area. Armed with this data, the Bureau was now certain of its appropriate urban mission: it should oversee the staged construction of a national system of interregional highways that included connecting routes within cities.

> Specifically, the needed improvements include the reduction of excessive curvature, the flattening of heavy grades, an opening of longer site distances, a general widening of pavement lanes, a construction of additional lanes and separation of opposing traffic where increased volume requires, and possibly also for the accommodation of slow vehicles on the heavier grades; the separation of grades at many railroad and highway intersections, and installation of protective cross traffic controls at others; the abatement of dangerous roadside conditions of all sorts; and a substantial improvement in the general directness of alignment between major metropolitan areas.[43]

But, most important, the 1939 plan declared that the construction of the trans-city connections of the main rural highways and other express routes into the center of the cities ranked first in the list of highway projects worthy of consideration by the Congress.[44] This was a significant departure from the initial priorities of the federal highway program, but one consistent with the traffic studies the Bureau performed for *Toll Roads and Free Roads*. Those studies gave the Bureau increasing confidence about the appropriate strategy for staging the development of expressways and freeways in metropolitan areas: Excess right-of-way should be acquired at the time of initial land purchase; divided highways should be built first and eventually succeeded by expressways with full grade separation.[45] In other words, the Bureau was endorsing national emulation of the ambitious construction programs that were under way in New York, New Jersey, and California, financed in part by the New Deal's provisional agencies. But it was also delivering a gentle critique of the minimal rights-of-way on which many of these new facilities were being built and making a strong case for urban highways of grade-separated design.

Congress received the 1939 plan, seems to have been largely pleased that the Bureau's report had scuttled the concept of toll financing, but did not hold hearings or conduct a focused review of the new direction in highway development that the Bureau was proposing. Nor was there any explicit endorsement of the Bureau's 1939 appraisal that the construction of express routes in cities should rank first in the list of highways worthy of congressional consideration. The Bureau, on the other hand, quickly incorporated the plan's basic precepts into its own policies and procedures. Thereafter, the Bureau encouraged the state highway departments to build highways of higher design and urged urban-industrial states to give higher priority to the construction of divided highways.[46] In turn, the Defense Highway Acts, which Congress approved in 1941 and 1943, included the first funding for projects on the interregional system, giving highest priority to those of military significance.

A second plan for interregional highways was prepared in 1944 in anticipation that a plan for postwar highway development should be ready and available to stimulate the economy in the aftermath of World War II. The Bureau's 1944 plan, Interregional Highways, argued that urban interstate projects should incorporate limited access design. Congress watered down the Bureau's recommendation in the process of including it in the Federal-Aid Highway Act of 1944. The 1944 act made "interstate" projects eligible to compete for federal funding, but did not specifically earmark funding for the interregional highway system as a system.[47] That would not occur until 1956. But clearly both the Bureau and the president made strong first commitments to the interstate in 1939 and again in 1944.

The Significance of the 1939 and 1944 Plans

Publication of Toll Roads and Free Roads in 1939 marked the first time that the Bureau of Public Roads had singled out a discrete tier of highways for designation as a system of national importance. In 1944, Interregional Highways proposed minor modifications to the system proposed in 1939, emphasizing the importance of staged development, limited access design, and the acquisition of right-of-way sufficient to eventually accommodate full grade separation and access control—the defining attributes of a freeway system. The 1944 plan also proposed a notable increase in design standards for the rural segments of the interstate relative to the conventional highways that the states had been building before World War II.[48] Most important, *Interregional Highways* endorsed design of the system's urban and metropolitan routes as expressways, singling out New York, Los Angeles, Cleveland, St. Louis, Jersey City, and Newark as exemplary cases of metropolitan expressway development.[49] With consummate realism, it also acknowledged that staged development would be necessary to gradually upgrade divided highways to freeways and expressways with full access control.

The ambition of the 1944 plan is best indicated by the fact that divided highways accounted for only 1 percent of the state highway mileage in urban areas when the Bureau's report was completed in 1944. Yes, a handful of states had begun to build divided highways, and New York and California had built a small first generation of metropolitan expressways, but no state had built a network of metropolitan expressways like those proposed in the Bureau's 1944 report. Nor had most states yet acquired the legal authority to build freeways with full access control. In other words, *Interregional Highways* was proposing an extraordinarily ambitious agenda for future highway construction both within and between U.S. metropolitan areas.

The Initial Reaction of Urban Planners to the Bureau's Plans

Urban planners and city engineers gave mixed reviews to the Bureau's 1939 and 1944 plans for urban expressway development. Most welcomed a long-term federal commitment to urban highway improvement, but many also voiced specific concerns about the urban impact of expressway development. For example, the Highway and Transportation Committee of the American Society of Planning Officials warned in 1940:

> A network of high-speed highways superimposed on the average American city in competition with existing mass transportation facilities is likely to have a number of results, some not readily apparent. It is possible that the new facilities may cause losses to [privately owned transit operations] sufficient to cause the discontinuance of those services. . . . There is likely to be an acceleration of movement to the suburbs, leaving behind new blighted areas. . . . Central District parking facilities would no doubt become still less adequate because travel would be increasingly by individual vehicles. [New parking facilities would be required.] And in order to avoid the exorbitant cost of providing sufficient off street parking facilities to meet the demand, numerous business establishments would probably move to [metropolitan] sub-centers. Industries of all kinds using [trucks] for the assembling of raw materials or the shipment of finished products could be expected to take advantage of locations on express highways, and in the absence of zoning regulations, new industrial plants are likely to spring up in unexpected places, even in the suburbs.[50]

On the other hand, ASPO also noted that express highways would present less competition for mass transportation "if they can provide for express bus operation."

> Transit experts are not all in agreement that this is a complete answer; they point out that the short haul, not the long haul, is the life blood of their business. The planner and traffic engineer will do well to consider these possibilities, not with the idea of throttling community growth, but with the idea of directing it towards a desirable pattern in which the various major residential, business, and industrial developments will be located in districts suitable for the purpose rather than scattered inefficiently and mixed inharmoniously throughout the urban region.[51]

A joint committee of AASHO, ASPO, and ITE was equally cautious in its appraisal of the Bureau's plan for urban expressway development:

> Expressways and major thoroughfares offer the means of reaching the downtown district from out-lying areas quickly either by private vehicle or by transit. That is only one phase of the problem, however. How to provide for movement within the area now clogged with parked and standing vehicles as well as moving vehicles is another but no-less important problem. Expressways and major thoroughfares by themselves do not solve the problem of congestion in downtown areas, nor is that their purpose. Coupled with a program of expressway or major thoroughfare construction must be a program for relieving the downtown area of its congestion if it is to survive and prosper.[52]

To this end, the joint AASHO, ASPO, and ITE committee proposed "making transit service more attractive" and making anticipatory investment in "suitable off-street parking facilities" for automobiles on the margin of the CBD.

As this gentlemanly debate suggests, there were serious planning issues to be resolved before expressways could be endorsed as an effective strategy of urban traffic management. These included the physical impact of expressways on the cities they were to serve, their impact on transit, transit's financial ability to play an evolved role, the availability of CBD parking sufficient to accommodate increasing automobile use, and the ability of urban streets to accommodate the concentrated volumes of traffic that freeways would eventually deliver to the center of American cities. None of these issues were resolved during the New Deal, nor had they been resolved when Congress finally authorized full funding for the interstate in 1956. What was different in 1956 was that World War II was over, motorization had surged, and Congress was finally ready to bite the bullet and authorize the increase in fuel taxes necessary to finance the interstate system.

Map 3.1 shows the interregional highway system as it was proposed in 1944. Clearly, the interregional system was little different from the interstate highway system as it was financed in 1956 and built in the decades that followed. What

Map 3.1. *The Bureau of Public Roads 1944 plan for interregional highways.*

changed from 1944 to 1956 was the priority Congress was prepared to give to highway investment, the bigger push that came from the Eisenhower White House, and a much larger sense of urgency about urban congestion, highway safety, and the increasing reluctance of suburban residents to drive "all the way downtown."

Beltways: The Undebated Routes of the Interstate System

Both the advocates of the interregional highway system and its gentlemanly critics were focused on the urban impact of the radial routes of the interregional system—those that would serve downtown. The Bureau expected salutary impacts in terms of both traffic service and downtown revitalization, while urban planners were more likely to have reservations about the disruption that expressway-scale facilities could produce in the central city, including downtown traffic and parking problems and the displacement of housing and households. Given these make-or-break concerns in the central cities, neither the Bureau nor most big-city planners focused on the likely impact of the circumferential routes of the interstate system—those known as the metropolitan beltways. Planners who voiced broader concerns, such as Harland Bartholomew, were most concerned about the potential exodus of the middle class from the central cities and the likely decline of urban buying power.[53] But even these planners do not seem to have anticipated any wholesale changes in the geography of metropolitan commerce, industry, and employment.

The Bureau proposed beltways on the premise that these circumferential routes would allow cross-metropolitan and transcontinental traffic to avoid the city center, thus mitigating traffic congestion downtown, a proposition that was widely endorsed by city and county traffic engineers. As anticipated, the beltways have diverted pass-through traffic away from the urban core. But with the benefit of hindsight, we also know that the beltways produced impacts that neither the Bureau nor urban planners anticipated. Most significantly, the freeway-to-freeway interchanges where the beltways and radials intersect created high-accessibility locations where relatively low-cost land could be acquired to accommodate future suburban employment growth. As suburban population growth surged in the 1960s, major developers began to bet on the marketability of office space, office-industrial parks, and the profitability of shopping centers built in these high-accessibility locations—one of many reasons that suburbs now account for well over half of all employment in U.S. metropolitan areas.

Neither the Bureau's engineers nor the city planners who critiqued the Bureau's 1939 plan seem to have anticipated the magnitude of future employment growth that would occur in beltway suburbs or the higher-order jobs that would cluster in beltway settings. Indeed, they seem to have been focused on downtown. Thus the gentlemanly discussion of future plans for metropolitan highway development gave only glancing consideration to the prospect that the beltways would attract business and industry to outlying suburbs. Viewed, on the other hand, from the perspective of the twenty-first century, the industrial and commercial development that has occurred in beltway suburbs since 1970 has to be seen as one of the interstate's most significant metropolitan impacts.

What seems surprising is that these dynamics were not widely anticipated by planners and urbanists in the 1930s. They recognized that "decentralization" was rapidly increasing the share of the population that *lived* in the suburbs and that decentralization had already begun to spread the population "over an extremely wide area of suburban territory."[54] But in 1939, there was no correspondingly articulate concern that major employers would follow in large numbers or that beltway suburbs would eventually become a primary locus of metropolitan employment growth.

Figures 3.1 and 3.2 show an artist's rendering of an urban expressway and a beltway, both featured in *Toll Roads and Free Roads* in 1939. These illustrations effectively communicate the role that expressways and beltways were expected to play in metropolitan area transportation systems. That message had two parts: that expressways would allow cross-town traffic to move smoothly and safely through cities without entanglement with the local traffic on surface streets,

Figure 3.1. *Artist's rendering of an expressway serving downtown.* U.S. Bureau of Public Roads, *Toll Roads and Free Roads* (Washington, D.C.: Government Printing Office, 1939), plate 54.

and that the beltways would provide a future framework for the orderly development of residential suburbs in greenbelt settings. In other words, the message that seems to have been intended is that a network of expressways could keep urban traffic moving without intrusive impact and that beltways would channel through-traffic around cities while anchoring green-acre development of high quality.

This was a timely message, because big city planners were painfully aware that the residential populations of their home cities had declined during the Depression and that their downtowns had surrendered both sales and employment. In this context, many urban planners welcomed and endorsed urban expressway development, seeing the metropolitan radials as a unique opportunity to bring customers back downtown and reinvigorate central city economies suffering from the loss of jobs and retail sales that had occurred during the Depression.

But with the benefit of hindsight we now know that central cities with more than a million people have accounted for a declining share of the nation's population since 1930, that this was not a short-term phenomenon, and that it was not primarily a consequence of the Great Depression. As John F. Long reported in a 1981 census report, "After 1930, suburbanization and the [spatial]

Figure 3.2. *Artist's rendering of a metropolitan beltway and its surroundings.* U.S. Bureau of Public Roads, *Toll Roads and Free Roads* (Washington, D.C.: Government Printing Office, 1939), plate 55.

deconcentration of the metropolitan system began to reduce the percentage of the population [living] in the very largest cities so that by 1970, although 73 percent of the U.S. population was urban, only 27.8 percent of the U.S. population was in cities of over 100,000, and the percentage in cities over 1 million had declined to 9.2 [percent by 1970 and 7.7 percent by 1980, down from 12.3 percent in 1930.][55]

With the benefit of 25 additional years of hindsight, we also know that the beltways became the focus of both population and employment growth in most U.S. metropolitan areas between 1980 and 2005. The reason is straightforward: given the opportunity to buy affordable homes in the suburbs, large numbers of urban renters have chosen home ownership and suburban residence when they reach the age for settling down, marrying, and raising children. In turn, both retailers and light industry have followed the middle class to the suburbs. In this sense, it is the size and buying power of the American middle class, the large share of American households that can afford both home and automobile ownership, and the large share of Americans who live and work in suburban settings that accounts for the intensity of U.S. motorization.

These outcomes were not anticipated in the Bureau's 1939 and 1944 plans for the metropolitan extensions of the interregional highway system. Instead, the Bureau and most urban planners seem to have focused on the impact that expressways would have on the urban core and not on their impact on the future distribution of metropolitan employment. Figures 3.1 and 3.2 spoke to planners using visual images that would have been considered futuristic in 1939. Figure 3.1 showed an urban expressway that has been carefully integrated with the cityscape of a revitalized downtown—the kind of downtown revival that planners envisioned at the end of the Depression. Figure 3.2 showed a beltline highway that offers an alternative route designed to siphon off pass-through traffic that would otherwise have overloaded those radial expressways designed to carry commute traffic from outlying suburbs through the central city to downtown. In other words, these exhibits offered planners a plausible visualization of the ways in which a comprehensive network of expressways and beltways could simulta-neously contribute to both downtown revival and orderly suburban develop-ment. What was not anticipated in 1939 or 1944 was that freeway development would also provide both the impetus and framework for large-scale suburbaniza-tion of employment.

By 1980, 50 years of federal expenditure for urban highway development had combined with suburban population and employment growth to produce an evolved metropolis, a polyopolis, in which personal, commercial, and light industrial location choices had created a polynucleated settlement pattern. This metropolitan settlement pattern was enabled by mass motorization and freeway development and then reinforced by the collocation of households and employ-ment opportunities in beltway suburbs. This characteristically American form of metropolis is automobile dependent, access efficient for those who own a car or truck, but hard to navigate for those who do not drive.

These outcomes are in large measure a by-product of the buying power of the American middle class, America's early motorization, and the housing and location choices favored by the middle class. But they are also the legacy of highway plans that were conceived during the Great Depression, though not fully funded until 1956. In this sense, the Depression and the New Deal, taken together, were a transformational epoch in the history of American motorization —an epoch in which a bold federal plan for expressway development was con-ceived with the intention of bringing customers back downtown.

The Great Depression as a Hinge Event

At the end of World War II in 1945, only 892 miles of divided highway had been built in American cities, and only 1,456 additional miles had been built by 1955. Of this mileage of divided highways, only 355 miles had been built to true freeway standards by 1956. With the federal government paying for 90 percent of interstate construction expenses and 70 percent for other primary highways, another 24,432 miles of true urban freeway with full access control were built between 1956 and 1995.[56] Thus it is clear that construction of the metropolitan interstates did not get under way in earnest until 1956. But it is equally clear that it was the Depression and the New Deal that engaged the federal government and the states in urban highway construction and first mobilized the federal government and the Bureau of Public Roads to take an activist role in promoting the construction of urban expressways, which laid the groundwork for eventual funding and development of the interstate highway system.

Together, the Depression and the New Deal transformed the financial and institutional context in which future decisions about metropolitan transportation investment would be reached. Streetcar companies, already hobbled by financial difficulties, were further debilitated by the direct impacts of the Depression on their ridership and financial position. Later, aggressive enforcement of New Deal antitrust policies severed the financial relationships that weaker properties had developed with electric utilities and with National City Lines. These antitrust policies compromised transit's access to the private capital that it would have needed for reinvestment and renewal. On the other hand, the provisional agencies of the New Deal supplied funding for rail transit improvements in Chicago, Cincinnati, San Francisco, and New York, but these were onetime grants, not a long-term programmatic commitment.[57]

The aspect of New Deal policy that was fully institutionalized and therefore longest lasting was the change in federal highway policy that made cities eligible for federal highway funds. Given this push by Congress, the states moved to assign their highway departments urban construction duties. After reevaluating its own role in highway development, the Bureau of Public Roads emerged from the New Deal as an active champion of federal funding for urban expressways. It also developed its first plans for an interregional highway system—the precursor of the interstate—and financed the construction of a few hundred miles of showcase projects after World War II. State and federal highway funds displaced property taxes and revenue bonds as the primary sources of revenue for urban highway construction. With this shift in financing came a fundamental shift in governmental responsibility for urban highway construction from the cities and counties to the states and the federal government. With this shift in responsibility came a shift in focus from building urban thoroughfares to building freeways and moving more traffic more safely over longer metropolitan distances.

What the New Deal and Congress did not do was commit funding of the magnitude that would have been necessary to make any significant progress on construction of the interstate. That was ruled out by the death of President Roosevelt in 1945 and the relatively constrained agenda that could be pursued by his successor, Harry Truman. What the New Deal did do was commit the federal government and motivate the states and their highway departments to play a permanent role in urban highway development. During World War II, they also provided initial funds sufficient to build urban segments of the interstate system that were judged to be essential for the production of armaments and the movement of military supplies. Some of these segments were built as divided highways, and a few made provision for eventual reconstruction to freeway standards. No comparable long-term commitments were made to mass transit, but neither were substantial long-term funding commitments made to the interstate until 1956.

How Important Were the Depression and the New Deal?

Asked to identify the major events in the history of American motorization, most historians would surely nominate mass production of the Model T Ford and the passage of the Interstate Highway Act of 1956. Based on the discussion above, we would add the Great Depression because it permanently debilitated the street-car industry and produced a new majority in Congress that favored a long-term commitment to federal funding for state highway investment in cities. Tasking the state highway departments to play a principal role in urban transportation—the principal role, as it turned out—was a hinge event. It shaped the philosophy of highway development that would prevail in U.S. metropolitan areas and provided the institutional wherewithal to execute the interstate highway program, which with full funding in 1956 became the primary focus of transportation investment for the next 35 years and an important focus to this day.

State highway departments brought two overriding concerns to the metropolitan arena: the speed and safety of motor vehicle travel and the development of highways capable of serving the cross-metropolitan movement of cars and trucks both safely and efficiently. Necessarily, the highway departments were also concerned about project delivery within budget and meeting the expectations of governors and state legislators. On the other hand, the highway departments were less concerned about the complex relationship between highway investment and the financial health of downtown than the cities and their planners had been.

Thus the construction of metropolitan freeways and urban expressways was informed by different concerns from those which had informed local planning for boulevards and parkways before the Depression—and from different concerns flowed different outcomes. The most obvious were the most direct. Freeways and expressways displaced parkways and thoroughfares as the focal technologies of metropolitan road programs, and the responsibility for planning urban highways was uncoupled from planning for adjacent land use, although this was not the intention of *Interregional Highways*: it proposed metropolitan oversight of freeway planning.[58]

A less direct but equally important consequence was that most large cities abandoned their efforts to secure local tax financing for rapid transit for at least a generation. Los Angeles, Detroit, and Cincinnati were cases in point. Thus most of the burden of funding trunk-line transportation investment in metropolitan areas was shifted from local property taxes to state and federal fuel taxes. And with these shifts, neither the central cities and their downtowns nor their primary suburbs could exert commanding influence over metropolitan development or regional transportation priorities.

Under the leadership of the state highway departments, the movement of traffic became the focal concern of metropolitan transportation planning, and the construction of metropolitan highways and expressways became the principal output. Initial movement in this direction was slow but decisive. Only 355 miles of expressway had been built before Congress provided the funding to accelerate the construction of the interstate highway system in 1956. But another 12,378 miles of urban freeway were built between 1956 to 1980, most under the auspices of the interstate program.[59] Such was the eventual result of plans and policies first incubated in the context of the New Deal and the Great Depression and later endorsed by urban mayors, most planners, and the downtown establishments of most cities.

Only later did downtown, urban mayors, and big-city planners come to fully understand the democratization of accessibility and the diffusion of locational advantage that freeway networks and free parking would produce in U.S. metropolitan areas. These outcomes were advantageous for the vast majority of middle-class Americans, but produced decidedly mixed results in many of America's older central cities.

The New Deal and Mass Motorization: A Summation

The New Deal waged a two-front war against the Great Depression. On the programmatic front, it engaged the federal government in financing urban highway construction and other urban public works in order to generate employment and economic-multiplier effects. On the macroeconomic front, it sought to reflate the national economy and renew the growth of GDP. Both stimulated economic activity and produced job growth, but the New Deal was unable to generate employment sufficient to restore per capita GDP to the levels that prevailed before the Depression. Recovery came eventually, but primarily because of the full employment generated by World War II and the brevity of the recession that followed the world war.

This macroeconomic context is important for understanding the impact of the New Deal on the intensity and pace of motorization. Knowing that the New

Deal was not successful in restoring per capita GDP to the high levels that prevailed in the late 1920s is important for our analysis because growth in per capita GDP and increasing affordability had been the driving forces behind increasing motor vehicle ownership in the 1920s. But factory sales of motor vehicles remained depressed through the 1930s, and consumers were not fully confident that a durable prosperity had been restored until 1949. In this sense, the New Deal did not prove as successful in restoring economic confidence as its macroeconomic planners had hoped. For the same reason, the level of U.S. motorization increased, but only from 219 per 1,000 population in 1930 to 242 per 1,000 in 1940. During the 1920s, the U.S. motorization level had increased from 86 in 1920 to 219 in 1930. Clearly, the increase in motorization that occurred from 1920 to 1930 was vastly greater than the increase that occurred from 1930 to 1940: 145 percent versus 11 percent.[60]

Using the 1920s as our yardstick, we must conclude that the New Deal did not have much immediate impact on the intensity of U.S. motorization. But the New Deal did have a profound impact on public policy. It engaged the federal government and the state highway departments in urban highway construction, it produced the first plan for the interstate, it secured congressional authorization for that plan in 1944, and it financed the first expenditures on interstate projects during World War II.

Despite this effort, the total miles of urban highways that had been built to full expressway standards by 1956 summed to only 355. Nonetheless, the United States crossed the threshold of mass motorization two years later. Given the small mileage of expressways in place by 1958, mass motorization cannot be attributed to expressways in general or the interstate in particular. Instead, it must be attributed to the prosperity of the 1920s, social expectations established in the 1920s, increasing auto ownership in small towns and metropolitan suburbs, and eventual recovery from the Depression—primarily due to World War II—and the resulting increase in confidence, buying power, and automobile sales that followed the war.

The implication of this analysis is that the United States was already on a trajectory that was trending toward mass motorization in the 1920s. In the absence of the Depression, mass motorization would have occurred earlier. But in the absence of both the Depression and the New Deal, we can speculate that the national commitment made to metropolitan freeway development would have been substantially less aggressive. Absent the national economic crisis and the political realignment that it produced, it seems unlikely that the federal government would have assumed such a proactive role in financing urban highway development. And in the absence of both the Depression and the New Deal, obviously a counterfactual, we can guess that the federal government's role would have remained a more limited one and that some cities would have pursued expressway development, others parkway development, and still others a more transit-oriented strategy of metropolitan transportation investment. Some, perhaps many, would have continued to rely on wider streets for moving heavy traffic. In other words, it seems likely that both the pace and character of metropolitan transportation investment could have differed substantially from city to city.

In this postulated alternative history, it is unlikely that funding levels for urban highway development would have matched those of the New Deal or the interstate era. Thus inertia would have prevailed more often, producing less investment in the aggregate, more congestion, and less mobility. This is what occurred in Canada and what also occurred in London where plans for urban expressway development have been stalled by controversy and in effect repudiated by inaction. Given this array of might-have-been outcomes and the pattern in other nations, it seems reasonable to conclude that the economic crisis produced by the Great Depression was a special circumstance which combined with the financial troubles of the streetcar industry and early motorization in the United States to produce an ambitious and uniquely standardized approach to metropolitan highway development driven by federal funding. We would argue that events played out as they did in the United States because motorization was already well advanced before the Depression, which, in turn, recommended highway investment as a useful job creation and economic stimulus measure.

In any case, we must emphasize that mass motorization would have occurred in the United States with or without the New Deal and with or without an aggressive program of metropolitan expressway construction, just as it has in Europe. But what might not have occurred without the Depression and the New Deal was such uniformly active engagement of the states in urban freeway development or such thorough standardization of highway design and investment on a national basis. Nor is it likely that metropolitan areas could have financed and developed such comprehensive freeway networks if they had had to rely on a combination of state fuel taxes, bonds, and local property taxes to pay the bill.

Absent freeway development on the scale made possible by state and federal funding of the interstate, it is unlikely that multinucleation, suburban employment growth, and the three-car household would have become such prominent features of metropolitan life in the United States by 1980. And in this slower motorization, slower suburbanization, less pronounced multinucleation scenario, the United States might have posted year-2000 motorization levels only moderately higher than those reported in Canada, say, 725 motor vehicles per 1,000 population in the United States versus Canada's 676.

Readers can decide for themselves whether this represents a large or small difference in motorization. We conclude that the interstate made a difference that is significant, but not the vast difference that urbanists assert today.

In any event, it is crystal clear that the interstate and urban highway investment were legacies of the Depression and the New Deal. It is also clear that the New Deal's commitment to a nationwide program of metropolitan highway development that was financed with state and federal funds derived from fuel taxes and executed by highway departments with a statewide perspective and at least some insulation from urban politics was the only institutional framework that could have produced metropolitan freeway development of the ambition and ubiquity achieved by the interstate program. In turn, the long-term effects of urban expressways and the metropolitan beltways on household location options and urban development patterns—many beneficial, others not so beneficial—nominate the Great Depression and the New Deal, taken together, as another hinge event in the American history of motorization.

Summing Up

1. The Great Depression compounded the financial difficulties of street railways and accelerated their abandonment. The antitrust policies of the New Deal also contributed to further difficulties for street railways by forcing electric utilities to divest their street railway holdings.

2. Transit's competitiveness was enhanced in a handful of cases where the temporary agencies of the New Deal provided federal funding for urban subway construction. But the New Deal also preempted local interest in transit by making a long-term commitment to federal funding for urban highway construction.

3. The financial difficulties of the cities during the Depression led state legislatures to authorize state highway construction within municipal boundaries. The Depression also led to profound changes in federal highway policy. Most important, the National Industrial Recovery Act authorized the use of federal funds for state highway construction within cities. Previously federal highway funds had been reserved for rural construction.

4. The first plan for the interstate—then called the interregional highway system—was drafted in 1939. This plan was the first to recommend an extensive national program of expressway construction within metropolitan areas. A trickle of initial funding was made available in 1941 and again in 1944. By war's end, the state highway departments had built 826 miles of divided highway within metropolitan areas, but most of this mileage was not grade-separated.

5. Circumstances conducive to mass motorization were already in place by the 1920s. But with the Depression, the pace of motorization was slowed by economic hardship and a sharp decline in the volume of new

car sales. Depression-era highway construction stimulated employment but does not seem to have had much impact in terms of buoying new car sales. On the other hand, state and federal funding for urban highway development had decisive implications for the future. It laid the groundwork for the interstate highway system and metropolitan freeway construction.

6. The Great Depression delayed mass motorization, while the New Deal incubated the development of a national plan for interregional highways and metropolitan freeway development. In turn, the engagement of the state highway departments in urban highway development and the eventual funding and execution of the interstate highway program contributed significantly to the transformation of metropolitan settlement patterns and location options and thus to the present intensity of U.S. motorization. But we should also emphasize that the present motorization differential between the United States and other advanced industrial nations is gradually closing and that the residual differential reflects not only differences in metropolitan highway policy but also differences in aggregate and per capita GDP, the greater age and density of European cities, and the relative youth of the U.S. population vis-à-vis the European nations in its G-7 peer group.

FOUR

World War II and Its Immediate Aftermath: The End of the Streetcar Era and the Beginnings of the Freeway Era

The years during and immediately after World War II marked the end of the streetcar era and the beginning of the freeway era. For the transit industry, World War II was a period of extraordinary ambivalence. Transit carried its highest passenger volumes during the war (1941–45). Patronage reached these high levels because transit carried servicemen in large numbers and because auto and truck use was substantially diminished by gasoline rationing and the temporary unavailability of new tires and spare parts. Transit was clearly essential on the home front, but the war years also proved the streetcar industry's final undoing, because the volume of patronage and the demands of the war effort literally wore out the industry's track and rolling stock. With the streetcar companies' physical assets and credit both exhausted, wholesale abandonment of trackage and service followed from 1945 to 1955.[1]

The war years also saw the designation of the first urban routes of the interregional highway system and the specification of highway design standards that foreshadowed those of the interstate system. As a first step toward full freeway design, the Bureau of Public Roads articulated standards which required that projects on the interregional system be built as divided highways with the potential for upgrade to freeways with full access control. The first such projects served ports, military bases, and the armaments industry. Thus the war effort accelerated the development of divided highways within cities and engaged state highway departments in the design and construction of a next generation of highways that were forebears of the interstate system. The war effort also wore out street railways, accelerating both their abandonment and their replacement by buses.

Transit during and after World War II

Chart 4.1 shows the long-term trends of transit ridership from 1902 to 2004. Our immediate interest is in the huge surge in transit ridership that occurred during World War II and the devastating slump that followed. Clearly, this was both a tumultuous and defining period in transit's history, and so it is important to understand why ridership increased so dramatically during the war and plunged so far and so fast after the war.

Economic historians agree that the conversion of large parts of the economy to a wartime footing brought an end to the Depression and that wartime gasoline and tire rationing combined with the cessation of automobile and auto parts production to discourage automobile use during the war and the two-year reconversion period that followed it. In turn, economic expansion and gasoline and tire rationing combined with billeted travel by servicemen to produce a very high level of ridership that the transit industry acknowledges was a wartime anomaly. Thus the plunge that followed the war can be described as "postwar normalization,"[2] and transit's wartime service was the "last hurrah" for many streetcar companies.

Streetcars performed yeoman's service for the duration of World War II, but ridership collapsed immediately after the war. Operators providing subway and elevated service also experienced declining ridership, but at a much slower pace than the streetcar companies. Bus ridership actually increased during the first three years of the postwar period, but joined the general decline after 1949. Ridership stabilization was not achieved until federal funding made conversion to public ownership possible on a nationwide scale, and it took the OPEC oil embargo and a first generation of federal operating subsidies to produce sustained nationwide gains in transit ridership.

The net result for 1946–72 was a 72 percent decline in transit's nationwide

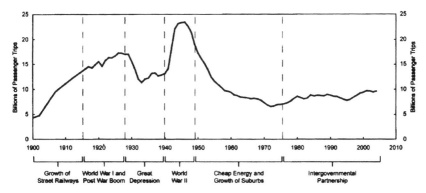

Chart 4.1. *The trends of U.S. transit ridership, 1902–2004.* "Major Trends of Transit Ridership," *Transit Factbook,* 2006. Used with the permission of the American Public Transit Association.

ridership. During this 26-year period, streetcar operators lost 98 percent of their riders, bus operators lost 60 percent, and rapid transit systems collectively lost 39 percent. Most of this decline occurred before Congress fully funded the interstate highway program in 1956.

Transit's market share declined even more precipitously. Measured in terms of rides per capita, transit's market share peaked at 167 rides per capita in 1945, then tumbled to 104 rides in 1950 and 65 in 1956—the year the interstate highway program was fully funded. In other words, most of transit's postwar ridership decline occurred before the interstate was fully funded. Table 4.1 shows that bus transit and heavy rail fared better than the streetcar companies in terms of retaining ridership after World War II, but total transit rides per capita nonetheless declined from 167 in 1946 to 70 in 1955 and bottomed out at 31 in 1972. In all, 53 percent of the postwar decline in transit ridership was associated with the wholesale abandonment of streetcar service. Subways and buses lost ridership, too, but not as fast as the streetcar companies.

The precipitous postwar decline of transit ridership and the subsequent abandonment of streetcar service pose numerous questions: Why did transit's postwar decline occur so quickly and, for streetcars, so completely? Why was streetcar service abandoned, but not bus service or rapid transit? Why were the streetcar companies, local governments, and state regulatory agencies unable to craft a strategy for renewal and recovery? And finally, why were so many streetcar companies allowed to fail without serious discussion of public ownership? To provide the context necessary for answering these questions, we must examine the dynamics of the war years in greater detail.

Table 4.1 *Transit's ridership losses after World War II*

	Total rides (in millions)	Streetcar rides (in millions)	Heavy rail rides (in millions)	Bus and trolley bus rides (in millions)
1946 peak	23,463	9,027	2,835	11,601
1972 bottom	6,567	211	1,731	4,625
Ridership lost	16,896	8,816	1,104	6,975
	72%	98%	39%	60%

SOURCE: APTA, *Transit Fact Book*, 2006.

The Impact of World War II

Streetcar ridership increased from 5.9 billion in 1940 to 9.5 billion in 1944. This wartime recovery was largely due to gas and tire rationing, a shortage of spare auto parts, and the inclination of recreational motorists to let their registrations lapse during the war. Billeted travel by servicemen also increased ridership and played a major role in sustaining ridership during the 1946–47 demobilization period.

With the wartime increase in streetcar ridership and revenues, streetcar companies began to rebuild their depreciation reserves and transit managers began to hope that the future could include reinvestment and renewal. In the interim, the demands of wartime service and the limited availability of steel for replacement rails and streetcar parts took a heavy toll on the condition of both cars and tracks. In fact, many streetcar companies reported that their rolling stock and tracks were literally worn out from overuse by war's end.

By 1945, transit workers were feeling the same way—that they, too, were being worn out by overuse. Due to wartime labor shortages, streetcar workers put in long hours of overtime. Demands for wage increases were also deferred. At war's end, unions sought catch-up wage increases that were, by then, long overdue. But management resistance was fierce because the industry's ability to finance reinvestment and renewal was clearly at stake. The result was a period of intensely bitter conflict between labor and management that produced an unprecedented number of strikes and work stoppages during the first years of the postwar period.[3] Strikes served to accelerate the decline of postwar ridership already under way due to postwar normalization.

The eventual outcome was a series of postwar labor settlements that restored labor peace, but these same agreements forced most properties to reallocate their depreciation reserves and thus trade away the potential for reinvestment in streetcar track and equipment. Fare increases followed, as did service reduction. These combined with the end of gasoline and tire rationing, the resumption of automobile use, and the completion of postwar demobilization to produce sharp losses in ridership after 1947. In turn, declining ridership and revenues foreclosed any realistic opportunity for reinvestment in new track and rolling stock, expenditures that were essential if streetcar service were to be sustained.[4]

The final outcome varied from company to company. Many smaller properties abandoned service altogether; most larger ones converted from streetcar to bus operation; a few were acquired by public agencies newly created to sustain urban service. In other words, the legacy of long-term financial distress, long-term disinvestment, the punishing demands of wartime service, and the streetcar industry's adversarial labor-management relations finally came home to roost. Outright abandonment of service and the replacement of streetcars with buses were the two most common outcomes. Conversion to public ownership occurred in only a handful of cases, but those were relatively important cases that involved midsized to large cities such as Oakland, California, one of the first to effectuate public ownership.

Conversion to bus operation was forced by necessity, but it was also economically sound. By the late 1940s, when the abandonment of streetcar service reached its climax, there was a consensus that, on an annualized basis, "a new diesel-powered bus was considerably cheaper to operate than a streetcar, old or new. Performing all the necessary calculations . . . leads to the conclusion that a bus was a cheaper vehicle to buy than a streetcar—annualized on a per seat basis."[5] In the highest density markets, such a conclusion requires qualification, but in most markets, conversion to bus service offered a far better alternative than outright abandonment or continued operation of worn-out track and obsolete rolling stock, and these were the choices facing most streetcar companies after World War II.

Some would still argue that replacement of World War I vintage streetcars with streetcars of the PCC generation would have been the industry's best long-run decision. But that was ruled out by the initial cost of the PCC car and new tracks and by the failed credit of most streetcar companies. Thus conversion to bus operation was often the best of the unhappy alternatives that were realistically available to American streetcar companies.

Why Abandonment? Why Not Public Ownership?

Public ownership and operation are now the accepted norm for public transportation and have been since federal funds became available for cities, transit districts, or transit authorities to acquire transit properties and convert them to public ownership. But conversion to public ownership did not occur on a widespread basis until federal funding became available to finance public acquisition of failing private operations in the mid-1960s. At the end of World War II, state regulators still expected transit companies to recoup their operating expenses from the fare box and other sources of operating income. Most transit properties were still privately owned and capitalized, with the significant exception of public systems in Boston, Chicago, Cleveland, Detroit, New Orleans, New York, San Francisco, and Seattle. Even by 1960, only 59 transit systems were publicly owned, subsidized, or operated, whereas some 1,200 properties remained under private ownership. On the other hand, the publicly owned properties were the industry's largest, and they accounted for almost half of all U.S. transit ridership by 1960.[6]

Most of the investor-owned properties were in financial trouble, but they were operated without subsidy and were opposed to public takeover. Indeed, the American Transit Association, the industry's foremost trade association, favored public investment but opposed outright public takeover until the 1960s. Likewise, transit unions opposed public takeover unless it came with ironclad guarantees that existing work rules and wage scales would not be tampered with. Downtown business associations liked the idea of public investment in rapid transit, but downtown property owners remained vehemently opposed to paying a fair share of the acquisition cost through special assessments. Nor were most mayors or county supervisors eager to push for tax-financed acquisition of public transit. After all, the states were mobilizing to build urban highways and freeways with federal funds, and downtowns had signaled that they weren't interested in sharing the cost of transit's acquisition and conversion to public ownership. Thus there was little realistic prospect of converting most transit properties to public ownership until Congress agreed to foot the bill in the 1960s.

For all of these reasons, most transit properties remained in private ownership and their ridership declined sharply after 1947. In these years, only a few transit properties emerged as promising examples of how to go about renewing and revitalizing transit systems. One such example was AC Transit in Oakland, which parlayed public ownership and a state-authorized property tax into a noteworthy revival. The most often cited success story from the early years of public ownership was also an Oakland–San Francisco transit system, Bay Area Rapid Transit.[7] BART could be touted as a success story precisely because it was a wholly new organization starting with new technology, a fresh slate, and thus no legacy of bad credit, adversarial labor-management relations, demoralized management, unreliable service, shabby equipment, or disgruntled passengers. In this sense, BART's success in attracting ridership was the exception that proves the rule. The rule is that the task of reorganizing and revitalizing a distressed industry is very difficult—technically, financially, organizationally, and politically—because most distressed industries bring with them the institutional baggage and market mismatches that produced their financial difficulties.

In most American cases, the conversion of transit properties to public ownership that occurred in the 1950s was a matter of last resort. Ridership was spiraling downward, and service reductions showed no prospect of producing eventual financial stability. To stop the bleeding, local governments acquired failing properties and used public credit to begin the process of reinvestment. But transit needed more than the backing of public credit to replace aging equipment. For years, American Transit Association economists had also been saying that transit needed to rationalize its work rules, fare policies, and cost structure so that it could operate efficiently despite patronage that was increasingly concentrated in peak commute hours. But these "technicalities" of economic recovery were not widely acknowledged in the 1950s when municipal acquisition gathered momentum, nor were they put front and center in the 1960s when Congress first took interest in the financial problems of mass transit and commuter railroads.

What was accomplished in the 1950s was the conversion of some operations to public ownership. The number of properties converted was relatively small—only 52 nationwide. But many of these were large properties, and thus the potential for impact was great. However, it would have taken much more than public ownership, public credit, and renewed capital investment to restore transit to a stable competitive footing. What would have been necessary was thoroughgoing industrial reorganization—and that was not forthcoming.

In any event, transit became a matter of secondary interest in most American cities after 1956, as the focus of public interest and governmental attention shifted to the construction of freeways and expressways. Most American cities welcomed the state and federal funding for metropolitan freeway construction that began to flow in the late 1950s, and they shied away from the more difficult task of rethinking how transit is financed and rationalizing how transit service is provided. With public funding for freeway development in prospect and then in progress, public interest in mass transit faded, at least temporarily, from the public agenda.

Planning for Express Highways

The 1939 plan for interregional highways provided an inventory of highways critical to the national defense, including those serving ports, military bases, and industrial plants converted to war production. Even before U.S. troops were engaged in combat, the Bureau of Public Roads was working with the War

Department and the state highway departments to upgrade those routes deemed most likely to be critical in the eventuality of renewed conflict in Europe.

Late in the war, the Bureau of Public Roads was asked to revise its 1939 plan so that it could serve as the centerpiece of the Roosevelt administration's program of postwar public works. The 1944 plan was endorsed by the White House as a major piece of its planning for postwar stimulus and received congressional authorization and an initial appropriation.[8] Thus the requirements of postwar economic conversion and stimulus provided one of the major rationales for White House endorsement of the program that was later renamed the interstate. Many of the defense highways built during this period—especially those in California, New York, Pennsylvania, and Massachusetts—were built as divided highways without full access control, but on rights-of-way wide enough to permit later reconstruction as expressways.

Before World War II, no state had built a true metropolitan freeway. Some had built a small mileage of elevated highways, others had built expressway segments with partial access control, and still others had used abandoned railroad or streetcar rights-of-way to build metropolitan highways without grade crossings—highways that mimicked the limited access that is the signature characteristic of an expressway. In other cases, local governments had used park and parkway development to shield roads from cross-traffic and abutting development, but no state had built any substantial mileage of true freeways of limited access design. In fact, no state had even acquired the legal authority to purchase urban rights-of-way and deny access to abutting property owners until Rhode Island did so in 1937. Between 1937 and 1944, an additional 16 states acquired the legal authority to build highways of limited access design, but fewer than 350 miles of true urban freeway had been built before the interstate highway program was fully funded in 1956.

The Postwar Explosion of Motor Vehicle Ownership

Gas and tire rationing and wartime controls on automobile production discouraged automobile use during World War II, and the nationwide level of motorization fell to a wartime low of 221 per 1,000 in 1945 as Americans garaged their cars and allowed their registrations to lapse.

The old prewar peak of 243 per 1,000 was matched in 1946, and a succession of new peaks was reached every year from 1946 to 1952. During this same period, the U.S. motorization level increased from 243 in 1946 to 371 in 1952, an increase of 53 percent over six years. Over the next six years, motorization increased only 9 percent—just enough to produce mass motorization in 1958. From 1958 to 1964, the U.S. motorization level increased from 404 to 427, a gain of only 6 percent. Clearly, most of the postwar growth in auto ownership that led to mass motorization occurred during the six-year normalization period that stretched from 1946 to 1952. The inescapable conclusion is that most of the increase in per capita motorization that led to mass motorization in 1958 occurred well before the acceleration of the interstate highway program in 1956. This further confirms that it was the push of per capita GDP and the pull of pent-up demand—not postwar highway investment—that initially propelled the United States over the threshold of mass motorization. This should not be surprising. During the early postwar period, the pace of urban highway development was insufficient to provide much stimulus for motorization.

In 1956, Congress finally made the financial commitment to "complete" construction of the interstate and finance 90 percent of the cost of construction. Over the next 40 years, this commitment to urban freeway construction enabled the state highway departments to build some 24,000 miles of metropolitan freeways and expressways. But until Congress made its commitment to "full funding" of the interstate on a 90–10 matching basis, the development of urban freeways required a financial commitment that most state legislatures were unwilling or unable to make. Thus in the early postwar era, the construction of urban freeways was caught in a financial and political stalemate that was almost as disabling as transit's. The problem was how to finance urban freeway construction in a manner that did not produce interminable delays in the improvement of other long-promised road projects, especially those in rural counties with sparse populations and a limited property tax base.

The Highway Program's Old and New Constituencies

The first legislation establishing state highway programs was authorized in the early twentieth century. This legislation tasked state highway departments to build rural roads, leaving cities to make their own road improvements because they had the financial wherewithal to do so. This arrangement broke down during the 1930s, because the Depression withered the property tax base on which cities had relied to finance infrastructure and services. In turn, Congress and the states made highway funds available for urban road programs—programs designed to produce both highway improvement and economic stimulus. Temporary sweetheart programs were also authorized to ensure that urban funding did not reduce the funds available for rural road construction. Thus the question of long-term funding and long-term priorities was papered over but not resolved during the New Deal. This is the question that came home to roost in state legislatures and in Congress during the late 1940s and early 1950s.

Rural communities and their legislators were understandably concerned

that the cost of urban freeway construction would interminably delay the construction of rural roads. At the same time, cities and their legislators were equally
concerned that ongoing development of cities and their suburbs would preempt
metropolitan freeway development if commitments to land acquisition and
urban construction were not made on a timely basis. For their part, the oil, auto,
and tire companies were concerned that excessive taxes on tires, gasoline, diesel
fuel, and vehicle registrations would diminish the salability of their products, a
concern that was heightened by the decelerating pace of motorization that was
evident after 1952. Truckers were similarly alarmed by proposed increases in the
diesel fuel tax. With hindsight, we know that these concerns were exaggerated.
Nonetheless, many stalwart members of the "highway lobby" initially opposed
the user-tax increases that were the most appropriate revenue source for financing construction of the interstate highway system—the same way downtown
property owners had opposed tax increment financing for rapid transit.[9]

The same kind of shortsighted self-interest prevented the development of
interregional highways until 1956, when Congress finally reached consensus on
user financing, the creation of a so-called highway trust fund, and federal contributions that would minimize the impact of the interstate on rural highway
improvement. With the interstate stalemated, a consortium of states proceeded
with the development of toll roads from New York to Boston and from New York
to Chicago, ventures inspired by the financial success of the Pennsylvania Turnpike.[10] Upon full amortization of their bonds, these turnpikes were converted to
toll-free operation, incorporated into the federal aid system, and turned over to
the state highway departments for maintenance.

Early Leadership in the Construction of Divided Highways

The late 1940s saw seven states establish early leadership in divided highway
construction under the auspices of the postwar highway program. In ranked
order of the mileage built, these states were California, New York, New Jersey,
Ohio, Texas, Connecticut, and Maryland. Together, they accounted for 63 percent of the divided highway mileage that had been built in the United States by
1950. The total mileage, both urban and rural, was less than 4,200—not much of
an economic stimulus. New York, California, Massachusetts, and Pennsylvania
established themselves as national leaders in metropolitan expressway development during this same period, using funding provided under the auspices of the
postwar program. Urban expressways built in these four states accounted for
71 percent of the expressway mileage built in the United States before the
interstate was fully funded in 1956. New York and California accounted for half
of the urban expressway mileage built before 1956.[11]

There are many reasons for California and New York's leadership, but the most important reason is that they were among the first states in which legislatures were able to reach postwar consensus on state gas tax increases to finance urban expressway construction. Most other states—and Congress— remained stalled over the cost of urban freeway development and divided by the concern that the cost of urban freeway construction would preempt the funding of highway projects long promised to rural counties. These concerns were resolved in California by ensuring every county a minimum appropriation for road projects. The concerns voiced by the oil, auto, and tire companies were also resolved by sequestering highway-user taxes in an account reserved for highway purposes. The same concerns dominated the congressional debate over the interregional highways, and these were finally resolved by Congress in 1956 on much the same terms as in California. In both cases, legislative leaders were eventually successful in creating a program that was sufficiently balanced for competing stakeholders to feel a sense of shared ownership, common interest, and appropriately equitable contribution. State and federal engineers called their relationship "The Partnership."[12] Together, the gas tax and the federal government's 90 percent revenue contribution to each interstate project provided sufficient glue to keep the interstate coalition together for the 40 years necessary to "complete" the construction effort outlined in *Interregional Highways* in 1944.

Thus financial stalemate did not postpone metropolitan freeway development the way transit development was stalled in the 1920s. The basic reason is that Congress and the state legislatures were able to work out the equities of a financial partnership that proved capable of sustaining both urban and rural highway investment for the next 40 years. The national highway program was based on two partnerships—one financial, one technical—both involving federal-state cooperation. Transit, on the other hand, remained a distressed industry that continued, for the most part, to be operated under private ownership until the mid-1960s. In 1964, with Lyndon B. Johnson succeeding John Kennedy in the White House, Congress finally hammered out the equities of an investment partnership that made federal funds available for public transportation and for the conversion of transit properties to public ownership, creating an appearance of symmetry between federal transit and highway policy. Federal funding paid for transit's conversion to public ownership and for modernization of the industry's capital stock. But it cannot be concluded that federal investment has been successful in restoring transit to a footing that can be described as vigorously competitive—a subject to which we will return in chapter 6. Nor is it likely that the nation's highway-building partnership can be sustained on the priority basis that it enjoyed in the twentieth century—a subject to which we will return in chapter 7.

Summing Up

1. During World War II, gasoline and tire rationing and a shortage of spare parts for automobiles combined with billeted travel by servicemen to produce all-time highs in transit ridership.
2. Wartime revenues allowed streetcar companies to replenish their capital accounts and make hopeful plans for reinvestment and renewal. But by 1945, streetcar replacement had become unavoidable because wartime service had literally worn out streetcars and trackage. At war's end, streetcar workers were in no mood to postpone long-deferred wage increases. The industry capitulated after a season of long and bitter strikes. Thus revenues that had been set aside for streetcar replacement were used instead to reach postwar labor settlements that paid for higher wages. Wholesale streetcar abandonment followed, and buses became transit's predominant technology after World War II.
3. War production in the industrial cities of the North and West combined with fair employment practices instituted by the federal government to produce a significant exodus of African Americans from the agricultural South to seek jobs in the urban North and West.
4. Congress first authorized both the designation of the interregional highway system and the use of existing federal funds to finance interstate projects in 1944, but only 355 miles of true urban freeway were actually built before 1956.
5. Auto and truck ownership increased rapidly in the early postwar period as Americans gained confidence that the economic recovery would prove a durable one. The resulting surge in motorization that occurred from 1946 to 1952 was much greater than the subsequent increases in the level of motorization that accompanied freeway development during the first dozen years of the interstate program.
6. In many states, increases in state funding for postwar highway improvements were stalemated by disagreement over the priority of urban and rural highway projects. Rural legislators were concerned that the funding required for urban freeway construction would preempt construction in rural areas.
7. New York and California were the first states to work out legislative compromises that increased gas taxes to finance a balanced program of urban and rural highway improvements. Two compromises were essential. Guaranteed minimum expenditures for individual counties assured rural legislators that their home counties would receive a fair share of statewide highway funding, while the segregation of highway-user taxes in a separate highway development assured the oil and tire companies

that such taxes would be reserved for highway construction. This state legislation provided the model for later congressional action on interstate funding.

8. The keys to congressional passage of the interstate highway program were fuel-tax financing, 90 percent federal funding for interstate projects, and the creation of the highway trust fund. The size of the federal contribution assured rural senators and congressmen that the matching requirements of the interstate would not preempt rural road construction in their home states. The trust fund mechanism assured the oil, auto, tire, and trucking industries and the automobile clubs that highway-user revenues would be set aside for highway improvement. In turn, the growth of motor vehicle ownership and use ensured that there would be sufficient money to complete the interstate, although not on the ambitious schedule that Congress had first established in 1956.

FIVE

The Interstate and Pervasive Motorization, 1956–80

In 1956, Congress authorized full funding of the interstate highway program. Over the next 24 years, state highway departments built 12,377 miles of freeway in U.S. cities and metropolitan areas.[1] In 1958, the United States crossed the threshold of mass motorization. In 1980, the United States became the first nation to boast pervasive motorization. The United States' aggressive commitment to metropolitan freeway development and the contemporaneous growth of auto and truck ownership raise an obvious question: To what extent was pervasive motorization a by-product of the interstate highway program?

For many planners and urbanists, the causal nexus between the interstate, suburbanization, and pervasive motorization appears so direct and obvious as to require no systematic explication or critical appraisal. In turn, this comfortable assumption has led to the faulty conclusion that unbalanced public policy explains the pervasiveness of U.S. motorization.

The Trajectory of U.S. Motorization before and after the Interstate

The diffusion of cars and trucks first accelerated rapidly in the United States during the 1920s. Indeed, the per capita increase in motorization that occurred from 1920 to 1929 was 157 percent. Much of this increase in automobile ownership occurred in small towns and midsized cities, producing the first wave of transit's ridership losses. Only the largest cities experienced continuing growth in transit ridership.

From 1947 to 1980, U.S. transit systems lost 62 percent of their ridership, and motor vehicle registrations increased 160 percent—actually a smaller increase on an annual basis than the increase that occurred during the 1920s. Both periods saw significant increases in vehicular travel and in traffic accidents and fatalities. The 1950s, 1960s, and 1970s also saw the acceleration of metropolitan decentralization in its many forms. These included the loss of central city employment, the development of outlying shopping and activity centers, and the continuing erosion of downtown's once-elevated position as a singularly dominant commercial and cultural center. By 1980, there had also been a decided shift in both population and buying power to metropolitan suburbs and sufficient growth in motor vehicle ownership to produce pervasive motorization.

Motorization increased in the 1920s and following World War II because owning a car vastly increased the horizon of spatial opportunity for most Americans, enabling increases in personal mobility, home ownership, and the "elbow room" most Americans seem to need. But in the 1960s, the third-order impacts that came with this opportunity became increasingly apparent. These included increasing congestion, air pollution, fuel consumption, and (after 1973) increasing demand for imported vehicles. A fourth-order impact is increased CO_2 emissions.

Funding the Interstate

Dwight D. Eisenhower is widely credited with the presidential push that produced full funding for the interstate highway system in 1956. Eisenhower clearly played a key role, but not a decisive one. He requested a plan for funding the interstate on an accelerated basis, but the plan developed by his aides called for bond financing and was largely ignored by Congress. On the other hand, the popular president's call for action was not ignored, and the chairs of the House and Senate subcommittees on roads seized the opportunity to hammer out the 1956 legislative compromise that finally allowed a highway bill to pass after 10 years of failed attempts to break the urban/rural deadlock in Congress.[2] The artful compromise of 1956 increased highway-user taxes and created the high-way trust fund. It simultaneously mollified the toll road states, the auto clubs, and the oil, tire, and trucking industries while balancing the interests of the populous industrial states and the land-rich, lightly settled states. This compro-mise proved durable long enough to finance and finally build the highway network that Congress had first approved in 1944.

As proposed by *Interregional Highways* in 1944, the interstate was "a na-tional system of rural and urban highways totaling approximately 34,000 miles." The proposed network comprised "only 1 percent of the total road mileage of the United States," but it was expected to carry 20 percent of the nation's traffic. This expectation was fulfilled. In 2000, the interstate system accounted for 24 percent of all vehicle miles traveled in the United States.[3]

Another way to scale the ambition of the interstate program is to compare highway investment at the peak of the freeway era with railroad investment at the peak of the railroad era. At its peak in 1910, capital outlays for railroad investment accounted for 2.0 percent of U.S. GNP.[4] In the much larger U.S. economy of 1964, state outlays for highway capital investment accounted for only 1.1 percent of GNP.[5] The interstate was an ambitious undertaking, but in relative terms it was not outsized. We also know that the methodology used to size the system and choose its routes was a discriminating one that was attentive to both cost and serviceability. Indeed, the engineers who developed the inter-state plan viewed the proposed system as "very close to the optimum mileage which will afford the greatest possible service per mile."[6] In other words, the initial conceptualization of the interstate was cost-conscious as well as am-bitious. But this economy-minded view of the interstate's logic has lost currency today as urbanists champion the revisionist view that the interstate was an out-sized public works program that propelled the growth of automobile ownership, sapped the vitality of central cities, and spurred suburban sprawl, creating the most auto-dependent nation on earth.

Still another way to measure the impact of the interstate is to report the miles of urban freeway already in place when the program was financed in 1956, by 1980, and in 2000 at the program's sunset. As table 5.1 indicates, large-scale development of metropolitan freeways in the United States was the direct result of the funding generated by the interstate highway program. The total mileage of express highways built from 1956 to 2000, including rural interstates, freeways, and expressways, exceeded 52,000. The urban mileage at the end of 2000 was 20,270. In turn, our analysis is framed by the question: What outcomes have flowed from this significant increase in metropolitan highway capacity?

In the pages that follow, we will challenge key elements of the revisionist view of the interstate. The preexisting demand for home and auto ownership, the buying and borrowing power of the American population, and the relatively

Table 5.1 *Urban freeway mileage in place in 1956, 1980, and 2000*

Urban mileage of true freeway before Congress authorized full funding of the interstate system in 1956:	355
Urban freeway mileage in 1980 when the United States crossed the threshold of pervasive motorization in 1980:	12,733
Urban freeway mileage at the program's sunset in 2000:	20,270

SOURCE: *Highway Statistics, Summary to 1985* and *Highway Statistics 2002*, table HM-36.

small increment in motorization that can be attributed solely to the interstate all indicate that the United States would have become the world's most thoroughly motorized nation with or without a highway program as ambitious as the interstate. On the other hand, we can concur with the view that the interstate contributed to the spatial transformation of U.S. metropolitan areas, to the usefulness of automobile ownership, and to an outsized increase in per capita VMT.

The Interstate and Increasing Automobile Ownership

The United States experienced initial motorization in 1925 and mass motorization in 1958—year two of accelerated investment under the 1956 act. Thus motorization already had substantial momentum before any significant mileage of metropolitan freeways had been built. This momentum was attributable to the United States' leadership in per capita GDP, in household buying power, in automobile manufacturing, and in petroleum refining and its early dominance in oil exploration and petroleum reserves, which translated into gasoline prices much lower than those found in the other G-7 nations. Early motorization was also attributable to the development of installment financing arrangements that propelled the automobile's early acceptance and rapid diffusion in small towns, farm country, and streetcar suburbs.

This recitation of ground that we have already covered is a reminder that motorization had gathered momentum after World War I and again after World War II without any significant supply-side push from urban freeway development. Yes, slow but steady highway improvement occurred, making auto use safer and more convenient, but "slow and steady" wasn't what produced the surge in automobile ownership that occurred between 1947 and 1957. The increment in vehicle ownership that produced mass motorization was the result of postwar recovery, renewed economic confidence, and pent-up demand for automobile ownership.

What about pervasive motorization? Wasn't this globally unique level of motorization the by-product of the interstate? James Flink argues that the "irrational proliferation of the post–World War II automobile culture occurred less because of consumer demand than because of the government's massive indirect subsidization of the automobile and oil industries, especially through the Interstate Highway Act of 1956."[7] We would respond, no, not primarily. Here is our reasoning. If the interstate were the primary reason for the pervasiveness of U.S. motorization, we would expect to find outsized increments in motor vehicle ownership occurring as the interstates were completed. We would also expect to find an outsized increment in U.S. motorization vis-à-vis that of Canada, which has pursued a much more restrained approach to metropolitan highway development. Neither outcome is evident from the trends of motor vehicle ownership in the United States or the comparison of such trends in the United States and Canada. On the other hand, the serviceability of the interstate, the development of successive generations of new suburbs, the growth of suburban employment, and the growth of the trucking industry sustained the demand for cars and trucks and contributed to an explosive increase in motor vehicle travel.[8] Thus it was increased VMT that was the most significant impact of the interstates and suburbanization.

Comparing the Pace of Motorization in the United States and Canada

Table 5.2 shows the increase in motor vehicles per 1,000 population in the United States during each of six decades that were free of both major warfare and severe recession. The table shows that the single largest increase in U.S. motorization occurred between 1967 and 1977, the second decade of interstate construction, when the United States added 181 motor vehicles per 1,000 population. But in no other interstate decade did the increase in motorization exceed the overall average for peacetime decades. In fact, the increase in motor vehicles per 1,000 population was below the historic average: 71 per 1,000 population during the first interstate decade and 97 per 1,000 population during the second.

On the other hand, well above average increases in motor vehicle ownership occurred immediately after both world wars, when highway construction was proceeding at a sluggish pace. The increment for the decade following World War I was 147 motor vehicles per 1,000 population; following World War II it was 130 per 1,000. Both were substantially larger than the increment in vehicle ownership that occurred during the three peak decades of interstate construction, which averaged 116 per 1,000 population. The implication of table 5.3 is that the peak years of the interstate, 1957–87, were not a period of exceptional increase in the intensity of U.S. motorization, despite the extraordinary commitment that was made to the construction of metropolitan freeways. This

Table 5.2 *Timing of all U.S. motorization*

Decade	Incremental motorization per 1,000 population	Miles of freeway built in urban areas
1919–1929	147 per 1,000	0
1947–1957	130 per 1,000	274
1957–1967	71 per 1,000	4,665
1967–1977	181 per 1,000	3,682
1977–1987	97 per 1,000	8,000
1987–1997	18 per 1,000	2,800
Average per decade	107 per 1,000	NA
Average per decade for 1957–87	116 per 1,000	5,449
Average for non-interstate decades without war or depression	139 per 1,000	NA

SOURCE: MVMA, *Motor Vehicle Facts and Trends*, and *Highway Statistics.*

suggests that the rapid growth of GDP and GDP per capita and pent-up demand were sufficient to account for U.S. leadership in motor vehicle ownership, both in the 1920s and after World War II.

Table 5.3 shows the increase in cars and trucks per 1,000 population for both the United States and Canada during the peak period of freeway construction. The Canadian increase was 406 motor vehicles per 1,000 population, while the U.S. increase was only 349 per 1,000. In other words, the Canadian increase was substantially greater, despite the fact that Canada pursued a notably restrained approach to metropolitan highway development. There is a convincing explanation for this outcome: Canadian GDP increased faster during this period than U.S. GDP on a per capita basis. The appropriate conclusion is that the link between highway improvement and auto ownership is relatively weak, while the link between auto ownership and per capita GDP is relatively strong. In other words, the revisionists have made too much of the link between the interstate, urban freeway development, and U.S. motorization. The interstate had a significant impact, but it is only one of many reasons that the United States has become the world's most pervasively motorized nation.

Table 5.4 reinforces this appraisal. It shows that the United States had experienced more motorization than any other G-7 nation up to 1956 and that it experienced less after 1956. The European increments in motor vehicle ownership are just what one would expect as second-generation adopters of a new technology gradually catch up.

Table 5.5 uses index values to show the 1957–87 trend of U.S. vehicle registrations, VMT, and GDP all on a per capita basis. The increase in vehicle registrations per 1,000 population closely tracks the trend of GDP per capita during the peak years of the interstate program. This suggests that increased

Table 5.3 *U.S. and Canadian increases in motorization and GDP per head, 1957–87*

	U.S. increase	Canadian increase
Numeric increase in vehicles owned	349 per 1,000	406 per 1,000
Increase in GDP per capita	99.5%	113.2%

SOURCE: MVMA, *Motor Vehicle Facts and Trends*, and Maddison, *World Economy: Historical Statistics*.

Table 5.4 *Motor vehicles per 1,000 population in the G-7 nations, 1956 and 2000*

	Vehicles per 1,000 pop. in 1956	Vehicles per 1,000 pop. in 2000	Increase per 1,000 pop.
United States	384	784	400
Canada	262	676	414
Great Britain	106	511	405
France	113	574	461
Germany	30	576	546
Italy	29	626	597
Japan	4	651	647

SOURCE: MVMA, *Motor Vehicle Facts and Figures*, 1956 and 2000, and Maddison, *World Economy: Historical Statistics*.

buying power would be sufficient to account for most of the growth in vehicle registrations that occurred during the peak years of interstate construction. Certainly, highway investment made auto and truck ownership more useful, but the implication of tables 5.4 and 5.5 is that increasing GDP per capita provides a sufficient explanation for most of the increase in auto and truck ownership that occurred during the peak years of interstate highway construction.

Table 5.5 also shows that the growth of VMT per 1,000 population substantially exceeded the growth of vehicle registrations and GDP per capita. This is another strong indication that the most significant impact of the interstate was on the geography of location, on travel patterns and distance traveled rather than on the decision to own a car or truck. But there was very little increase in VMT on a per vehicle basis. This suggests that what increased VMT during the peak years of interstate construction was the increasing share of the population that lived in the suburbs and the increasing number of two-car and three-car households that accompanied suburban population growth. In turn, this suggests that pervasive motorization is a by-product of the growth of suburban population and employment and that it is intimately connected with suburban lifestyles, suburban borrowing power, and the felt need for a second and third car in two-worker suburban households. In turn, this would indicate that (1) it is the uniquely large number of American households with two and three vehicles

Table 5.5 *Per capita trends of U.S. GDP, vehicle registrations, and VMT*

	GDP per capita	Vehicles per 1,000 pop.	VMT per 1,000 pop.	VMT per vehicle
1957	100	100	100	100
1967	131	124	128	103
1977	161	164	176	107
1987	200	186	231	112
Change	100%	86%	131%	12%

SOURCE: *Highway Statistics*, and Maddison, *World Economy: Historical Statistics*.

that accounts for the intensity of U.S. motorization; (2) it is the internationally exceptional share of the U.S. population that lives in suburban settings which accounts for the high level of U.S. VMT per capita; and (3) it was postwar prosperity, the borrowing and buying power of the American population, increasing women's workforce participation, the interstates and a longer commute, the GI Bill, and the mortgage income-tax deduction which had made home ownership affordable for 66 percent of the U.S. population by 1980, up from 51 percent in 1945.[9]

The Emergence of Two-Car Households

In 1960, the average American household owned one car and wealthier families owned two. In this author's home neighborhood, roughly half of the families in the neighborhood had two cars, and the rest wanted a second car as soon as it was financially possible. This observation from personal experience in the early 1960s is a reminder that peer group norms and peer group expectations play an important role in shaping how individuals and households make use of gains in their buying power. In the United States, owning a car had become a well-established household "aspiration" by 1925. By 1950 it had become "essential."

In 1960, the national average for auto ownership stood at 1.03 per household for all households. Household levels of auto ownership increased rapidly during the 1960s and 1970s as incomes increased and as an increasing number of middle-income households moved to the suburbs and purchased a second car, setting a new standard by which neighbors and peers began to assess and reappraise their own needs. By 1980, the average American household owned 1.61 vehicles, and higher-income households and many suburban households with two breadwinners were beginning to model a still-higher level of need—a car for each adult in the household and "a reliable used car" for teenagers with a driver's license.[10] Most of this increase can be attributed to increasing parity between men and women in terms of both driver's licensing and labor force participation. From 1950 to 1980, the number of women who were licensed drivers increased threefold, while the number of men who were licensed drivers increased less than 40 percent, but on a larger base.[11] Likewise, much of the increase in the buying power necessary to purchase a second or third car in family households was attributable to increasing women's workforce participation, which surged from 38 percent in 1960 to 52 percent in 1980.[12]

A significant increase in three-car households was paired with these trends. In 1960, only 2.5 percent of American households owned three or more vehicles; by 1980, that share had increased to 17.5 percent.[13] It was in the context of rising real incomes, increasing women's workforce participation, increased borrowing power, increasing home ownership, the increasing suburbanization of the American population, and keeping up with the Joneses that the United States became the world's first pervasively motorized nation.

The growth of women's labor force participation and the resulting increase in household income seems to have accounted for much of the increase in motor vehicles. Part of this dynamic is simply and directly attributable to women working outside the home, part to the increased buying and borrowing power of a two-worker household, and part to the increased need for a second car that arises when two household members work. Intra- and interregional shifts in national population shares also contributed: the transit-oriented central cities of the frostbelt lost population, while their auto-oriented suburbs and the auto-oriented cities of the sunbelt both gained population. All of these dynamics—plus the growth of beltway population and employment—contributed to the resulting increase in the number of motor vehicles owned by the average American household in 1980.

A different factor was the quality and affordability of the generation of import cars brought to market in the United States after the OPEC oil embargo of 1973. These affordable imports broadened auto ownership among young adults, especially among the generation of young women who became first-time job holders and first-time car buyers in the 1970s. U.S. women's workforce participation rate increased from 34.5 percent in 1955 to 51.5 percent in 1980. This accounted for much of the increase in household buying power that enabled increased home and automobile ownership. Thus suburban households, two-income households, beltway workers, and young women who were first-time car buyers made a substantial contribution to the increase in household ownership of motor vehicles during the decade that closed with the United States achieving pervasive motorization in 1980.

Canada achieved an almost comparable level of motorization a generation later, with the result that Canada is now approaching the threshold of pervasive motorization. Pervasive motorization will not come to Canada because highway investment has given it a strong supply-side push. Rather, it will come because of the continuing growth of both GDP and GDP per capita, because of the conviction of an increasing number of middle-class households that husbands and wives each need a car of their own, and because of the increased buying power and auto ownership rates that have become the group norm for many working women in Canada.

The implication of this analysis is that pervasive motorization occurred earliest in the United States because it was here that household income, household borrowing power, and public policy first combined to make both a home and two cars affordable for most households with two working adults. Clearly, the interstates had a significant impact on the spatial organization of U.S. metropolitan areas and thus a significant but indirect impact on the affordability of home ownership and the need for a second or third car in suburban households. But just as clearly, the seeds of such aspirations were sown in the 1920s and reached fruition in the 1980s. This indicates, in turn, that the push of highway policy should be viewed as only one among many factors that produced pervasive motorization in the United States. The same is even more obviously true for Canada. It is now approaching pervasive motorization without having made an aggressive commitment to metropolitan freeway development.

The Interstate and VMT

A different conclusion arises when we examine the complex relationship between the interstate, suburbanization, and VMT. Here the impacts of highway investment seem to have been more decisive.

During the first 24 years of the interstate era that led up to pervasive motorization in 1980, increases in U.S. motorization were roughly in line with the increase in personal buying power produced by the growth in GDP per capita. Motor vehicles per 1,000 population increased 77 percent from 1956 to 1980, while per capita GDP increased 72 percent.[14] This was a growth rate much higher than the growth rate of both the urban population (47 percent) and the population as a whole (35 percent), but substantially lower than the growth rate of aggregate GDP (129 percent). These trends were in line with historical experience, but another trend was not: the postwar trend of vehicle miles traveled. VMT and especially urban area VMT increased at an exceptionally rapid pace from 1956 to 1980. Nationwide, VMT increased 142 percent, while urban VMT increased a stunning 198 percent.[15] The urban increase seems to have been a by-product of the interstate and other intertwined postwar dynamics: the growth of GDP, increased buying and borrowing power, and large-scale development of affordable middle-income housing in suburban settings, which made possible the resulting growth of suburban population and employment. Each of these trends contributed to increasing auto and truck travel over increasing distances and hence increased VMT.

In the revisionist view, increased VMT is the statistical indicator that points to the most important second- and third-order effects of the interstate and motorization: more travel by motor vehicles over longer distances to more widely dispersed destinations in sprawling suburbs, a chain of impacts that has vastly increased urbanization's "ecological footprint" on the natural environment. In the traditionalist view, on the other hand, the interstate created the opportunity for the development of affordable suburban housing that has enabled successive generations of Americans to afford home ownership in comfortable suburban settings by making commutes that are relatively long in terms of the miles traveled but still relatively brief in terms of time spent on the road. Traditionalists focus on home ownership, the quality of suburban schools, a safe child-rearing environment, and a still-convenient commute. Revisionists focus on long commutes, suburban sprawl, automotive pollution, and those left behind to attend substandard urban schools. In this case, the coin has two sides, and both are accurate descriptions.

Suburban Growth in Historical Perspective

Motorization has had a profound influence on the pattern of metropolitan development, but suburban growth is not a new phenomenon, nor was it a by-product of motorization. The first generation of commuter suburbs was developed during the railroad era and the second during the streetcar era.

The commuter suburbs of the railroad era were typically stand-alone communities that catered to a population that was wealthy by urban standards. In many cases, steam railroads or interurban electric lines instigated and promoted the development of these suburbs by building suburban stations and subdividing the adjacent land for suburban development. Some of these nineteenth-century railroad New Towns became fabled outposts of American wealth.

The suburbs of the streetcar era more typically catered to would-be home-owners of the middle and upper middle classes who bought a lot and contracted with a builder and his small crew to build a family home. In many instances, the development subsidiary of a streetcar company would build homes for sale on spec. Volumes were typically low, and the typical mode of operation was for a development company to install utilities, sell lots, and build under contract with future owners one at a time.[16] With low volumes, unit costs were relatively high, and profitability hinged on purchasing land that would appreciate once streetcar service was provided.

Most streetcar companies had withdrawn from the speculative business of housing development by World War I because it had become so easy for rival developers to exploit the value added by a streetcar line without incurring the initial cost of streetcar development. Any residual financial synergy between streetcar development and suburban housing development was destroyed by the rapid diffusion of the automobile in streetcar suburbs. Thereafter, most extensions of transit service were provided by buses, which made use of the improved roads being built by counties and state highway departments.

Deductibility for mortgage interest was part of an omnibus tax bill that Congress paired with the Sixteenth Amendment to the Constitution, which imposed the federal income tax in 1913. The Tariff Act of 1913 authorized companion-piece deductions for property taxes and mortgage interest payments. The tax deductibility of mortgage interest—and other interest expenses—was paired with the income tax to ensure that the economy would not lack fiscal stimulus due to the tax increase—or so its proponents said.[17]

The prosperity of the 1920s fueled a third suburban development boom. This came with the maturation of the automobile into an all-weather utility vehicle, federal tax deductions for mortgage interest payments, and more robust commercial arrangements for home and auto financing.

At the turn of the century, roughly half of all debt for home ownership had been noninstitutional, most of it carried by family, friends, or business associates. But by the mid-1920s, a substantial majority of debt was being carried commercially by banks, mutual savings banks, savings and loan associations, and life insurance companies. Thus the maturation of commercial lending combined with rising incomes, tax deductions for mortgage payments, and initial motorization to fuel the suburban housing boom of the 1920s. The development of this third generation of American suburbs was associated with the tax deductions for mortgage interest payments—but not the development of freeways and expressways. In terms of motor vehicles added per 1,000 population, this was the second most vigorous period of motorization in American history (as was shown in table 5.2).

There were other ways that the underpinnings of the 1920s housing boom were different from those of the railroad era and the earlier years of the streetcar era. No longer was the developer providing transportation for would-be home-buyers, and no longer was developable land limited by adjacency to a train station or convenient walking access to a streetcar or bus line. But the stimulative impact was less than the reader might expect. This was because the cost of land limited suburban employment opportunities, while the cost of utility extension and the relatively short term of the commercial mortgages available in the 1920s all served to constrain the pool of would-be homeowners who could actually secure mortgage approvals and afford a home of their own.[18] Nonetheless, credit became overextended, and the collapse of the development boom, mortgage defaults, and the financial distress of overextended households contributed to the severity and duration of the Great Depression.

The New Deal and Mortgage Insurance

The interstate and federal mortgage insurance were both initiatives of the New Deal. Federal mortgage insurance was designed to prevent a recurrence of the meltdown that occurred when homeowners defaulted on their mortgages, leading to the failure of banks and savings and loans. FHA insurance was also intended to provide an instant boost in public confidence in the banking system, encouraging deposits and priming the pump of economic recovery. More important for the long term, FHA insurance made home loans a much safer investment for banks and mortgage companies, laying the groundwork for the lending boom that underwrote the housing boom that followed World War II. With federal insurance in case of default, banks and other financial institutions could justify dramatic postwar increases in lending. In turn, new housing starts intended for the rental market declined from 44 percent of all new starts in 1927 to 8 percent in 1956.[19] It appears that the federalization of the financial risk associated with lending for home mortgages profoundly increased the production of homes for owner occupancy while reducing both the need and the incentive for commercial lenders to finance the development of multiunit housing. The postwar demand for owner-occupied housing was further stimulated by the GI Bill, which provided veterans with up to $25,000 to finance home ownership. With these finance measures in place, the postwar housing boom got under way long before Congress authorized the additional highway funding necessary to accelerate metropolitan freeway construction in 1956.

Metropolitan Expressways, Home Ownership, and Suburban Growth

New York and California increased their state gasoline taxes in 1946 and 1947, respectively, and established an early lead in postwar expressway construction and the development of a first generation of outlying suburbs premised exclusively on transportation by car and truck. After 1956, interstate funding provided the stimulus necessary to jump-start metropolitan freeway development in other states that had not reached legislative agreement on postwar increases in state gasoline taxes. New York and California provided models to emulate in building freeways and expressways.[20] Just as important, their new suburban developments and building codes also provided models that were widely emulated. Driven by economic recovery, rising incomes, unprecedented demand for home owner-ship, mortgage assistance, the development opportunities created by freeway access, and the affordability of housing built on less costly outlying land, the housing sales volumes of the 1950s and 1960s dwarfed the sales volume of the streetcar era.[21]

The signature housing product of the postwar era was a tract home built in the suburbs near a newly built expressway for getting to work. Perhaps the most seminal marriage of expressway and subdivision was Levittown, a 17,500-home subdivision development in Hempstead, Long Island. Still one of the largest subdivisions ever built, Levittown was located on 7.3 square miles of land that was transformed into a planned community of two-bedroom ranch and Cape Cod homes designed and priced for first-time homebuyers. Located on the Wantagh Parkway between the Southern and Northern Parkways, Levittown's instant success was made possible by pent-up demand, the affordability of its modest homes, and its parkway connections to Queens, Brooklyn, Manhattan, and the Bronx. Levittown's contribution to suburban development has been well described in Robert Sobel's *The Great Boom*. No other builder, Sobel wrote, "is more closely associated with the post–World War II building boom than William Levitt. No one has done more than he to revolutionize the [hous-ing] industry or to smash the notion that [public housing] projects were the best solution to the [postwar] housing shortage." As Sobel emphasizes, Levitt and Levittown were trailblazers for a new housing product—the tract home—and a new kind of housing production process that borrowed from Henry Ford's ap-proach to assembly-line production.

The typical homebuilder of the 1920s and 1930s was "an ambitious carpen-ter, bricklayer, or plumber who had amassed a little capital and started out by building a single house. If successful, he might hope to put up a half dozen homes a year with the aid of subcontractors." After the war, Levitt sensed much earlier than other builders that VA mortgages and mortgage insurance had the potential for transforming the owner-occupied segment of the housing market, creating the opportunity to use mass production methods to develop housing tracts with hundreds or even thousands of homes for sale. As Sobel reports, Levitt saw that "the market was there and the government was providing the financing. How could we lose?"

As Sobel tells the story, Levitt quietly amassed 7.3 square miles of land in the Island Trees area of Nassau County, not far from the Queens Border, much of which had been potato fields. Between mid-1947 and late 1951, Levitt put up 17,500 homes in two basic models, "ranches" and "Cape Cods." Levitt accom-plished this by adapting mass-production techniques that had been developed in the automobile industry and by purchasing materials in bulk, again like the automobile industry. As Levitt put it: "What it amounted to was a reversal of the Detroit assembly line. There the car moved while the workers stayed at their stations. In the case of our houses, it was the workers who moved doing the same job at different locations." Levitt's workers were deployed in teams, each of which was charged with a different task: These were not "factory-built" houses, but rather on-site construction. The only part of the house that was manufactured in a factory was the windows. The workers would put up the houses in a little more than a week, after which they would move on to the next unit of the development. As Levitt told *Time* magazine, "Each team or worker had specific tasks to perform. . . . Each crew did its special job and hurried on to the next site. A new [house] was finished every fifteen minutes."

As Sobel sums it up, "These 'Levitts' were purchased by individuals who were often the first in their families to own their own homes. . . . Most of these homes were purchased with FHA and GI mortgages, and the veterans who qualified for the latter could purchase their Levitts with no down-payment. . . . [T]hey were grateful to William Levitt for what they received."[22]

We have quoted Sobel at length because his commentary tells us a great deal about the kind of innovation that led to American leadership in the production of both motor vehicles and single-family housing. Both William Levitt and Henry Ford rethought and rationalized production processes so as to transform a luxury good into a consumer durable that could be profitably mass-produced at a price that was affordable for a broad swath of the American middle class. In other words, Levitt did for housing what Ford had done for cars. He industrialized housing production and made home ownership affordable for a larger swath of middle-income households.

In the 1960s, these and other innovations in housing construction combined with rising incomes, federal mortgage insurance, the tax deduction for mortgage interest, and expressway access to outlying acreage to lay the groundwork for suburban development on a massive scale. Such development could be financed because the results from Levittown and other large developments convinced commercial lenders that there was a huge reservoir of pent-up demand for home ownership and tract housing and that housing development was a good investment in terms of risk.

Much of the tract housing built during the 1960s and 1970s benefited from Levitt's production techniques. But the design and marketing methods used by later developers were more like those pioneered by General Motors. Later housing developers learned to use style and price differentiation as they were used by GM, to differentiate homes in ways that were responsive to style trends and to the demand for upgrades and amenities. Levitt and Ford were both pioneers of the art of mass production, but both were eventually eclipsed by rivals with a knack for styling and the profitable exploitation of product differentiation.[23]

The Interstate and the Development of a Next Generation of Suburbs

With the interstate, large but affordable parcels of outlying land—sometimes in current agricultural use, sometimes wasteland—became accessible for purchase, subdivision, and development as suburban homesites. Their distance from the city made these large parcels affordable for developer acquisition, while the interstates and the growth of suburban employment reduced the time it took to drive from these peripheral locations to metropolitan job centers. The size of these parcels and their relatively low acquisition cost made possible the replication of Levitt's industrial approach to housing production in metropolitan areas across the nation. Together, these synergies made home ownership affordable for a broad swath of the middle class. Thus the interstates were essential to the calculus of both home ownership and suburban development that followed World War II.

Initially, a long commute came with the purchase that many new homebuyers made, but freeways and the speed of freeway travel compensated by compressing the time it took to get to work or go shopping. And as the interstate beltways were built and linked with connecting arterials, additional opportunities for both commercial and residential development were created. In turn, these new shopping centers, industrial parks, and office parks created intervening employment and shopping opportunities for suburban residents. Over time, this array of new origins and destinations transformed the pattern of metropolitan travel and produced suburban population and employment majorities in U.S. metropolitan areas.

The development of beltway greenbelts into metropolitan employment centers was largely unanticipated when the Bureau of Public Roads drafted its 1939 and 1944 plans for the interregional highway system.[24] Nor was it a focus of attention when leading traffic engineers such as Wilbur Smith & Associates described the purpose and function of metropolitan freeways in the 1960s.

> Urban freeways are a vital part of the modern city's transportation system. They structure the transportation network; coordinate with land use planning; increase regional accessibility for all trip purposes and linkages; serve rapidly expanding and diffused urban travel patterns; provide rights-of-way for passenger cars, motor trucks, and public transit vehicles; afford many aesthetic opportunities; substantially relieve arterial street volumes, thereby reducing travel through residential neighborhoods; and constitute a prerequisite framework for organizing urban renewal projects and new community development.[25]

The vocabulary and phrasing of this 1966 description of the role of freeways in metropolitan transportation tells a transportation historian quite a bit about the expected outcomes of metropolitan freeway development. Most interesting is what's left out. This recitation places essentially no anticipatory emphasis on suburban *employment* growth, multinucleation, or the evolution of beltway suburbs into major employment centers that can rival many older central-city downtowns. The reason is that highway engineers did not anticipate the future magnitude of suburban employment growth.

Oral history interviews that this author has conducted on and off since the 1960s suggest that the extent of beltway shopping center and industrial park development caught the central cities, metropolitan newspapers, consulting engineers, and even the state highway departments largely by surprise.[26] This is not altogether surprising because the generation of suburbs built up in the late 1940s and early 1950s had been largely residential and therefore not widely perceived as a serious competitive threat to downtown. That perception began to change dramatically in the 1960s because the next generation of suburbs— with their shopping centers, their industrial parks, and the cantonment of their residential neighborhoods—was capable of competing effectively with the CBD for employers, for jobs, and for retail sales. This is the generation of suburbs that now accounts for substantially more than half of the population and employment in most U.S. metropolitan areas.

Traffic Engineering for Postwar Suburbs

The hallmarks of those suburbs that grew up in the 1960s and 1970s included the segregation of residential and commercial land use to protect residential areas from the noise and traffic associated with commercial and industrial activity; the cantonment of residential areas to shelter neighborhood streets from the intrusion of through traffic; the imposition of rigorous requirements for off-street parking, so as to allocate parking costs to merchants and employers, while protecting residential areas from spillover parking; the elimination of sidewalks in residential areas, so as to reduce housing costs and increase the yard-space available for private use; and the development of a street network with a hierarchy of facilities designed to serve the specialized functions of neighborhood access, local distribution, and arterial movement.[27]

The concept of "cantonment" was crucial to the workings of this hierarchy of streets and highways.[28] Los Angeles County traffic engineer Harold Marks told an Institute of Traffic Engineering conference in 1961 that neighborhood streets should be designed to provide access to a residential neighborhood but discourage travel through it. He added that "a basic guiding principle for all modern residential street design is the provision of 'built-in' protection against through traffic. The street pattern should allow for penetration of the neighborhood only by vehicles with destinations inside. Direct connections between boundary thoroughfares should be avoided or made circuitous to discourage undesirable through traffic." In turn, design features, such as curvilinear align-ment, cul-de-sacs, short street runs, and elbow turns, should be used to dis-courage the intrusion of through traffic.[29]

The intended result of this reform movement in traffic engineering was the development of communities in which the automobile could be used safely and conveniently without impinging on the safety, quiet, privacy, and parking supply of residential areas—problems that are notoriously obvious in former streetcar suburbs that are now inhabited by an auto-owning population and workforce. A second intended result was the specialization of arterial streets to serve relatively large volumes of local traffic as safely and efficiently as possible. Both of these results were largely achieved. But with this improvement in the safety and efficiency of traffic movement came an unintended side effect: the creation of a land use pattern and street layouts that are inhospitable to walking and transit use. In this sense, the dependence of postwar suburbs on the automobile was a by-product not of sprawl but of systematic and orderly planning for the safe use and the contained parking of the automobile.

The Interstate and Pervasive Motorization

By 1980, the construction of many of the most important urban radials on the interstate system could be characterized as well advanced, and the development of the metropolitan beltways was well under way. Together the construction of the radials and beltways and the development of suburban housing and employ-ment centers created communities and travel corridors that were hospitable to the safe and convenient use of the automobile. Many of these outlying suburbs were wholly dependent on cars and trucks for day-to-day transportation, and most were largely so. For families in outlying suburbs, getting to work, getting to the market, and getting the kids to school all required ready access to an auto-mobile. This "requirement" defined the auto-ownership expectations of most suburban residents: Every adult needed one.

In turn, the growth of the suburban population ratcheted up the share of American households in which one car for each adult had become a social expectation and a felt "need." The resulting increase in households with two and three cars—and the declining share of the population that was able to get to work by walking or using mass transit—was sufficient to propel the United States over the threshold of pervasive motorization in 1980. In this sense, we can say that the interstate laid the groundwork for pervasive motorization. But with the next breath, we must also emphasize that increasing home ownership,

Table 5.6 *Scaling the presence of cars, trucks, and transit in the United States*

	1956	2000	Change
U.S. GDP per capita	$10,914	$28,129	158%
U.S. population (in millions)	168	281	67%
Vehicle registrations (in millions)	65	222	240%
Vehicle registrations per 1,000 pop.	387	786	103%
Vehicle miles traveled (per capita)	3,947	9,808	248%
VMT (aggregate in trillions)	664	2,760	316%
Transit ridership (in billions)	10,981	9,363	−15%
Population of top 8 U.S. transit markets in 1956 (in millions)	18.1	15.2	−16%

SOURCE: *Statistical Abstract of the United States*, 1962 and 2003.

suburbanization, and pervasive motorization would not have occurred in the absence of postwar economic growth, increasing GDP per capita, and the rising expectations of American households. Nor would they have occurred if they had not matched the social norms and lifestyle expectations of the American middle class. In fact, the outcome that was achieved after World War II was not unintended: it was hoped for.

In 1937, Harvard scholars John Nolan and H. V. Hubbard specifically artic-ulated the hope that "Parkway systems, if broadly and widely conceived, may give form to a new type of 'regional city.' [Parkways] may become the framework for a new town-and-country community by providing a practical means for a better distribution of population."[30] Nolan and Hubbard's desired outcome has been largely achieved, but many contemporary planners and urbanists regret the metropolitan transformation that has accompanied it.[31] This author's view is that Americans have voted with their wheels and their checkbooks.[32]

Table 5.6 scales the increasing presence of cars and trucks in American life since the interstate was fully funded in 1956. The difference between table 5.6 and table 5.5, which examines the period between 1957 and 1987, is striking. Table 5.6 shows that both vehicle registrations and VMT increased almost 3.6 times faster than the U.S. population between 1956 and 2000. It also shows that aggregate VMT increased 4.7 times faster. Finally, it shows that the population of the six cities that were the prime transit markets of 1956 declined by 16 percent from 1956 to 2000, while transit's nationwide ridership was declining 15 percent.

Other major dynamics of this period were the explosive growth of both suburban employment and suburb-to-suburb commuting and a dramatic in-crease in the teenagers with driver's licenses, especially teenage girls, which produced correspondingly rapid growth in the number of households with three vehicles. These outcomes were, of course, contemporaneous with the growth of beltway suburbs and beltway employment. Taken together, we suspect these factors account for most of the differences between tables 5.6 and 5.7, but the data necessary to fully test this hypothesis are fragmentary. In any case, another conclusion is unavoidable. The United States was already the world's most thoroughly motorized nation in 1956 and had become much more so by the year 2000, thanks largely to the concentration of national population and employment growth in the sunbelt and the beltway suburbs of U.S. metropolitan areas.

Which Came First?

Which came first: income gains, motorization, or suburbanization? This sounds like a "chicken or egg" question, but it is not. Rising incomes and suburbanization came first in the railroad and the streetcar eras. The suburban estates of the railroad era established housing expectations to which only the wealthy could aspire. The suburban homes of the streetcar era ranged from gracious family homes to modest bungalows affordable to skilled members of the working class, a widening of home ownership opportunity that could now include a larger swath of the middle class. Thus both home and auto ownership had become expectations of the middle class by the late 1920s.

The suburban homes of the freeway era range from grand estates to modest two-bedroom homes like those that Levitt built on Long Island. The trend from the railroad era to the freeway era is fourfold: increasing breadth of American buying and borrowing power; increasing democratization of the potential for home ownership; increasing aspirations on the part of the middle and working classes to own homes; and increasing reliance on transportation—first railroads and streetcars, then automobiles, highways, and freeways—to fulfill these aspirations.

Home ownership was the prize; increasing incomes created the possibility; and in turn streetcars, the tax deductibility of interest payments, the GI Bill, efficiencies in housing construction, freeways and expressways, women's participation in the workforce, and increased household buying power made it possible for more Americans. A substantial mortgage, a longer commute in terms of mileage, and a sprawling settlement pattern are all part of the price that Americans have paid. The result can be described as sprawl or the democratization of home and automobile ownership. The extent of both is uniquely American—a reflection of personal and social aspirations that are deeply felt, buying and borrowing power that is widely distributed, and the income-tax deductions for mortgage interest that date from 1913. Nowhere did these dynamics play out more powerfully than in Los Angeles.

America's First Thoroughly Motorized Metropolis: A Los Angeles Case Study

In 1970, Los Angeles was self-described and widely known as "the freeway capital of the world," but its national leadership in motorization was of much longer duration. In 1936, Los Angeles was already the United States' third most populous metropolitan area. It trailed only New York and Chicago. In 1936, Los Angeles reported 357 motor vehicles per 1,000 residents. Chicago had 122, and New York only 86. In 1936, the aggregate nationwide level of motorization was 222 per 1,000 residents, thanks primarily to relatively high levels of auto owner-ship in metropolitan suburbs, midsized cities, small towns, and farm country. The only other large metropolitan area with a motorization level close to that in Los Angeles was Detroit with 227 per 1,000 residents.[33]

This barrage of statistics raises an obvious question: Why did motorization occur so much earlier and more thoroughly in Los Angeles than in any other U.S. metropolitan area? The answer is counterintuitive, and it lies in the timing of L.A.'s development. Los Angeles experienced exceptionally vigorous invest-ment in street railways and exceptionally rapid growth in both population and motor vehicle ownership during the streetcar era. Streetcar lines were installed in anticipation of population growth and the demand for housing that would accompany it. More specifically, they were built to exploit the development potential of a largely vacant coastal plain. The population growth that followed was extraordinary. The population of metropolitan Los Angeles increased from 190,000 in 1900 to 2.3 million in 1930. Thus Los Angeles became the first American city to grow up with both the streetcar and the automobile. The result, by 1920, was a multinucleated settlement pattern best described as a hori-zontal city with a town-and-country weave. There was room in the weave of this settlement pattern for the interurban streetcar network, a vast network of thor-oughfares, and eventually the nation's most extensive metropolitan freeway system. There was insufficient density of settlement in Los Angeles to deflect mass motorization or to make surface parking an uneconomic land use—a de-velopmental difference that sharply distinguishes Los Angeles from New York, Chicago, Philadelphia, and Boston, all of which experienced initial urbaniza-tion two centuries earlier than Los Angeles.[34]

In each of these older American cities, street railway electrification and extension were superimposed on the streets of an already dense and populous city that had grown up with walking and horsecars as its primary means of urban movement. In these cities, street railways and subways reinforced the domi-nance of downtown. In turn, the limited parking supply of these densely cities served to deflect motorization. No such deflection of motorization occurred in Los Angeles or other cities that grew up primarily reliant on the automobile.

Other factors also contributed to the intensity of motorization in Los An-geles. One was Southern California's mild Mediterranean climate, which meant that winter snow provided no deterrence to the growth of outlying suburbs. Another was the distribution of the metropolitan population: Los Angeles devel-oped as a constellation of communities with numerous shopping districts and activity centers and a downtown that was central in location but largely vestigial in function. Thus, in terms of both urban form and the intensity of motorization, Los Angeles in 1936 was already America's first thoroughly motorized metropolis long before the freeway era. Others cities in this class of motorized metropoli now include Austin, Dallas–Fort Worth, Houston, Jacksonville, Oklahoma City, Orlando, Phoenix, Sacramento, San Antonio, San Diego, San Jose, Tampa, and Tucson. These sunbelt cities were America's primary growth centers of the interstate era.

As the first of this kind, Los Angeles was a metropolis of its own invention, embracing both streetcar and freeway development more aggressively than any previous city of its size. In the 1930s, Los Angeles followed New York's lead in developing parkways. It built its first expressways during and after World War II, and then pursued the nation's most aggressive program of freeway development, beginning early in the 1950s. It was able to do so because interstitial open space was still widely available for acquisition as freeway rights-of-way following World War II. In turn, public policy gave motorization in Los Angeles a forceful push: the California legislature increased the statewide gas tax in 1947 and again in 1953. The 1953 legislation was especially timely because it enabled the state to reserve rights-of-way for freeway development despite the continuing rapid growth of Los Angeles in the 1950s, allowing L.A. to make the most of the federal highway funds that became available under the auspices of the interstate pro-gram in 1956.

The outcome of freeway development in Los Angeles is not what its plan-ners and engineers had expected. Los Angeles has become the nation's most congested metropolitan area, despite building the nation's most comprehensive freeway network. Table 5.7 shows that the delays now experienced by freeway users in Los Angeles are longer than those in any other metropolitan area on a per capita basis. In fact, those delays were nearly two times longer than those experienced in other large sunbelt cities in the year 2002. Los Angeles also led the nation in terms of the fuel wasted and the pollutants emitted due to conges-tion and stop-and-start driving. In other words, the nation's most aggressive freeway construction program has been unable to sustain the reductions in delay and stop-and-start driving that it initially achieved.

But table 5.7 also shows that San Francisco ranks second in the nation in terms of congested delay per capita, despite having made one of the nation's most aggressive commitments to transit investment. Obviously, this is not the

Table 5.7 *Delays in the nation's most congested cities in 2002*

MSAs	Hours of delay per capita
Los Angeles	62
San Francisco	41
Dallas/Ft. Worth	37
Houston	36
Washington, D.C.	35
Denver	35
Seattle	34
Miami	33
San Jose	33
Atlanta	33

SOURCE: Schrank and Lomax, 2002 *Urban Mobility Study.*

outcome that the Bay Area expected from its ostensibly "balanced" program of investment in freeways and rapid transit.

What the Bay Area should have anticipated is that the region's topography and development pattern would concentrate traffic flow and lead to an exceptionally dense concentration of traffic on its skeletal freeway network. Anticipating and seeking to avoid this outcome, the California Division of Highways proposed a second generation of parallel freeways in the region's most congested bayside corridors. With San Francisco in opposition to continuing freeway development within its boundaries, the highway department's plan for offshore freeways was rejected by local authorities on both sides of San Francisco Bay, and the region bet on BART instead. As tables 5.7 and 5.8 show, the result is not what the Bay Area expected. It has become the nation's second most congested metropolitan area.

On the other hand, table 5.8 does show that delays per capita are substantially lower in most of the transit markets of the Eastern Seaboard than in Los Angeles and San Francisco, despite population densities that are substantially higher. One implication of table 5.8 is that older cities with limited parking and densities that are sufficient to deflect motorization can be more effective in delimiting congestion and excess fuel consumption than cities like Los Angeles and the San Francisco Bay Area, which have tried to prevent congestion by pairing extensive freeway development and extensive transit investment. But a second implication of the same table is that a metropolitan area like the Bay Area may not be able to rely on transit and high densities and limited parking in the urban core to dampen highway congestion if most of its population growth has occurred in the freeway era and its freeway network is too sparse to effectively distribute and disperse metropolitan traffic flows.

Table 5.8 *Traffic delays and fuel wasted in Los Angeles and other large cities in 2002*

Prime transit markets	Hours of delay per capita	Fuel wasted in gallons per capita
Philadelphia	15	44
New York	23	39
Chicago	27	43
Boston	28	45
Seattle	34	56
Washington, D.C.	35	56
San Francisco	41	67
Los Angeles	62	94

SOURCE: Schrank and Lomax, 2002 *Urban Mobility Study.*

Thus four cautions are in order before planners embrace the new direction in land use and transportation planning that Kenworthy and others propose. The first of these cautions is that transit-friendly settlement patterns are historically conditioned. In the United States, there are only seven cities with sufficient density to sustain close-to-European levels of transit use.[35] Four are major financial centers that had surpassed the population threshold of 1 million by the year 1900: New York, Chicago, Philadelphia, and Boston. Two other major U.S. transit markets are financial centers that anchor metropolitan areas with unique topography: San Francisco and Seattle. The last is a city with a unique role: Washington, D.C.

The second caution is that cities with high rates of transit use may, nonetheless, experience high levels of congestion and fuel waste if their expressway networks are as sparse as those in San Francisco, Seattle, and Washington, D.C. The third caution is that prolonged congestion does not have to translate into long commutes if most workers live relatively close to their place of work. In this regard, Los Angeles and San Francisco compare favorably with New York, Chicago, and Washington. Their year-2000 work-trip travel times averaged 29 minutes, compared with 34 for New York, 32 for Washington, and 31 for Chicago.[36] Seattle bested its peer group with an average journey-to-work travel time of just 28 minutes.

Our conclusion is that when it comes to transportation investment and traffic management, one-size-fits-all doesn't work very well. Transportation planning is most likely to produce its best results when it is tailored to fit local circumstances and local needs. Neither highway nor transit investment is intrinsically "better." A mix of transportation investments that fits local circumstances is likely to be the best local alternative.[37]

The Growth of Suburban Employment

In most U.S. metropolitan areas, major employers followed the middle class to the suburbs during the interstate era, and by 1980 suburban employment exceeded central city employment in most of the United States' largest metropolitan areas. Table 5.9 reports the suburban share of employment in eight major metropolitan areas for 1982, two years after the United States crossed the threshold of pervasive motorization. As it shows, suburban employment accounted for more than half of all metropolitan employment in every one of these major metropolitan areas and more than 60 percent in four of the seven. This was largely attributable to the growth of major shopping and employment centers in beltway suburbs and main street shopping districts in other suburban communities.

After World War II, the mix of suburban employment was dominated by retailing and manufacturing, but it also included a healthy endowment of business services, wholesale trade, and finance, insurance, and real estate activities. The evolving character of suburban employment opportunities is indicated by the fact that 178 Fortune 500 corporations were headquartered in suburban locations by 1980, up from only 47 in 1965.[38] The increased collocation of households and job opportunities in suburban settings was obvious by 1980—a strong indication that the interstate, the affordability of suburban housing, and the buying power of the suburban population have all had a profound impact on the geography of employment and commercial activity in U.S. metropolitan areas. The result is an increasingly sprawling but polycentric settlement pattern that is simultaneously horizontal, automobile-dependent, and access-efficient. It is access-efficient because the collocation of jobs and housing in nearby suburbs has made home-to-work travel more time-efficient, even if work trips are somewhat longer in terms of miles driven.

The Evolved Metropolis of the Interstate Era

Most geographers agree that increases in home and automobile ownership have combined with the growth of suburban population and employment to create a settlement pattern that is no longer "metropolitan" in the traditional sense of the word. Instead, the desire for home ownership and the increasing collocation of jobs, services, and employment in suburban settings has transformed the downtown-centered metropolis of the streetcar era into the sprawling but polynucleated metropolis of the freeway era. This evolved metropolis remains access-efficient because the collocation of households and employment in suburban settings still allows most commuters to get to work by freeway in 15–

Table 5.9 *Suburban employment shares in U.S metropolitan areas in 1982*

St. Louis	69.4%
Washington	69.1%
San Francisco	64.0%
Philadelphia	63.2%
Baltimore	58.8%
New York	53.7%
Denver	52.7%

SOURCE: Wheeler et al, *Economic Geography*, 181–82.

30 minutes even if their journey is 10–20 miles.[39] This suburbanized metropolis can be aptly described as a polyopolis, comprising a multitude of cities, suburbs, and outlying towns.[40]

Urban mayors complain that this evolution has diminished downtown and the central city's standing in the metropolitan economy, while the critics of urban sprawl emphasize the low density and auto dependence of the post-interstate metropolis. But an increasing number of geographers now emphasize that collocation and motorization have produced a settlement pattern that is simultaneously sprawling and access-efficient.[41] In any case, what seems clear is that the interstate has combined with the growth of suburban population and suburban employment to enable the development of a new kind of American metropolis that is access-efficient for the vast majority of American households that own an automobile, but increasingly difficult to navigate for those who do not.

The evolution of the prototypical American city from a downtown-centered metropolis to a multicentered polyopolis went hand-in-hand with increasing motorization and the growth of suburban employment. In turn, VMT have increased significantly, but journey-to-work travel times have increased only moderately. Nationwide, the average worker can still get to work in roughly 25 minutes.[42] The increase in VMT is directly associated with the increase in travel speed that the interstates have enabled and the corresponding ability of the metropolitan motorists of the last quarter of the century to travel much longer distances in half an hour than their peers of the 1920s, 1930s, and 1940s. Thus the combined effect of motorization, freeway development, suburban housing development, and suburban employment growth has been to make home ownership possible for a much larger slice of the American population without substantially increasing commuter travel time. This—along with the decline of the frostbelt's share of the U.S. population—explains why public subsidies for mass transit have been unable to reverse the continuing decline in transit's share of the commute market, and why continuing motorization has produced such significant increases in both freeway congestion and metropolitan VMT.

What Is the Bottom Line?

This author believes that metropolitan freeway development has produced both social opportunities and environmental liabilities. The most significant opportunity was the increased ability of the middle class to afford home ownership. This opportunity reached full bloom in the late 1980s as the development of the metropolitan beltways combined with increasing women's workforce participation to enable a tidal increase in suburban employment, household buying power, and home ownership. The resulting impacts included a significant acceleration of suburban population growth and resulting increases in urban sprawl, VMT, and automotive fuel consumption. An unexpected side effect was that the highway capacity installed under the auspices of the interstate program became congested much sooner than highway engineers had forecast. Still another side effect was the diminished usefulness of transit in an operating environment transformed by freeways and subdivisions.

One of the most obvious reasons that public ownership has not enabled transit to regain metropolitan market share is that suburban land use patterns are not conducive to intensive transit use, but the more telling reason is that freeways and an auto-oriented land use pattern work well for the vast majority of adults who own a car. This is especially true for the majority of metropolitan commuters who now live *and* work in nearby suburbs. Thus as sprawling and sometimes congested as American suburbs may be, freeways, multinucleation, and collocation have produced a settlement pattern that is time-efficient for most adults who drive.

For all of these reasons, many urban geographers believe that "a critical mass of leading economic activities has irreversibly suburbanized and the polycentric freeway city has become the urban morphology of the foreseeable future.[43] For the same reason, it is likely that pervasive motorization will remain the American norm as long as automobile ownership and use remain broadly affordable for most of the working population. The seemingly unavoidable correlate of this conclusion is that changes in motor vehicle technology and fuels will prove more effective than mass transit and mode shift in resolving the future economic and environmental problems that will otherwise be associated with the gradual depletion of the world's oil supplies and the increasing burden of CO_2 emissions associated with global motorization and global industrialization.

Summing Up

1. After a decade of political stalemate, Congress authorized full funding for the interstate highway program in 1956. The legislative logjam was broken after Congress reached agreement that the federal government

should finance 90 percent of the cost of construction through an increase in gasoline, motor fuel, and tire taxes and that such funds should be reserved exclusively for highway investment. Over the next 44 years, almost 20,000 miles of urban freeway were built under the auspices of the interstate highway program.

2. It is widely believed by urbanists and planners that the metropolitan freeways built and financed by the interstate program are the primary reason that the United States became the world's most pervasively motorized nation. But Canada experienced more intensive motorization during the interstate years than the United States, despite pursuing a notably restrained approach to metropolitan highway investment. During these same years, Canada experienced greater percentage increases in GDP and GDP per capita than the United States and greater increases in motor vehicle ownership per 1,000 population—a strong indication that household income growth was the more decisive factor determining per capita levels of motor vehicle ownership in both the United States and Canada.

3. The interstate was instrumental in opening up opportunities for middle-income and working-class households to own a home of their own. The interstate's principal contribution was bringing large swaths of outlying farmland and open space within the convenient commute radius of U.S. metropolitan areas. Simultaneous advances in home construction methods enabled developers to achieve economies of scale in housing production. This enabled builders to develop and market suburban housing at prices that made home ownership affordable for middle-income families. The GI Bill further contributed to the affordability of home ownership during the postwar years.

4. Since 1956, congestion has increased more rapidly in cities like Los Angeles that were aggressive in building freeways than in major transit markets that have the density to deflect pervasive motorization. But caution is in order in interpreting this finding, because high levels of U.S. transit use and downtown employment are only found in a special class of cities—the nation's longtime banking and finance centers.

5. Increasing incomes, increasing automobile ownership, the interstate, suburbanization, and the growth of trucking all contributed to the extraordinary 198 percent increase in urban VMT that occurred in the United States from 1956 to 1980.

6. The outlying suburbs built during the interstate era are largely dependent on motor vehicles for transportation. In turn, the growth of the suburban population has ratcheted up the number of households likely to own more than one car.

7. Commerce and light industry followed the middle class to the suburbs

during the interstate era, and by 1980, suburban employment exceeded central city employment in most of the nation's larger metropolitan areas. Thus, as sprawling and pervasively motorized as American cities may be, freeway development, multinucleation, and collocation have produced a settlement pattern that is access-efficient when measured in terms of the time it takes to get to and from work by car.

8. The social dynamics of the postwar era—the decline of central city population, the decline of industrial employment in frostbelt cities, the growth of both population and employment in the suburbs and sunbelt, and the seeming inability of transit to substantially rebuild market share—all suggest that changes in automotive technology and fuels will be more effective than transit expenditures in reducing U.S. oil import requirements, automotive CO_2 emissions, and motorization's contribution to global warming.

SIX

Transit's Conversion to
Public Ownership

Transit's conversion to public ownership occurred in the context of profound changes in the growth trends, spatial arrangements, racial composition, and economic prospects of American cities. In many of the nation's most populous and most transit-oriented cities, these changes included decline in the central city's white population, rapid growth of the central city's black population, quickening growth of suburban population and employment, a weakening of downtown's employment base, and increasing dilapidation and blight—both in the shadows of downtown and in lower-income neighborhoods. These trends accelerated white flight, alarmed urban mayors, and mobilized downtown support for urban redevelopment and federal investment in both rapid transit and urban renewal.

The mayors and downtown viewed rapid transit and suburban commuter service as essential preconditions for keeping employers downtown and luring suburban customers back downtown. Such was the context in which urban mayors began their push for federal aid for transit in 1958, first goaded by a round of railroad commuter service abandonments in the Northeast.

The effort to secure federal subsidies for railroad commuter service was led by a coalition of urban mayors and commuter railroads with a shared interest in securing federal funds to upgrade commuter rail systems, develop a next generation of rail rapid transit systems, and renew downtown growth and development. The specific legislative objective of this coalition of urban mayors and railroad executives was twofold: low-interest loans for the improvement of commuter rail services and federal grants for rapid transit projects like Philadelphia's Lindenwald Line. The coalition's principal talking points were the "imbalance" of the federal government's transportation policy with its exclusive emphasis on highway investment and the promised future potential of new rail rapid transit lines such as the Lindenwald Line and new systems such as San Francisco's BART.

By 1960, the railroads and the mayors had concluded that federal aid was more pragmatic than state funding for transit and commuter service. Urban Democrat John F. Kennedy had just been elected to the White House, and the mayors had found little receptivity to funding for mass transit in most state legislatures. Congress was receptive, and the eventual result was a federal transit program that gave priority emphasis to the conversion of mass transit to public ownership and federal funding for new rail systems.

With hindsight, we can say that public ownership and reinvestment were necessary but insufficient to restore transit's competitiveness. Missing was any serious effort to reorganize street transit in the process of its conversion to public ownership. Thus policymakers passed up a favorable opportunity to orchestrate change in transit's fare structure, work rules, and service mix—changes that were essential if transit were to compete on widely favorable terms with the automobile. Instead, Congress focused on recapitalizing transit and shied away from the kind of industrial reorganization that would have been necessary for buses to compete more cost-effectively with the automobile. Federal funding made a soft landing possible for transit, but the decades that followed have produced neither vigorous recovery of central city ridership nor a broadly based increase in transit rides per capita or transit's commute share.

These disappointing results reflect the fact that policymakers did not and have not come to grips with the many aspects of public transit's inherited cost structure that were incompatible with the new markets that transit has entered since its conversion to public ownership and with the new roles that transit has been asked to play under public ownership. As a result, public ownership and investment have proved insufficient to substantially reverse the long-term decline in transit ridership on a per capita basis.

Table 6.1 shows that transit ridership declined from its peacetime peak of 147 rides per capita in 1926 to 31 rides per capita in 1972, its most recent low. It then recovered to 36 rides per capita in 1980 and has since fluctuated narrowly. It appears that federal investment and local subsidy have, at best, stabilized transit's market share at a level very close to its low for the twentieth century. We cannot avoid the conclusion that neither public ownership nor federal investment

Table 6.1 *Transit rides per capita in peacetime, 1907–2000*

Year	Rides per capita	Index of rides per capita (1926 = 100)
1907	120	82
1920	143	97
1926	147	100
1940	99	67
1946	165	112
1950	113	77
1960	52	35
1970	36	24
1972	31	21
1980	36	24
1990	35	24
1995	30	20
2000	33	22

SOURCE: APTA, *Transit Fact Book*, 1997.
NOTE: APTA and its predecessor organization, ATA, did not define commuter rail, dial-a-ride, and ferry service as transit rides until 1990. The baseline for 1926 would be approximately 153 rides per capita if it were adjusted to include railroad commuter passengers.

has enabled transit to make steady gains in market share or to bounce back very far from its 1972 low in rides per capita.

Gains in market share have proved elusive for four primary reasons. One is that federal policy was premised on the historically faulty proposition that transit's difficulties were the result of unbalanced public policy, a premise that ignored the many forms of obsolescence that plagued the transit industry by 1945 and the financial difficulties it had experienced since World War I.[1] Another reason that gains in market share have proven elusive is that the population of the central cities has declined both in absolute terms and as a share of the national population. The third reason is that the sunbelt's share of the national population has increased, while the share of the population that lives in the frostbelt's transit-oriented industrial centers has declined sharply. The fourth reason is that increasing women's participation in the workforce has enabled an increasing number of households to afford both a second car and a suburban home. For all of these reasons, public ownership and federal investment have been unable to produce any broadly based or sustained increase in either transit rides per capita or transit commute share.

Thus it is our appraisal that Congress misjudged the underlying causes, the duration, and the severity of transit's competitive difficulties in the process of constructing transit policy. The result was legislation that pleased urban mayors, downtown business, and transit labor—but did not prepare or equip transit to rebuild market share. The unfortunate consequence is that transit's conversion to public ownership was missed as an opportunity to modernize and reorganize public transportation in more than cosmetic ways.

Transit's Problems and Their Underlying Causes

There is no doubt that many major cities and their transit systems were in trouble in 1960 when Congress took up the question of public ownership of public transportation. From 1950 to 1960, transit ridership had declined 46 percent on an aggregate nationwide basis.[2] Central cities of the nation's largest metropolitan areas had experienced net losses in residential population. These cities included Baltimore, Boston, Chicago, Cleveland, Detroit, Minneapolis, Newark, New York, Philadelphia, Pittsburgh, San Francisco, and Washington, D.C. Rapid transit systems lost 21 percent of their aggregate nationwide ridership, while surface lines in the largest cities lost 56 percent of their ridership between 1950 and 1960.[3] Even larger percentage losses were experienced in smaller cities and in suburban markets. Clearly, the combined impact of declining central city populations, ridership losses, service abandonment, and increasing automobile ownership was rapidly displacing transit use in cities both large and small. But race was another factor that complicates any easy or comfortable understanding of the reasons for transit's ridership losses.

During World War II, the federal government imposed wage and price controls while establishing fair employment practices that effectively outlawed discrimination in hiring. One by-product of these policies was a sharp increase in the number of black workers—especially tenant farmers from the cotton belt—who sought employment in the industrial states of the urban North and West where defense contracting was concentrated. The scale of this migration may be judged from the sectional trend of black migration that occurred in the 1940s. Emigration diminished the black population of southern states by 8 percent while increasing the black population of the northeastern states by 27 percent and the north central states by 36 percent. The increase in the West's black population was 300 percent on a very small initial base.[4] Thus World War II was clearly a critical event in terms of igniting the process of racial change in the population composition of America's industrial cities. In the 1950s, African Americans continued to leave the cotton belt. As Carol Heim reports, "Southern blacks displaced by mechanization in agriculture that migrated north in the 1950s found an economy less able to absorb them (and later their children) than had the wartime migrants of the 1940s. This problem worsened in the 1970s–80s as the number of good-quality manufacturing jobs open to those with less education or skill diminished."[5]

Table **6.2** *Black percentage of the 1960 population in U.S. cities that were major transit markets*

Newark	34
Detroit	29
Cleveland	29
St. Louis	29
Philadelphia	26
Chicago	23
Pittsburgh	17
New York	14
San Francisco	10
Boston	9
Seattle	5

SOURCE: *Statistical Abstract of the United States, 1962.*

Another reason that new arrivals experienced chronic underemployment in the central city is that many retail and service businesses followed the white population to the suburbs during the 1950s, 1960s, and 1970s. In turn, chronic underemployment contributed to the decline of central city buying power and the vigor of the retail sector of the urban economy. These domino effects of white flight further exacerbated the decline of urban employment, urban retailing, and big city transit ridership. Table 6.2 shows the major transit markets that experienced the largest proportional influx of African Americans during the 1950s.

Those northern cities that experienced the largest influx of African Americans experienced "white flight" on a larger scale than those that did not. We also know that present-day transit use rates are greater in those cities where neither black influx nor white flight were mass migrations. This suggests that white flight and other racial dynamics of the 1950s and 1960s contributed to the "hollowing out" of central city economies and the decline of urban buying power, employment, and transit use.

Major transit markets of 1960 that seem to have been relatively successful in avoiding these dynamics include New York, San Francisco, Boston, and Seattle. They have retained their standing as prime transit markets. In large measure, their exceptionalism can be attributed to their role as national banking and finance centers—a role that sustained both downtown employment and transit ridership, despite declining central city populations. Table 6.2 also suggests that it would have been easier for New York, San Francisco, Boston, and Seattle to maintain economic equilibrium because they experienced less black immigration and less white emigration than Newark, Detroit, Cleveland, St. Louis, Chicago, or Philadelphia. Hurting more than other major banking centers, Philadelphia was the city whose mayor instigated the initial push for federal funding for mass transit.

The Campaign for Federal Funding

Philadelphia mayor Richardson Dilworth and James Symes, the chairman of the Pennsylvania Railroad, initiated the campaign for federal investment in mass transit in 1959. Dilworth was looking for improvements in suburban commuter service that could be combined with urban renewal and downtown redevelopment to bring jobs, customers, and buying power back to downtown Philadelphia. Symes was looking for financial relief from the regulatory obligations that required the Pennsylvania Railroad to operate suburban commute service to Philadelphia, even though passenger service was losing money. Symes and Dilworth assembled a coalition of urban mayors and railroad presidents who were prepared to advocate for federal subsidies for mass transit and low-interest loans for railroad commuter service.[6] They proposed tax relief for commuter railroads, low-interest loans for capital improvements, and a study of capital grants for rail rapid transit—a proposal that was rebuffed by the congressional committees responsible for highway investment.

A tactical decision was made that federal aid for public transportation would be sought within the framework of federal aid for the cities rather than federal aid for public works.[7] With hindsight, we know that this had significant future implications. It meant that decisions about transit investment would be largely divorced from decisions about metropolitan highway development. It also meant that capital grants to transit agencies would be separate from formula apportionments to state highway departments and that it would be more difficult to coordinate the development and programming of synergistic projects such as bus service, high-occupancy vehicle lanes, and park-and-ride lots.

Turning to the Senate Urban Affairs Committee, the coalition of mayors and railroads received a warm welcome from the subcommittee responsible for urban renewal and redevelopment. Working with Senator Harrison "Pete" Williams of New Jersey, Dilworth and Symes further honed their proposal so that it would fall within the jurisdiction of the model cities and urban renewal programs over which the committee had legislative oversight. The heavy investment that the transit aid program has made in rail rapid transit and its lack of enthusiasm for bus-on-freeway transit is understandable in this context because the construction of rail systems was—and is—seen as an important strategy of urban renewal by HUD, city planners, redevelopment agencies, and downtown business.[8]

Thus the mayors' advocacy for federal funding was intensely focused on downtown, urban renewal, and subsidies for rapid transit and rail commuter service. As Michael Danielson observed, "By the spring of 1961, the federal mass transportation coalition bore a close resemblance to the urban alliance of downtown stores, real estate interests concerned with central city property values, commuter railways, central city banks, central city politicians, and others concerned with the implications of the worsening of the central city tax base."[9] Senator Williams broadened the proposal advanced by the mayors and railroads to include bus service, but no significant effort was invested in understanding the financial difficulties of urban bus and streetcar companies, the long-term duration of those difficulties, or the steps necessary to renew ridership growth and improve productivity. This orientation was reinforced by the consultants' report prepared by Lyle Fitch and Associates for the Kennedy administration. Both the administration and the Fitch report focused on planning at the metropolitan scale and the rail transit improvements needed to deliver suburban commuters and shoppers downtown.[10] No comparable interest was shown in bus and streetcar operations, even though they accounted for 80 percent of all transit passengers in 1960.

The Kennedy Administration's Prescription for Transit

The presidency of John Kennedy was the first headed by an urban Democrat since the New Deal. Thus it should not be surprising that the focus and priorities of the federal transit program as it first emerged in the 1960s were informed by the perceived needs of the central cities of the largest metropolitan areas.[11] As the administration's transit consultant concluded: "It is here that the deficiencies, both of private automobile and mass transportation modes, are most acute, the financial requirements the greatest, and the organizational problems most complex."[12] In turn, the recommended first priority in terms of "urgency of need" for transit investment was providing the infusion of federal funds necessary to stabilize and modernize transit service in the largest metropolitan areas, especially "financially shaky and partially obsolete suburban [rail] and rapid-transit rail services."[13] The emphasis on suburban rail and rail rapid transit was, of course, the emphasis sought by the commuter railroads and the big city mayors.

The legislation that finally emerged from Congress entailed a much broader commitment. It included the federal funding needed to finance local public acquisition of the hundreds of bus and streetcar operations still in private ownership; federal funding for the replacement of aging buses and streetcars, and labor-sponsored provisions that guaranteed labor contract continuity under public ownership. This broad-based commitment to public ownership of public transportation preserved transit service in communities large and small. It also enabled the introduction of service in suburban communities previously without service, but it included no specific focus on productivity improvement.

Table 6.3 details the expansion of the federal role in financing urban public

Table 6.3 *Congressional actions in the evolution of federal transit policy*

1961	Authorized loans and demonstration grants for urban mass transportation services.
1964	Appropriated general fund revenues for a program of capital grants for transit improvement, established a 67 percent federal match rate, and stipulated that no state was to receive more than 12.5 percent of the program's total outlays.
1970	Eliminated 12.5 percent ceiling and allowed multiyear commitments necessary to fund rail rapid transit systems.
1973	Authorized the use of federal gas tax funds for selected transit purposes; increased federal matching share to 80 percent for transit projects.
1974	Authorized federal funding for transit operating purposes on a 50/50 matching basis.
1978	Augmented operating assistance for cities with rail transit systems and extended operating subsidies to cities previously considered too small to support public transportation.
1980	Retreated from the federal commitment to transit operating subsidies, at the insistence of President Reagan. Only a few states provided funds to fill the revenue gap.
1991	Declared the sunset of the interstate highway program. Designated a new national highway system of 155,000 miles. Increased flexibility to use highway funds for transit projects and air quality programs, and increased the role of metropolitan planning organizations in programming federal funds.
1998	Extended the 1991 act and increased funding for transit and air quality purposes. Reinforced modal flexibility and regional decision making. Restored federal operating assistance in urban areas with a population under 200,000.
2006	Earmarked federal funds for paratransit operators providing transportation services for persons with disabilities.

SOURCE: APTA, *History and Provisions of the Federal Transit Act and Other Major Laws Affecting Public Transportation, 1961–2007.*

transportation since 1961. Transit and its advocates have been largely successful in cultivating the congressional support needed to expand federal transit investment. The sole exception to this generalization is the rescinding of federal funds for operating purposes that occurred during the Reagan administration.

Transit Ridership Trends since Federal Engagement

Despite public ownership and federal funding, transit ridership continued to decline from 1960 through 1973. Since the OPEC oil embargo of 1973, though, transit has been relatively successful in increasing ridership on an aggregate nationwide basis. From 1946 until the embargo, the trend of transit ridership had been short-term cyclic and long-term downward. Since the embargo, the

Table 6.4 *Transit rides and rides per capita, 1972–2001*

	1972	2001	Change
Rides (in billions)	6.6	9.7	+47.0%
U.S. population (in millions)	209.9	285.0	+11.0%
Transit rides per capita	31	32	+3.2%

SOURCE: APTA, *Transit Fact Book* and www.apta.com/research/stats.
NOTE: (a) Before 1977, APTA did not report the substantial ridership of commuter railroads, ferries, or dial-a-ride systems, which were not then considered transit services. To maintain comparability from 1972 to 2001, the 600 million rides generated by these modes are also omitted from the totals for 2001.

trend of transit ridership has remained short-term cyclic, but its long-term trend has been upward. Total nationwide transit ridership has increased from 6.5 billion passenger trips at its postwar low in 1972 to almost 9.7 billion trips at its most recent high in 2001.[14] In 2004, it stood at 9.6 billion trips. Stated more generally, transit ridership has exhibited two concurrent trends since the 1973 OPEC embargo: a cyclic trend that has generally mirrored the national employment rate, and a secular trend that reflects the growth of population and employment. Transit's upward secular trend is an encouraging sign that public ownership has positioned transit to make a sustainable, long-term contribution to urban transportation. But these trends are not as favorable they might appear on first inspection.

Table 6.4 shows that transit rides have increased 47 percent from the low they reached the year before the OPEC embargo. In fact, transit ridership has actually grown more rapidly than the U.S. population: it increased from 31 rides per capita before the embargo to 32 rides per capita after the embargo. However, rides per worker continued to decline because the growth of the workforce far outpaced the growth of the population, due primarily to increasing women's employment and the growth of suburban employment.

Table 6.5 shows that federal transit policy has been unsuccessful in rebuilding transit's share of the commute market despite the transition to public ownership and the infusion of federal funds. The number of workers using transit to get to work declined steadily from 1960 to 1970, 1970 to 1980, and 1980 to 1990. From 1990 to 2000, there was essentially no change—an improvement relative to the results for 1960 to 1990. But transit's share of commute trips continued to decline from 1990 to 2000, as it has every decade since 1960. The good news is that the decline from 1990 to 2000 was a small one. Also good news is that, for the first time since transit's conversion to public ownership, the census found that a significant number of the largest metropolitan areas had registered gains in commute share. These metropolitan areas included New York, Los Angeles,

Table 6.5 *U.S. workers using transit for the journey to work*

1960	7.8 million	12.1%
1970	6.8 million	8.9%
1980	6.2 million	6.4%
1990	6.1 million	5.3%
2000	6.1 million	4.7%
Change	−21.8%	−61.2%

SOURCE: McGuckin and Srinivasan, *Journey-to-Work Trends in the United States and Its Major Metropolitan Areas, 1960–2000.*

the San Francisco Bay Area, Washington, D.C., Boston, Seattle, and Portland. Nationwide, transit was unable to regain market share because in most metropolitan areas the workforce continued to grow much faster than transit's commuter ridership.

What was different in the 1990s that slowed the decline of transit's market share? The answer is not that transit regained ground. Quite the contrary, transit continued to lose resident commute share in most of the central cities that are prime transit markets.[15] These included New York, Chicago, Philadelphia, Washington, Los Angeles, and San Francisco. Major exceptions were Boston and Seattle; their central cities gained transit commute share from 1990 to 2000. Transit did make gains among workers living in the suburbs of the largest metropolitan areas, especially among those workers who lived in the suburbs but commuted to the urban core. Transit also made gains in many smaller, less transit-oriented metropolitan areas. Examined in modal terms, transit's 1990–2000 ridership gains were confined to four modes—heavy rail, commuter rail, light rail, and dial-a-ride.[16] These, of course, are the transit modes geared to delivering commuters from the suburbs to the central city and providing demand-responsive service in outlying suburbs. Bus and trolley bus ridership stagnated and declined relative to the size of the national workforce and population. In other words, those modes (commuter rail, heavy rail, and light rail) and that market (the suburbs to central city commute) that have been the focus of the federal capital program produced most of the ridership gains that enabled transit to "break even" in terms of passengers using transit for the journey to work. At the same time, it is clear that the nation's most transit-oriented central cities did not "break even." Transit continued to lose commute share in 20 of the nation's 25 prime transit markets.

These outcomes indicate that the federal transit program has delivered what the big city mayors, downtown, and commuter railroads sought in 1959: it has funded corridor transit services that bring suburban commuters and suburban customers back downtown. The federal program has also produced ridership and commute share gains for many midsized metropolitan areas that have implemented light rail transit. These include Denver, Minneapolis, Portland, Sacramento, Salt Lake City, and San Diego.[17] But federal investment and local planning have been largely unsuccessful in sustaining transit's commute share in America's prime transit markets—its oldest central cities.

Instead, light rail, the expansion of rail commuter service, suburb–central city ridership more generally, and the introduction of suburban dial-a-ride service account for the stabilization of transit's commute share in the 1990s. This was good news in the statistical sense, because the trend from 1960 to 1990 had been steadily downward. But the continuing decline of transit's commute share in 20 of the nation's most prominent central cities has to be described as a considerable disappointment.

Transit and the Geography of U.S. Population Growth

As table 6.5 shows, commuter use of transit declined every decade from 1960 through 2000. This trend reflects population dynamics that have literally overwhelmed the positive effects of public ownership and service expansion. These included (1) the decline of the central cities' share of the national population, (2) the growth of suburban and sunbelt population shares, and (3) increasing women's workforce participation, which has produced gains in household buying and borrowing power, which have, in turn, enabled continuing increases in both home and automobile ownership.

These and other large-scale geographic and demographic dynamics largely explain the continuing decline of transit's commute share. Table 6.6 shows that the Midwest and Northeast—the regions that once boasted the largest number of streetcar and subway riders—accounted for 60 percent of the nation's population in 1920. They still accounted for almost 54 percent in 1960, but that share had fallen to 42 percent by 2000. This population shift from the frostbelt to the sunbelt gained initial momentum with the rapid growth of California in the 1920s and with the billeting of American servicemen in West Coast cities during World War II. Further declines in transit commute share and in rides per capita were also associated with the migration from the heartland to the West Coast after World War II. Texas and Florida began to experience rapid growth during the same period. By 1970, the cities of the frostbelt were experiencing significant emigration, while the sunbelt was enjoying significant immigration. Since 1980, Hispanic and Asian immigration has accounted for a substantial share of U.S. population growth, and most of that growth has been concentrated in cities of the West and Southwest.

The relevance of these interregional population shifts to the decline in transit's market share will become obvious with inspection of table 6.7. Many of

Table 6.6 *Regional population shares in the United States, 1920–2000*

	Northeast and Midwest	South and West
1920	60.1%	39.9%
1960	53.7%	46.3%
2000	41.9%	58.1%

SOURCE: *Statistical Abstract of the United States*, 1922 and 2002, "Resident Population by Region."

the leading transit markets of 1920 were industrial cities or manufacturing centers that have since experienced significant deindustrialization and hollowing out, especially in their central cities. These include Detroit, Pittsburgh, St. Louis, and Cleveland. From 1950 to 2000, Detroit lost half of its central city population, and Pittsburgh, St. Louis, and Cleveland were displaced from the ranks of the nation's most populous MSAs by Houston, Atlanta, and Dallas. Boston was also displaced, not by hollowing out but by metropolitan areas that experienced more rapid population growth. These were Los Angeles and Washington. The table also shows each area's 2000 commute shares by public transportation. Predictably, those newer growth centers that were added to the list for 2000 have much lower transit commute shares than the older industrial centers that they displaced.

One implication of table 6.7 is that those *financial* centers that were prime transit markets of the streetcar era have been able to hold their own in terms of both population growth and sustaining relatively high levels of transit use. But those *industrial* centers that were once prime transit markets have not. These include St. Louis, Pittsburgh, Cleveland, and Detroit and smaller cities such as Baltimore, Buffalo, Hartford, Milwaukee, and Newark.[18] All of these have experienced significant losses in both central city population and transit market share. Detroit held its own in terms of metropolitan population growth, but not transit market share. This was due to the hollowing out of its central city employment base. St. Louis, Pittsburgh, and Baltimore experienced much the same dynamic. They lost population and were displaced in the pecking order of American cities by Los Angeles, Houston, Atlanta, and Dallas. Thus table 6.6 is an illustrative microcosm of how sunbelt job opportunities and rustbelt economic decline have contributed to the hollowing out of the frostbelt's central city population and industrial employment and to the decline of cities that were prime transit markets in the streetcar era. In turn, Los Angeles, Washington, Houston, Atlanta, and Dallas have displaced these older commercial and industrial centers in the pecking order of American cities. Of their replacements, only Washington can be described as a major transit market, and its ascendancy is of relatively recent origin. Thus deindustrialization, interregional population

Table 6.7 *Most populous metropolitan areas in 1920 and 2000*

Largest metro areas in 1920	Year 1920 population in 1,000s	Largest metro areas in 2000	Year 2000 population in 1,000s	2000 transit commute share (%)
New York	8,491	New York	21,200	24.9
Philadelphia	2,714	Los Angeles	16,374	4.7
Chicago	2,093	Chicago	9,158	11.5
Pittsburg	1,760	San Francisco	7,039	9.5
Boston	1,685	Philadelphia	6,188	8.7
Detroit	1,306	Washington, D.C.	4,923	9.4
St. Louis	1,140	Detroit	4,442	1.8
San Francisco	1,009	Houston	4,178	3.3
Los Angeles	998	Atlanta	4,112	3.7
Cleveland	972	Dallas	3,519	1.8

SOURCE: *Statistical Abstract of the United States*, 2002; Bogue, *Population Growth in Standard Metropolitan Areas, 1900–1950*, and McGuckin and Srinivasan, *Journey-to-Work Trends in the United States and Its Major Metropolitan Areas, 1960–2000*.

shifts, and the deconcentration of metropolitan population and employment have contributed significantly to transit's continuing loss of nationwide market share.

This shift is most evident for New York, Chicago, Philadelphia, Boston, San Francisco, and Washington. In 1920, these cities accounted for 16 percent of the nation's population. They still accounted for 9 percent as recently as 1960. But by 2000 they accounted for only 5.1 percent of the national total.[19] In the face of these population trends, transit has achieved a Pyrrhic victory. It has retained ridership more effectively than America's largest cities have proved themselves able to retain their once prominent share of the nation's population.

The principal implication of this analysis is that transit's ridership and work-trip market share have been diminished by economic forces and population dynamics well beyond transit's control. One of the most important of these dynamics has been the hollowing out of industrial employment in the central cities of the rustbelt. Another is the shift of employment growth to the suburbs and the sunbelt. These intra- and interregional population and employment shifts have been reinforced by the geographic pattern of international immigration. Since 1980, Mexico, Latin America, the Caribbean, Asia, and Southeast Asia have been the primary sources of immigration to the United States, and the destinations of these immigrants have tilted to the West, Southwest, and Florida. In turn, Hispanic and Asian immigration accounted for essentially all of the population growth in the largest U.S central cities from 1990 to 2000.[20]

The net effect of these population dynamics is that both population and employment growth have tilted to the sunbelt. In turn, those industrial cities of the Northeast and Midwest that were prime transit markets of the streetcar era now account for a substantially diminished share of the national population and workforce. Thus, the postwar geography of population growth, employment growth, and interregional migration has created a nation that is increasingly auto-oriented, despite federal and local transportation policies that were increasingly favorable to transit.

The Brookings Institution has succinctly reported how the 1990–2000 population trend has further reinforced the dynamics we have just described:

> Cities with substantial public transportation systems lost population during the 1990s. The average growth rate for those cities in which more than 10 percent of commuters took public transportation was nearly zero. The average growth rate for those cities in which less than 3 percent of commuters used public transportation in 1990 was almost 17 percent. A huge shift has occurred away from the older walking-oriented and public-transport-oriented cities of the past toward the driving-oriented cities of today.[21]

Almost all of the reasons for transit's persistent and continuing decline in market share are beyond transit's control. In order for public transportation to have retained market share in the face of these population dynamics and development trends, it would have been necessary for transit to retain ridership in frostbelt cities that were losing population and employment, while simultaneously increasing its market share in sunbelt cities with relatively low densities and widely dispersed destinations. Instead, the total number of U.S. workers that commute by transit declined from 8.1 million in 1960 to 6.1 million in 2000, a decline of 25 percent.[22] On first inspection, these aggregate data suggest that transit's decline is a relentless nationwide dynamic that will produce continuing declines in transit's work-trip market share in the future, despite continuing state and federal investment. A different picture emerges when we disaggregate the nationwide trend since 1980 and look at outcomes by metropolitan area.

Trends in Transit's Commuter Ridership, 1980–2000

Transit's commuter ridership declined 12.7 percent from 1960 to 1970 and an additional 9.3 percent from 1970 to 1980. Despite the rescinding of federal operating subsidies in 1980, commuter ridership declined only 1.7 percent from 1980 to 1990, and there was essentially no change in the number of commuters using transit nationwide from 1990 to 2000—a victory of sorts when compared with the significant downtrend of 1960 to 1980. But these nationwide aggregate statistics mask significant differences in outcome from city to city and from region to region.

Table 6.8 *Metropolitan areas experiencing large increases in transit commuting*

SMSA	Commuters gained, 1980–2000
New York	189,000
Los Angeles	54,000
San Francisco	39,000
Seattle	38,000
Houston	33,000
Boston	29,000
Las Vegas	24,000

SOURCE: McGuckin and Srinivasan, *Journey-to-Work Trends in the United States and Its Major Metropolitan Areas, 1960–2000.*

Tables 6.8 and 6.9 show the trend of transit's commuter ridership for those metropolitan areas that experienced the largest gains and the largest losses in commuter ridership from 1980 to 2000. The pattern of gains and losses is predictable but nonetheless instructive. In New York, San Francisco and Los Angeles, we can specifically attribute transit's gains in commuter ridership to major public investment. In Las Vegas, ridership gains reflect both service expansion and the use of competitive contracting to secure service from the lowest bidder, an innovation that enabled Las Vegas to increase both ridership and market share while reducing unit costs. In New York, ridership gains reflected successful completion of several major phases of the city's federally financed program of subway rehabilitation. Its completion produced a significant rebound in subway ridership.

In both San Francisco and Los Angeles, operating subsidies provided by the state of California enabled significant expansion of service despite the rescinding of federal operating funds in 1980. In the Bay Area, increases in metropolitan population combined with increases in downtown employment in both San Francisco and San Jose to produce increases in BART, light rail, and commuter rail ridership—projects substantially financed with state and federal funds. Los Angeles secured ridership gains from light rail and synergies between heavy rail planning and redevelopment efforts in the new Wilshire transit corridor. But more important in terms of ridership volume, gains in bus ridership in Los Angeles, Houston, and Phoenix seem to reflect the large-scale population growth and the demand associated with the day-to-day commuting needs of recent Hispanic immigrants. Indeed, sprawling Houston and Phoenix were the only major U.S. metropolitan areas to report gains in transit's work-trip market share from 1980 to 1990; not coincidentally, both enjoyed significant Hispanic immigration. Seattle's gains in commuter ridership reflect the combined effect of large-scale population growth and the serviceability of one of the nation's best-managed bus transit systems. But ridership gains also reflect Seattle's ascendant

Table 6.9 *Metropolitan areas experiencing large declines in transit commuting*

SMSA	Commuters lost, 1980–2000
Chicago	94,000
Philadelphia	49,000
Cleveland	47,000
St. Louis	27,000
Detroit	26,000
Milwaukee	16,000
Kansas City	14,000

SOURCE: McGuckin and Srinivasan, *Journey-to-Work Trends in the United States and Its Major Metropolitan Areas, 1960–2000.*

role as a port city that provides a gateway for Asian imports and U.S. exports, an economic role that has made Seattle the magnet for a rapidly growing Asian immigrant community accustomed to the use of public transportation.

Clearly, the trends of commuter ridership vary from city to city and mirror local circumstances. But just as clearly, local ridership trends reflect national megatrends. These include the decline of heartland industrial centers, the growth of the port cities of the West Coast, and the continuing ascendancy of cities that are anchored by finance, communications, and oil. Cities that are primary destinations for Hispanic and Asian immigrants are also experiencing growth in population and transit ridership.

We can also be reasonably sure that white flight contributed to the decline of transit ridership and urban buying power in many of the metropolitan areas listed in table 6.9 because the mean black population share for the central cities of these MSAs was 40 percent, compared with only 18 percent for their counterpart cities listed in table 6.8. Taken together, these tables suggest that the federal transit program was relatively effective in building transit ridership in cities that were experiencing continuing economic growth, but not very effective in sustaining or restoring transit ridership in cities not yet recovered from the combined effects of industrial decline and white flight. This observation entails a significant irony because one of the founding rationales of the federal transit program was the desirability of reinvigorating transit so that it could reinvigorate its host cities.

Commuting Trends in Chicago, 1980–2000

In 1980, almost 580,000 commuters used public transportation to get to and from work in the Chicago metropolitan area. Twenty years later, only 485,000 workers used transit to get to work in Chicago and the suburban counties that surround it, a 16 percent decline in transit commuting that occurred despite a 14 percent increase in Chicago's metropolitan population.

What happened in Chicago? One answer is nothing as traumatic as the deindustrialization that characterized many other industrial cities of the American heartland. The 16 percent decline in Chicago's transit's commuter ridership from 1980 to 2000 decline was substantially less than the losses that occurred in Kansas City (56 percent), Cleveland (50 percent), St. Louis (47 percent), Detroit (37 percent), and Milwaukee (36 percent), most of which were directly or indirectly attributable to the loss of industrial employment. But the common dynamic in all of these cities—Chicago included—was that the central cities lost population, transit use declined, and automobile ownership, suburban employment, and the suburban population all increased.

In 1980, more Chicago area households had one vehicle available at home than those that had two. Likewise, the number of households with no vehicle available exceeded the number of households with three. By the year 2000, these relationships had been reversed. More Chicago area households owned two cars than one, and more owned three vehicles than none. Both income growth and population shifts played a key role in increasing automobile ownership. In Chicago's case, the central city's population declined by some 109,000 from 1980 to 2000, while the population of Chicago's suburbs and satellite cities increased by some 917,000. In other words, the entirety of the region's population growth occurred outside the city of Chicago.[23]

Joel Garreau reports that from 1980 to 2000, four "edge cities" developed in Chicago's suburbs.[24] These "edge cities" included the O'Hare Airport nexus of industry and warehousing, the constellation of suburban job centers in the vicinity of Schaumburg, the Illinois Research and Development Corridor, which can be described as Chicago's answer to Boston's I-95 Corridor, and the Lakeshore Corridor defined by the Eden Expressway and the Tri-State Tollway. Each of these constellations of residential, commercial, and light industrial activity can be described as employment centers of metropolitan scale but suburban layout. Fueled by such development, Chicago's suburban collar counties accounted for 99 percent of Chicago's metropolitan job growth from 1980 to 2000. Conversely, Cook County lost 18,000 jobs from 1990 to 2000 alone. With Cook County employment in decline, central city workers necessarily looked to the suburbs for jobs. In turn, drive-alone commutes increased from 53 percent of all Cook County work trips in 1980 to 63 percent by the year 2000. In Chicago's collar counties, drive-alone work trips increased from 69 percent in 1980 to 79 percent in 2000. The net result for the period 1980 to 2000 was a 29 percent decline in the share of Chicago area commuters that relied on transit to get to work.

As this case study suggests, the decline of transit commuting in Chicago is a by-product of four dynamics: One is the growth of income and motor vehicle ownership, both urban and suburban. Another is the decline of central city population and employment. The third is the growth of suburban population and employment. The fourth is conventional transit's seeming inability to develop evolved suburban services that can compete effectively in serving the large number of workers now employed in beltway suburbs.

Why Hasn't Transit Been Able to Adapt and Evolve?

Part of the answer is that conventional transit's ability to operate productively hinges on serving markets with the limited parking and the characteristic densities and demography of America's older central cities. Another part of the answer is that transit's cost structure is mismatched with the relatively low ridership volumes of newly prominent commercial suburbs. Still another part of the answer is that both Congress and the urban advocates of federal investment in public transportation were focused on downtown, rapid transit, and capital investment during the decade of transit's transition from private to public ownership. That focus produced a federal program with a heavy emphasis on rail transit and the downtown commute—precisely what downtown, the big city mayors, and the railroads sought. The federal program has delivered significant gains in rail transit use and, in some cases, in transit's share of the downtown commute. But transit's market share has relentlessly declined in many metropolitan areas because urban employment has declined and suburban employment has increased.

With the advantage of hindsight, we can sketch a broader agenda that would have enabled transit to adapt to suburbanization more productively. That agenda would have paired the federal commitment to rapid transit with an equally vigorous commitment to rationalize the way urban and suburban bus service is provided. In this scenario, Congress would have brokered a win/win deal between the representatives of transit labor and local bus operators. In its broadest outline, the deal we are postulating would have been a national agreement with transit's unions to cash out transit's existing labor contracts and start fresh with a new contract, explicitly designed to fit the evolving temporal rhythms and spatial patterns of metropolitan travel in the freeway era. Such a contract would have explicitly endorsed the use of part-time labor and the contracting out of at least some peak service to the owner-operators of taxi-vans. It would also have paid workers a generous onetime settlement premium for accepting and endorsing contracting out and the right of transit agencies to hire part-time workers in specified numbers.

Obviously, the merit of this alternative is most apparent with the advantage of hindsight. At the time that the transit program was originally crafted, Congress, urbanists, and transit's mayoral advocates had high hopes that reinvestment would be sufficient to rebuild transit's market share and reduce the operating and maintenance costs that were associated with the use of aging equipment. They also hoped that reinvigorated transit would reinvigorate their host cities, starting with their central business districts. Transit operators, on the other hand, were cautious; their testimony acknowledged the long-term difficulties reported in this history. This testimony was dissonant with the testimony of the urban mayors and the advocates of urban redevelopment and future rail systems such as BART. Unfortunately, Congress ignored the seasoned bus company managers, who had spent time in the trenches and had the keenest understanding of the industry's problems.

Thus Congress endorsed federal engagement in transit improvement without understanding the difficulties that industrial renewal would entail and without thoughtful examination of the challenges posed by the growth of suburban employment. In turn, transit passed from private to public ownership still hobbled by work rules, fare structures, and operating policies that were inherited from the early years of the streetcar era when six-day work weeks were the norm, when American cities were more compact and densely settled, and when heavy off-peak and weekend ridership made transit operation a paying proposition. Today, the temporal composition of transit ridership and the growth of population and employment in outlying suburbs have made it difficult for transit to operate service that is simultaneously frequent, affordable, and well patronized more than three or four hours a day.

In the central cities, the critical challenges are work rules and fare structures that remain out of date, street traffic and congestion levels that make for unreliable service, and a riding public with incomes that make them sensitive to higher fares. In the suburbs, the critical challenge is a market that is inhospitable to transit for many more reasons than most land use planners are prepared to acknowledge. And that is doubly problematic because the suburbs have accounted for the lion's share of metropolitan population and employment growth since transit's conversion to public ownership.

Why Are Suburbs Inhospitable for Transit?

Most land use planners would say that the answer is settlement patterns that are sprawling and densities that are low compared with cities that grew up in the railroad and streetcar eras. But this is a partial answer that substantially underestimates the difficulty of the problem. Understood more broadly, there are eight reasons why most postwar suburbs generate low levels of transit ridership:

1. Most Americans who live in suburban households have the income and borrowing power to afford both home and auto ownership. The marginal cost of using a car is small, once households have made the financial commitment to own one.
2. Households with children—the norm for most suburban communities—have complex schedules and itineraries that transit cannot serve conveniently given the land use arrangements that are characteristic of suburbs built since World War II.
3. The planned characteristics of suburbs include ample off-street parking, the segregation of residential and commercial land uses, and the functional differentiation of road space in order to prevent the intrusion of crosstown traffic in residential areas. The intended result is quiet neighborhoods and a community compatible with the safe and convenient use of the automobile. The unintended result is an environment that is inhospitable to walking and transit use.
4. The characteristic suburban housing type is single-family detached. Most communities of single-family homes sized to meet the expectations of middle-class families lack the density needed to support frequent arterial bus service.
5. Auto use is an accustomed part of the suburban lifestyle. It is the way most suburban residents get to work, get to school, transport children, socialize, and take vacations. In other words, auto use is a social norm as well as a mode choice.
6. Most suburban residents work locally or in another suburb nearby. This makes it virtually impossible for transit to compete with the automobile for local or suburb-to-suburb commuting because suburban destinations are dispersed, most parking is free, and most local transit service is infrequent.
7. Even where suburban transit is well patronized for getting to work, almost all off-peak and weekend trips are made by motor vehicle.
8. For all of the reasons above, suburban ridership is usually insufficient to justify frequent local service, which poses another obstacle to suburban transit use.

If residential densities and proximity to a transit stop were the principal determinants of mode choice, so-called Smart Growth or Transit-Oriented Development would enable a larger share of suburban commuters to use transit to get to downtown worksites and other destinations conveniently served by transit. But most metropolitan workers no longer work downtown, and most other worksites are not conveniently served by transit. Thus most suburban commuters drive to work for reasons of convenience, habit, economy, and necessity.

Land use planning innovations such as Smart Growth can increase the number of households that live near public transportation, but the gains in transit use are not likely to be as large as Smart Growth advocates expect because such a large share of metropolitan jobs are now located in the suburbs, even in the nation's primary transit markets. By 1994, for example, suburban employment accounted for 76 percent of total SMSA employment in Boston, 74 percent in Washington, 72 percent in Philadelphia, and 68 percent in Chicago.[25] Even in New York, the suburbs accounted for 66 percent of metropolitan employment. Smart Growth and timed transfers can make it easier to commute downtown or make convenient bus-to-bus transfers at rail stations, but it has not been established that they can produce sustained decade-to-decade increases in transit's market share.

What they can achieve has been best demonstrated in Portland.

Smart Growth in Portland

The nation's first comprehensive demonstration of Smart Growth—sometimes called Transit-Oriented Development—was undertaken in Portland, Oregon.[26] Portland's experience with Smart Growth underlines both its potential and its limitations as a strategy for reducing automobile dependence and increasing transit use. Portland's approach has included a focus on downtown redevelopment, the diversion of highway funds to finance light rail transit, rezoning for higher density residential development in the vicinity of suburban rail stations, proactive efforts to promote both residential development near rail stations and new commercial development downtown, and the containment of urban sprawl through the designation of an "Urban Limit Line" designed to prevent premature development of outlying farmland and open space. Rail stations have been located where they can serve as a focus for mixed-use development or as a spur for redevelopment. Suburban stations also serve as transfer points for buses where a well-executed time transfer system allows passengers to transfer from bus to bus as well as from bus to rail.

Smart Growth along with the time-transfer system used by Portland's transit system and a 27 percent increase in the region's workforce combined to increase transit ridership by 56 percent between 1990 and 2000. Transit ridership per capita increased 26 percent, while transit's metropolitan commute share increased from 4.7 percent in 1990 to 5.7 percent in 2000, a 21 percent increase.[27] Thus the combined impact of collocating housing near rail stations, more effective coordination of bus and rail service, time transfers, the opening of a second rail line, the publicity associated with Smart Growth, light rail, and increasing congestion enabled transit to achieve a significant increase in both ridership and work-trip market share. As a result, Portland is now a leader among U.S. cities of its size class in terms of transit trips per capita, transit's commute share, and the percentage of workers who bicycle to work. These results are encouraging, but not all of the results of Smart Growth have been positive.

Because Portland had to curtail highway development in order to finance its first light rail line and because of the explosive population growth that occurred in the decade that followed, Portland experienced the largest increase in congestion of any city in its size class from 1989 to 1999. Portland also experienced an estimated 283 percent increase in congestion-related fuel consumption during the same period, again the largest in its size class.[28] Congestion-related increases in vehicular emissions typically increase in tandem with fuel use, but the net impacts of Smart Growth and increasing congestion on vehicle emissions and air quality have not, to our knowledge, been systematically examined in Portland. Adding to the difficulty of any bottom-line appraisal is the fact that Portland experienced explosive population and employment growth during the dot.com boom, making it difficult to disentangle the effects of population growth, employment growth, and Smart Growth.

Thus the most definitive conclusion that can be reached is the one drawn by Professor Jennifer Dill at Portland State: Portland's approach "may be working." What seems to be well established is that Portland's highly publicized efforts to promote Smart Growth have made transit use, walking, and bicycling both more salient and more convenient for more of Portland's metropolitan population. The publicity associated with Smart Growth has certainly made transit and transit use more salient, while Portland's time-transfer system has created a seamless network that accommodates bus-to-bus as well as bus-to-rail transfers.

What cannot be established in a decade is whether Smart Growth will enable Portland to sustain gains in transit's market share over time. In this regard, it is appropriate to note that Seattle achieved a 21.4 percent increase in transit's commute share during the same period without any new rail start and that Sacramento achieved a 17 percent increase in commute share during light rail's second decade of operation. Thus transit's 21 percent decadal increase in Portland market share does not stand out as particularly exceptional. Indeed, transit's most exceptional gains in 1990–2000 market share were realized in Las Vegas, which used contracting out to achieve a 128 percent increase in transit commute share, along with a significant reduction in operating costs per rider.[29]

What Portland has most clearly established is that a comprehensive approach to transit improvement—one that involves a regional commitment to transit, effective coordination of bus and rail operations, time transfers, and Smart Growth—can increase the visibility of transit, the convenience of transit use, and transit's ridership and commute share. But the sharp increases in both congestion and congestion-related fuel consumption that accompanied diminished highway investment make it impossible to conclude that Portland's approach to Smart Growth has been an unmitigated success. Housing prices in Portland also escalated sharply during the 1990s, but the extent to which this was attributable to Portland's Urban Limit Line or simply to vigorous housing demand associated with a surge in regional population and employment growth is a matter of continuing dispute, both in Portland and in the planning and academic communities more broadly. Also uncertain is the extent to which future increases in the density and concentration of development will increase traffic congestion, fuel consumption, and congestion-related emissions, despite future increases in transit ridership. Thus the jury is still out on the net benefits of Portland's pathbreaking approach to Smart Growth.

Across the United States, metropolitan freeway development and suburban population growth have produced a uniquely American conundrum.[30] One dimension of this conundrum is rooted in the nature of most outlying suburbs. They lack both the density and walkability to support frequent transit service. The other dimension is that the freeway networks which serve them lack the density of routes needed to prevent the concentration of traffic that leads to excessive congestion.

Portland's approach to Smart Growth is a strategic response to the first half of this American conundrum. It focused on higher density development both downtown and in the vicinity of suburban transit stations, contributing to a regionwide increase in transit's ridership and market share. But to reinforce the impact of Smart Growth and to generate highway transfer funds that could be used to finance light rail development, Portland had to defer metropolitan expressway investment. When planned expressway development is deferred, however, and investment is shifted to transit despite continuing growth of population and traffic, it is likely that transit use will increase, as it has in Portland. But continued population and employment growth will produce greater concentration of traffic on existing freeways and arterials. This occurred in Portland in the 1990s, producing the largest increase in congestion and fuel waste of any city in its size class.[31]

So what is the bottom line? Can Smart Growth be fine-tuned to produce an effective strategy for growth management? Our judgment is yes. But we doubt that Smart Growth and related transit improvement can substantially reduce vehicular emissions and automotive fuel consumption unless they are paired with highway operational improvements and an effective multimodal strategy for keeping traffic moving in the face of continuing population growth. The traffic management element of such a strategy might include ramp metering, high-occupancy vehicle lanes, flexible working hours, and the construction of a next generation of suburban parkways. This is not the European model of traffic management, but it is the domestic model most likely to be effective in managing traffic flow in that majority of American cities that have experienced most of their growth and development since World War I.[32] In other words, American cities require a locally tailored approach to Smart Growth and a multimodal approach to traffic management that is well tailored to fit local circumstances.

Yes, the Europeanization of an American city can increase transit use, but in the American context, it is also likely to produce more congestion, more congestion-related emissions, and more fuel consumption. And this means that the ability to secure significant environmental benefits from Smart Growth should be viewed as a situationally contingent outcome and not as a given. Thus we conclude that Smart Growth is most likely to produce productive results if it is paired with contracting out and a multimodal approach to traffic management.

Las Vegas and "Contracting Out"

In 1993, Las Vegas and its transit union hammered out a mutually agreeable strategy for expanding transit service and bidding out bus operation to private operators. In the first year of the new contract and expanded system, Las Vegas increased the miles of transit service it provides by 234 percent, while restraining its increase in operating costs to 135 percent. Since 1993, transit ridership in Las Vegas has increased from 15.0 million rides to 50.5 million, and transit's commute share has increased 128 percent. No other U.S. transit system came close to achieving such results.[33] In most U.S. transit agencies, tradition and Section 13c have combined to discourage transit operators from employing part-time labor or contracting out for transit service. But the Las Vegas experience suggests that it is precisely such innovations in service and methods that are necessary for transit to be successful in increasing its market share without incurring an uneconomic increase in costs per rider.

Las Vegas provides the premiere example of what transit can accomplish when both service and the methods of service delivery are adapted to fit the travel patterns of twenty-first-century America. Portland, on the other hand, provides the premiere American example of what can be accomplished when settlement of higher density is focused in the vicinity of transit transfer centers and the scheduling of bus and rail service is effectively coordinated. A fusion of the Portland and Las Vegas models of transit development—a new model that combines transit-oriented development, light rail, high-occupancy vehicle lanes, traffic management, conventional bus service, paratransit, and contracting out—would seem to offer the best chance of managing traffic flow and restoring transit's market share in America's midsized cities. This, we believe, is the essential lesson to be learned from more than 40 years of high expectations and largely disappointing results from public ownership of public transportation in the United States.

The Bottom Line

Federal transit policy has been based on the premise that transit's financial difficulties were a by-product of unfair competition created by unbalanced public policy. The commuter railroads in the Symes-Dilworth coalition made this case to Congress with specific reference to the suburbs–central city commute. In the segment of the transit market occupied by suburban rail commuter service, there is substantial merit to the proposition that the profitability of railroad commuter service was undermined by state and federal investment in metropolitan freeways.

But many planners and urbanists have generalized this case more broadly, arguing that subsidies for metropolitan freeways were the primary cause of the decline of bus, streetcar, and subway ridership. This conviction is misplaced. The decline began in the 1920s, long before the freeway era. Significantly, urban transit operators representing the American Transit Association told Congress the same thing in the early 1960s. They focused on the industry's long-standing credit problems and sought federally guaranteed loans that would enable properties still in private ownership to reinvest in new equipment and thus escape their punishing debt loads. Congress largely overlooked this testimony from urban bus operators, focusing instead on the testimony of the urban mayors, the railroads, and the advocates of new rail systems such as BART and Philadelphia's Lindenwald Line.[34]

As a result, the duration, complexity, and diversity of the many underlying reasons for the decline of transit ridership were largely ignored in the process of constructing federal policy. The resulting program was designed with rail transit and the commute from the suburbs to the central city in mind. Not surprisingly, this has proved the market in which transit has been most successful in using federal funds to recover ridership and rebuild market share, but at an exceptionally high cost per rider.

At the same time, federal policy has been conspicuously unsuccessful in rebuilding the market share of urban bus transit—in large part because the focus of federal policy has been on commuter rail, rapid transit, light rail, and the corridor commute. The result is a program that has built rail transit ridership at considerable cost but proved inadequate to the larger and more challenging task of modernizing urban street transit and enabling it to increase both ridership and productivity.

The continuing difficulties of urban transit systems should not be surprising. Their problems are much more complex, of much longer duration, and much more contentious than those presented by the corridor commute. Their underlying causes include the long-term decline of off-peak and weekend ridership, the increasing difficulty of bus and streetcar operation in congested city traffic, and the diminished income of a large share of transit's residual urban riders. These difficulties have been compounded by work rules that have prevented effective adjustment in service and methods. Adaptation has also been stymied by revenue shortfalls associated with declining central city populations, declining center city market share, and transit operating problems associated with increasing traffic congestion.

More might have been achieved if federal policy had been premised on a broader view of urban transit and its difficulties. Instead, the federal transit program that evolved in the 1960s was responsive to the big city mayors and their request for public investment in rail systems serving the suburbs–downtown commute. Congress also responded to the concerns that transit unions voiced about public ownership in the 1960s. Section 13c of the Urban Mass Transportation Act of 1964 gave transit unions effective veto power over any significant change in work rules, work hours, or the terms of employment without contract renegotiation and compensation, creating a new obstacle to the modernization of union contracts and squandering an opportunity to negotiate new work rules and new contracts that could have enabled transit to operate more productively.

Together, Section 13c and the availability of federal funds for capital investment explain much of the character of transit's subsequent evolution and development under public ownership. Capital investment has been the centerpiece of local efforts to improve transit service, rail starts have become a marker of a city's status and standing in its peer group, and most transit agencies have happily pursued federal capital grants. At the same time, most transit agencies have shied away from any thoroughgoing effort to modernize their work rules, fare structures, labor agreements, and wage scales. Thus federal funding has proved a double-edged sword. It has enabled modernization through capital investment, but seems to have discouraged those changes in work rules, operating procedures, and pricing policies that would be needed if transit were to break out of the narrow range of 33–35 rides per capita in which it is presently stuck. It has also encumbered suburban transit with labor contracts better suited to the 1920s than to the twenty-first century.

A handful of metropolitan areas have demonstrated the merits of contracting out. Since 1993, transit ridership in Las Vegas has increased from 15.0 million rides to 50.5 million and transit's commute share has increased 128 percent. No other U.S. transit system came close to achieving such results.[35] In most U.S. transit agencies, tradition and Section 13c have combined to discourage transit operators from employing part-time labor or contracting out for transit service. The Las Vegas experience suggests that such innovations in service and methods are absolutely essential if transit is to be successful in increasing its market share without incurring an uneconomic increase in costs per rider.

Public Ownership and Transit's Productivity

Table 6.10 shows the trend of conventional transit's ridership, operating costs, and costs per ride on an inflation-adjusted basis for 1964 and 2001. Congress first authorized federal funds in 1964 for transit capital investment and transit's conversion to public ownership; transit's most recent ridership peak occurred in 2001. Public ownership, federal investment, and service expansion have combined to produce an 8.5 percent increase in bus, streetcar/light rail, and rail rapid transit ridership between 1964 and 2001. During the same period, operating expenses for bus, rapid transit, and streetcar/light rail transit increased 159 percent in constant 1982 dollars. In turn, operating costs per ride increased 140 percent. In other words, public ownership and subsidy have produced a small increase in same-mode rides per capita at a very high cost.

There are six basic reasons that operating costs have outpaced the growth of same-mode ridership.

1. Federal investment has successfully encouraged commuter use of rail transit over relatively longer metropolitan distances. With this "success" has come a substantial increase in cost per rider due to the length of commute trips from the suburbs to the central city.
2. Many of the largest central city transit systems located in the largest cities of the northeastern and north central states have experienced both ridership losses and increased operating costs despite modernization and reinvestment. Declining ridership and increasing costs have also been experienced in the midsized cities of the industrial heartland where smokestack industries have been shuttered and central cities have lost population and employment.
3. Public ownership and federal subsidy have stimulated substantial expansion of transit service in suburban and sunbelt markets where per-rider costs are high because ridership is relatively low per mile of service rendered.
4. Operating subsidies now permit the operation of service that was considered "uneconomical" under private ownership. The most important example is local service provided in outlying suburbs.

Table 6.10 *Transit's same-mode ridership and operating costs, 1964 and 2001*

	Rides by bus, streetcar, and rapid transit	Operating expenses	Operating cost/ride
1964	8,328 million	$4,008 million	$.48
2001	9,032 million	$10,378 million	$1.15
Change	8.5%	158.9%	139.6%

NOTE: Author's calculations are based on APTA ridership and operating expense data. All costs are in 1982 constant dollars. Both 1964 and 2001 ridership and expenses exclude commuter rail, ferry, and dial-a-ride expenses and ridership for which APTA data are unavailable before 1984 (these services accounted for 9 percent of all transit trips in 2001); 1964 and 2001 ridership levels, costs, and cost per rider are fully comparable and thus appropriate for comparing the combined operating results of bus, trolley bus, heavy rail, and light rail in 1964 and 2001.

5. Conversion to public ownership has not resolved the problems underlying transit's financial difficulties. It has enabled transit to receive federal funding, replace equipment, and increase service, but it has not enabled transit to increase labor productivity or substantially restore midday, night, or weekend ridership.

6. Public ownership and subsidy have relaxed the revenue constraints on transit wages that had prevailed under private ownership.

The net result of these many dynamics is that bus and trolley bus ridership actually declined 3.1 percent on an aggregate nationwide basis from 1964 to 2001. During the same period, light and heavy rail operations—the showcase technologies of the federal transit program—increased their ridership 41.5 percent. Thus rail service accounts for the entire increment in same-mode ridership that was achieved between 1964 and 2001. And with transit operators proposing 37 new rail-starts and extensions, 23 of them in sunbelt cities, future increases in rail ridership are all but certain.[36]

Table 6.11 shows how these many dynamics affected the transit industry's operating results from 1990 to 2000. It shows the percentage of increase in miles of service rendered on an aggregate, nationwide basis and the combined increase in the ridership of rapid transit, light rail, buses, and streetcars. It also shows the percentage of increase in the number of rides provided per mile of service rendered, the operating expense per rider served, and the increase in operating subsidy required from 1990 to 2000.

In round numbers, it required a 10 percent increase in service to achieve a 5 percent increase in same-mode ridership from 1990 to 2000. Thus ridership declined 10 percent per mile of service actually rendered, while operating expenses increased almost 11 percent in real dollar terms for each rider served.

Table 6.11 *Trends of five transit indicators, 1990–2000*

Vehicle miles of transit service rendered	+10.1%
Riders served	+5.2%
Riders served per mile of service rendered	−10.0%
Operating expense per rider served in 1982 constant dollars	+10.6%
Increase in operating subsidy in 1982 constant dollars	+17.0%

SOURCE: APTA Web site: 1990–2003, "Unlinked Passenger Trips and Operating Expense," both by mode, 1990–2003, www.apta.com/research/stats. Data are for bus, heavy rail, light rail, and trolley bus. Thus the service mix is comparable to that shown in table 6.10.

During the same decade, the governmental subsidy for operating purposes increased 17 percent, again in real dollar terms. Clearly, federal investment has not reduced aggregate costs per rider, nor has federal investment resolved the productivity problems of the urban and suburban bus operations that have inherited the cost structures and labor contracts of the streetcar industry. Reinvestment and operating subsidy have increased same-mode ridership but not transit's productivity.

A further implication of table 6.11 is that it is unlikely that transit's present 4.7 percent share of the commute market can be sustained without increasing future subsidy. Still another implication is that it will take much greater subsidy or a sustained increase in gasoline prices to make any significant inroads in the share of trips made by automobile. Thus transit subsidies that are large enough to make any significant difference in CO_2 emissions or the nation's oil import requirements could well prove politically unacceptable.

Expectations vs. Outcomes

The Senate committee that crafted federal transit policy in the 1960s expected public ownership and federal investment to improve service and create substantial efficiencies that would enable transit to attract more riders and reduce unit costs. Tables 6.10 and 6.11 show that these expectations have not been met. Quite the contrary, the per-rider expense of providing transit service has increased substantially under public ownership. This was due to the continuing decline of ridership in many of the nation's largest cities, increased dispersion of the metropolitan population, the relatively low productivity of local bus service in suburban settings, the increasing concentration of transit ridership in peak commute hours, the increased share of riders using suburban rail and rail rapid transit services that are more costly on a per rider basis, the increased route mileage now served by both bus and rail, and the increased political clout that transit unions have come to enjoy under public ownership.

In the first 40 years of public ownership, there was a nationwide increase in the size of the transit fleets, the size of the transit workforce, and the cost of serving each residual transit rider, without any correspondingly significant increase in total bus, streetcar, and rapid transit ridership. In 1964, year one of the transit capital program, bus, streetcar, and rapid transit ridership summed to 8.3 billion passenger rides. Downward momentum carried ridership to a postwar low of 5.3 billion rides in 1972. Bus, streetcar, and rapid transit ridership gradually recovered after the OPEC embargo and reached a high of 9.0 billion in 2001, the peak of the new economy bubble.

Public ownership, federal investment, and local subsidies have enabled a net increase of only 8.4 percent in bus, streetcar, and rapid transit ridership since the inception of the federal assistance program in 1964. During the same period, the U.S. population increased 46.7 percent while the U.S. workforce increased 95.1 percent.[37] Clearly, transit's same-mode ridership has not kept pace with the growth of the population or workforce.

Yes, public ownership has enabled transit to rebuild ridership, but nowhere near enough to maintain the commute share it enjoyed in 1960. Nor has it enabled transit to achieve any aggregate increase in nationwide productivity. Most of transit's ridership gains have been realized in those segments of the metropolitan market that are most costly to serve on a per rider basis—the suburbs and the commute to the central city. Clearly, the federal transit program has produced what the urban mayors and downtown asked for in 1961, but the net result has been a steady increase in transit costs per rider and continuing decline in transit's nationwide and central city commute shares.

Why Hasn't Public Ownership Produced Better Results?

The federal transit program as it emerged in the 1960s was a Senate committee's answer to the question: How can the federal government help downtown rebound from the twin problems of deteriorating transit service and declining sales? The committee's answer was low-cost loans for commuter railroads and grant funding for rapid transit provided under the auspices of the federal agency responsible for urban renewal and redevelopment. This answer was an on-target response to the concerns of the big city mayors, downtown, the commuter railroads, and the advocates of rail rapid transit and downtown redevelopment. But it was off-target if the more important questions were as follows: How should public transportation be reorganized, refinanced, and repriced so that it can deliver the wide variety of transit and paratransit services that are needed to serve central cities, metropolitan suburbs, and midsized cities nationwide? What is the appropriate role of government—local to federal—in transforming a distressed industry like transit into a financially sustainable public service? What are the appropriate roles of the private and public sectors in the planning and delivery of transit service? What can be done to rebuild transit ridership as cost-effectively as possible? What simultaneous steps can be taken to improve the productivity of labor and equipment and the efficiency of street operation, especially in the largest cities with the most intense traffic congestion? And finally, what can be done to simultaneously increase both transit's ridership and its productivity?

In most American cities, these difficult questions have been left unasked and unanswered, because the Senate committee that established the federal transit program's mission and focus took its cue from that handful of mayors and cities considering plans for rapid transit. Congress eventually endorsed the rail coalition's agenda and broadened it to include every form of transit, both urban and suburban, without addressing these issues. The result was a politically salable program that was based on high hopes for rail transit—but very little understanding of the persistent, long-term difficulties of the transit industry.

With ISTEA and TEA-21, congressional enthusiasm for rail transit has reached new heights. In fact, the Federal Transit Administration was actively considering 37 rail capital projects, 23 from sunbelt cities.[38] The number of projects presently in the funding pipeline indicates that a rail renaissance is in progress. It may also indicate that TEA-21 and congressional earmarking have created an irresistible opportunity to fund high-visibility projects that can burnish a city's image. If this rail revival can stimulate a downtown renaissance in a next generation of rail cities, the cost could well prove justifiable. But whether that renaissance will actually occur remains to be seen.

What Is the Bottom Line?

Except for the years during and immediately after World War II, transit rides per capita of the U.S. population have been downward trending since 1926, the year that peacetime ridership peaked at 147 rides per capita. Following its World War II peak, transit rides per capita fell to 104 in 1950, 52 in 1960, and 43 in 1964, which was the year that Congress authorized federal capital grants for transit improvement. Transit rides per capita bottomed out at 31 rides per capita in 1972, and since the OPEC embargo they have oscillated in the relatively narrow range of 33 to 38 per capita.[39] Thus we can conclude that public ownership, federal investment, and state and local operating subsidy have more or less stabilized transit ridership on a per capita basis, but at a level very close to its historic low.

Unfortunately, transit's commute share has continued to decline under public ownership—from 12.1 percent in 1960 to its recent low of 4.7 percent in 2000. Perhaps more worrisome for the long term, transit's operating expenses have risen steadily under public ownership. Calculated on a same-mode basis, aggregate nationwide operating costs per bus, streetcar, and rapid transit rider have increased 140 percent in real dollar terms since 1964 as transit has expanded service into increasingly marginal markets.

Given transit's diminutive commute share in 2000 and the upward trend of transit's unit costs, it seems unrealistic to expect that continuing expansion of transit service into increasingly marginal markets can produce ridership gains sufficient to substantially reduce U.S. oil import requirements or the automobile's contribution to CO_2 emissions. In fact, it seems all too likely that tasking transit to play a significantly larger role in reducing oil imports or CO_2 emissions would distract transit managers from more important local priorities, including productivity improvement.

In the American context, those transit improvements that are most likely to be productive are those that have been tailored to fit local circumstances. Portland and Salt Lake City, for example, have demonstrated that light rail systems can play a significant role in energizing downtown redevelopment programs and rebuilding transit's market share. But tables 6.9 and 6.10 and the recent explosion of rail projects in the planning pipeline also suggest that the TEA-21 budgeting process and suburban service expansion are creating dynamics that could lead to an unsustainable increase in transit operating costs on a per rider basis.

In the context of increasing costs per rider, we have argued for a focused effort to increase transit's productivity. Recent experience suggests that the most promising way to do so would entail broad-based diffusion of the lessons learned from the Las Vegas experience with paratransit and contracting out. Selective replication of Portland's pairing of Smart Growth with light rail and timed transfers is also in order. So too is continuing investment in the modernization of big city transit fleets and the boulevards on which they operate. These would be appropriate priorities for a transit program that is focused on sustaining transit's usefulness while increasing its productivity and cost-effectiveness.

Summing Up

1. In 1961, with Democrat John F. Kennedy in the White House, big city mayors sought congressional funding for mass transit, most of which was privately owned and in precarious financial condition. Mayors and commuter railroads joined forces to emphasize the need for coordinated federal investment in both rail transit and urban redevelopment.

San Francisco's planned BART system and Philadelphia's planned Lindenwald Line were offered as models for future federal investment. In turn, Congress focused on capital grants for rail transit and the link between commuter transit and downtown redevelopment.

2. Urban street transit was largely ignored in building support for the federal aid program, and little attention was paid to understanding transit's problems or its financial requirements for recovery and renewed ridership growth. The focus was on downtown, rapid transit, and commuter rail—even though buses were then (and are now) the workhorse mode of the transit industry in terms of the miles of service rendered and the number of passengers carried. Provision was eventually made for public ownership of transit properties operating bus service, but as an afterthought in a study and hearing process that had focused on commuter rail, rapid transit, and downtown.

3. Federal funding was authorized for loans and demonstration projects in 1961 and for capital grants in 1964. Federal funding was first used to acquire transit systems and convert them to public ownership and operations. Conversion proceeded without prior renegotiation of work rules, pay scales, and fare structures. Thus conversion to public ownership was missed as an opportunity to modernize street transit and its labor agreements, operating policies, and fare structures in ways that could have enabled transit to retain more riders and serve them more cost-effectively.

4. Transit's conversion to public ownership and the infusion of federal investment short-circuited the relentless abandonment of transit service that had occurred in the 1950s, but public ownership and investment have not enabled transit to achieve the ridership gains that Congress expected. In fact, the combined ridership of buses, rapid transit, and light rail systems in 2000 was less than it was at the inception of the mayoral lobbying effort in 1960. Transit's share of work trips is also lower: it has declined from 12.1 percent of all work trips in 1960 to 4.7 percent in 2000.

5. A substantial proportion of transit's long-term decline in market share is attributable to economic and social dynamics that were well beyond the industry's control. These have included the growth of suburbs and the suburban population and the net losses in central city population due to the postwar emigration of white households—the dynamic that came to be known as "white flight." Other dynamics that compounded the loss of transit ridership included the hollowing out of industrial employment opportunities in many of the frostbelt's old-line manufacturing centers due to import competition and the obsolescence of plant

and equipment, the loss of manufacturing employment, and the corresponding decline in consumer buying power, retail sales, and retail employment in many frostbelt cities. In the 1980s, these dynamics were further compounded by migration from the frostbelt to the sunbelt. These many dynamics have diluted transit's nationwide share of commute trips and are likely to continue to do so, given the geography of economic growth.

6. From 1980 to 1990, transit achieved gains in commute share in only three cities: Phoenix, Houston, and Austin. More auspiciously, transit gained market share in 12 of the nation's 50 largest metropolitan areas between 1990 and 2000, including New York, Los Angeles, Washington, Philadelphia, and Seattle. On the other hand, transit continued to lose commute share in the central cities of many of the nation's prime transit markets.

7. Portland's widely publicized experiment with Smart Growth has created conditions conducive to an increase in transit's market share. These include investment in light rail transit, up-zoning for higher density residential development in the vicinity of rail stations, timed-transfer arrangements that facilitate passenger transfers from bus to rail and bus to bus, and high visibility in local media. The net result has been a 26 percent increase in rides per capita and a 21 percent increase in transit's work-trip market share. These are significant gains, but Portland has also experienced increases in congestion and congestion-related fuel consumption that were larger than those of any other city in its size-class. Smart Growth can be fine-tuned to produce an effective strategy for growth management, but that will also require a selective commitment to highway operational improvements and a more sophisticated approach to freeway operations and management.

8. Las Vegas achieved much greater gains in ridership and market share by selectively contracting out transit and paratransit service to private operators. Most significantly, transit posted a 128 percent increase in Las Vegas market share between 1990 and 2000.

9. Federal investment and local subsidy have enabled transit to modernize its fleets and expand service significantly, but the recovery of ridership has been slow and uneven. Federal grants for transit capital investment were authorized in 1964 when transit's nationwide ridership stood at 8.3 billion; ridership bottomed out at 6.6 billion in 1972 but reached a new postwar peak of 9.7 billion rides in 2001. Since the inception of federal capital investment in 1964, transit's nationwide ridership has increased 8.5 percent while the U.S. population was increasing 49 percent. During this same 1964–2001 period, transit's operating expenses per ride increased 140 percent in constant 1982 dollars.

10. Transit's nationwide results for the most recent decade were not much improved. It took a 10 percent increase in transit service to achieve a 5 percent increase in ridership. Thus ridership declined 10 percent per mile of service actually rendered, while operating expenses increased almost 11 percent per rider served. During the same period, governmental subsidy for operating purposes increased 17 percent. Such results indicate that public ownership and subsidy have increased transit ridership but not transit productivity.

11. Federal investment has enabled transit to sustain its contribution to urban mobility. But the recent escalation of transit operating expenses is unsustainable. This leads to the conclusion that transit properties should focus on improving productivity. It also leads to the conclusion that transit's present cost structure and its diminutive market share will, at the margin, make it difficult for public transportation to make a contribution to the reduction of CO_2 emissions or U.S. oil import requirements that is both substantial and cost-effective.

12. Our conclusion is that federal transit policy should discourage continuing role inflation that entails further geographic dispersion of transit service and increasing dilution of transit funding. Instead, federal transit policy should focus transit investment in those markets that transit can serve most cost-effectively, those cities where the demand for transit is greatest, and those metropolitan areas where investment is paired with an explicit plan for improving transit's productivity.

SEVEN

U.S. Motorization since the OPEC Embargo

The OPEC oil embargo of 1973 and the Iranian revolution of 1979 were hinge events in the history of U.S. motorization, events that rocked the industrial world and the global economy. Higher oil prices and uncertain oil supplies affected motorists, truckers, transit operators, the fuel tax revenues of the state highway programs, and the sales and production volumes of the world's automakers. These economic shocks produced a one-year pause in the economic growth of the industrialized nations. They also produced gasoline lines and spurred increases in transit ridership. The aftershocks affected the U.S. highway program and the automobile industry in less direct but more lasting ways. In the case of the automobile industry, they triggered the beginnings of a long-term shift in consumer loyalties that eventually enabled imported cars to capture a substantial share of the passenger car market in the United States. In turn, declining sales volume reduced the economies of scale essential to the profitability of the domestic automakers. The oil shocks also produced short-term declines in VMT, which resulted in a significant loss in fuel tax revenues and the cessation of highway right-of-way reservation in many states. In turn, the present difficulties of right-of-way acquisition pose a largely unacknowledged constraint on the potential for future highway development, which in turn signals the likelihood of continuing increases in metropolitan congestion.

Responding to the 1973–74 oil shocks, Congress imposed mandatory fuel efficiency standards for cars and trucks and made transit eligible to compete for funds previously earmarked for highway purposes. The oil shocks also led Congress to authorize what proved to be a short-lived program of federal operating subsidies for mass transit. More significant over the long term has been the financial damage that the oil shocks have done to the U.S. automobile industry. Vehicle ownership and registrations have continued to increase, virtually without pause, but the year-to-year predictability of the mix of vehicles that Americans will want to purchase has been affected profoundly. Since the OPEC embargo, U.S. consumers have signaled that they want more imports and fewer domestics, more fuel-efficient small cars and fewer "gas-guzzlers," and more trucks and SUVs a few years later. In turn, this variability and volatility has wreaked havoc with the product and production planning of the U.S. automakers. Together, the oil shocks, "the import invasion," and the volatility of demand for full-size vehicles and sport utility vehicles have substantially reduced both the sales volumes and the profitability of the U.S. automakers.

Significant import penetration in the U.S. passenger car market is a direct consequence of both the oil shocks and the quality of the second wave of imports that arrived in the 1980s. Imports gained and have substantially retained a sales edge with the 75 million U.S. baby boomers, the generation of Americans who bought their first cars after the OPEC oil embargo. The size of this cohort and its bifurcated preferences for SUVs and for small and midsized cars with European styling have had profound impacts on the U.S. auto market and the U.S. automakers, as have the succession of oil shocks that occurred, first in 1973, then again in 1981, and still again in 2004–2006.

The Oil Shocks

In February 1973, the price of a barrel of imported oil stood at $6.41 in 1992 dollars.[1] By July 1974, at the price peak associated with the OPEC embargo, a barrel of imported crude reached $24.53 in 1992 dollars. Over the next 12 years, oil prices retreated from their 1974 peak but remained relatively high and quite volatile. The monthly low for the next seven years was reached in September 1978, when the price of oil retreated to $20.48 in 1992 dollars. Clearly, the OPEC cartel was effective in maintaining oil prices at levels much higher than the price that prevailed in February 1973.

With the Iranian revolution and the displacement of the shah of Iran, the import price of oil reached a new high of $40.18 per barrel in June 1981. Production was restored quickly, and a new low of $9.21 was achieved by April 1983, but volatility remained the norm as the price of imported crude reached a new peak of $29.40 per barrel in 1983. By 1986, oil prices had collapsed again, due to new crude oil supplies found in the North Sea. In August 1986, the import price of oil had declined to $8.41 per barrel in 1992 prices.

A new high was reached after the Iraqi invasion of Kuwait and the subsequent UN-sponsored incursion in Iraq. Crude oil import prices reached an interim high of $23.16 a barrel in November 1990. The price level was restored to $12.03 per barrel in April 1991, and eventually it reached new lows of $10.28 per barrel in February 1992 and $9.80 in January 1994. Intermittent volatility took the price of crude as high as $11.46 in June 1996, but the price range was narrow after April 1991, and the price of imported crude reached its all-time low in January 1999. U.S. gasoline prices reached their all-time low a month later.[2]

Higher oil import prices followed in the run-up to the 2004 war in Iraq, and a new interim peak of $32.36 per barrel was reached in September 2005 and superseded in early 2006. This discussion illuminates two contradictory trends. The long-term trend of gasoline prices was downward in real dollar terms through 1999, but since 1973 that downward trend has been punctuated with extreme price volatility associated with both political instability and U.S.-led interventions in the oil-rich Middle East.

Oil Shocks and the U.S. Automobile Industry

One of the most important indirect impacts of the OPEC embargo and the later Iranian revolution was the opportunity that higher gasoline prices created for Japanese automakers to establish a beachhead in the passenger segment of the U.S. auto market. The oil shocks also provided baby boomers with the impetus they needed to test-drive smaller, more fuel-efficient import cars. The baby boomers' lasting affinity for imports, both Japanese and European, has reduced both the market shares and the profitability of the domestic automakers. Most significantly, the import share of U.S. passenger car sales increased 79 percent between 1973 and 2003, while their share increased from 15.3 to 27.4 percent.

During the same period, the truck share of total U.S. motor vehicle sales increased from 21.3 percent in 1973 to 55.7 percent in 2003, a net increase of 155.1 percent over 20 years. Most of these trucks were purchased for personal use or joint personal and occupational use, and many others were SUVs.[3] Increased sale of trucks and SUVs compensated, but not fully, for the U.S. automakers' loss of domestic passenger car sales. Increasing truck sales have not fully compensated for the loss of passenger car sales because the oil shocks and other sources of market volatility have intermittently depressed their sales and made it increasingly difficult to anticipate what mix of trucks and passenger vehicles and small and large cars will prove saleable from one year to the next. In turn, sales

Table 7.1 *U.S. passenger car production volumes, 1973–2003*

1973 all-time high	9.7 million
1975 short-term low	6.7 million
1978 short-term high	9.2 million
1982 short-term low	5.1 million
1985 short-term high	8.2 million
2001 short-term low	4.9 million
2002 short-term high	5.2 million
2003 short-term low	4.5 million

SOURCE: "U.S. Production of Passenger Cars, Trucks, and Buses," *Ward's Motor Vehicle Facts and Figures*, 2003, 3.

volatility has diminished the production volumes and production line efficiencies that were once the hallmark of the U.S. automobile industry.

Table 7.1 shows the cyclic nature of U.S. passenger car production over the past 30 years. Closer examination also reveals that the domestic auto industry's short-term cyclic trends sum to a long-term secular trend that has been downward trending since the OPEC embargo. Each new low in passenger car production volumes has established a lower low, and U.S. passenger car production declined 54 percent from its all-time high in 1973. During this same period, the U.S. population increased 69 percent.

Much of the extreme sales volatility that is shown in table 7.1 is the result of the external shocks created by the volatility of the Middle East and world oil prices. It is also the result of the cyclic favor that Americans have accorded fuel-efficient imports, on the one hand, and SUVs and pickup trucks, on the other. In turn, extreme volatility in new vehicle sales has brought an end to the period of lush profitability that the Big Three manufacturers enjoyed during the 1950s, 1960s, and early 1970s. And as a result, intermittent financial difficulty has been the U.S. auto industry norm since the OPEC embargo.

Cyclic movement from highs to lows has been more pronounced for trucks and SUVs than for conventional passenger cars. But the long-term secular trend for SUVs and light trucks has been upward trending, while that for passenger cars has been downward trending. The salability of SUVs and pickup trucks is precisely why the U.S. automakers have increased their production despite persistent criticism from those concerned with energy conservation and CO_2 emissions.

The volatility shown in tables 7.1 and 7.2 underlines the dilemma facing U.S. automakers. The long-term upward sales trend of trucks and SUVs justifies the priority that the U.S. automakers have assigned them in their production and marketing plans. On the other hand, the salability of characteristically "American" vehicles that are roomy and powerful but relatively fuel-inefficient

Table 7.2 *U.S. truck and SUV production volumes, 1973–2003*

1973 short-term high	3.0 million
1970 short-term low	2.3 million
1978 short-term high	3.7 million
1980 short-term low	1.6 million
1988 short-term high	4.1 million
1991 short-term low	3.4 million
1999 short-term high	7.4 million
2001 short-term low	6.5 million
2003 short-term high	7.6 million

SOURCE: "U.S. Production of Passenger Cars, Trucks, and Buses," *Ward's Motor Vehicle Facts and Figures*, 2003, 3.

is now intermittent. These vehicles have proved eminently salable when gasoline prices are low, as they were in the mid-1980s and mid-1990s, but fall out of fashion when gasoline prices turn volatile. This, of course, is precisely what happened in 1975 and 1982 and what has happened again during the second war in Iraq, which has produced another run-up in gasoline prices along with credit downgrades for both GM and Ford. At the same time, we must emphasize that the oil shocks have not had any appreciable long-term impact on the trend of U.S. motorization: motor vehicle ownership has continued to increase gradually.

Crossing the Threshold of Pervasive Motorization

As we have defined it, the threshold of pervasive motorization is reached when a nation's combined commute share for transit and walking falls below 10 percent. The United States crossed this threshold in 1980 when the nationwide motorization level reached 685 vehicles per 1,000 population. No uniquely significant event or singular dynamic pushed the United States over the threshold of pervasive motorization in 1980. It was a mediocre year for U.S. vehicle sales that followed a string of very good years from 1976 through 1979. It was a mediocre sales year because of the oil shock associated with the 1979 Iranian revolution. Thus pervasive motorization did not occur in 1980 because of favorable circumstances. Instead, the United States crossed the threshold of pervasive motorization because there had been a long enough string of consecutive years of low unemployment, steady growth in per capita GDP, stable gasoline prices, and robust motor vehicle sales to bring the nation to the brink of pervasive motorization.

In any event, the United States crossed the threshold of pervasive motorization in a down year for per capita GDP, an up year for unemployment, and a predictably lackluster year for automobile sales. Just enough Americans bought cars and trucks in 1980 to push the United States over the statistical threshold of pervasive motorization. Indeed, with an OPEC oil shock suppressing the sale of domestic cars, it was import sales that carried the United States over the threshold of pervasive motorization.

From 1980 to 2000, motor vehicle ownership increased an additional 100 vehicles per 1,000 population. The sales volume of full-sized domestic passenger cars declined, while the sales volume of fuel-efficient imports increased. Rebuffed in the compact car market, the U.S. automakers successfully timed the introduction of a next generation of passenger vans, SUVs, and other light trucks that appealed to the baby boomers as they entered their parenting years. Contrary to what might have been expected in the wake of the oil shocks, trucks increased from 19 percent of all vehicles in operation in 1973 to 41 percent in 2000.[4] This increase was almost entirely attributable to sales growth in the passenger segment of the truck market, which includes vans, SUVs, and light trucks. Others in the boomer generation continued to prefer fuel-efficient import cars. These bifurcated preferences have proved durable, which has forced the domestic automakers to reduce sharply the production of the full-sized passenger cars that were once the auto industry's bread and butter. In turn, intermittent oil shocks have increased sales volatility in the automotive marketplace, making it difficult for the automakers to anticipate the mix of cars and trucks that U.S. customers will want to buy in any given year. This is problematic given the long lead times that are required to bring each generation of motor vehicles to market. Tables 7.1 and 7.2 showed how sales volatility has influenced the demand for cars and trucks, including SUVs. Inevitably, such volatility has made it difficult for the automakers to anticipate what mix of vehicles will sell from one year to the next. And that is problematic in the extreme because production planning was the essential underpinning of the auto industry's profitability in the heydays before the OPEC embargo.

Table 7.3 tells a somewhat different story. It shows that the oil shocks of 1973 and 1980 did not prevent continuing motorization. In each case, vehicles per capita continued to increase after a brief pause. But the table also shows that motor vehicle ownership is no longer increasing at a pace substantially faster than the growth of the driving-age population. This would seem to indicate that the United States is approaching saturation in terms of motor vehicle registrations per 1,000 population. The declining size of each successive decadal increment suggests that U.S. motor vehicle registrations per 1,000 population would peak relatively soon, probably somewhere between 784 and 800 vehicles per 1,000 population

On the other hand, table 7.3 does not indicate that total vehicle registrations or the total number of vehicles in operation will peak any time soon. The

Table 7.3 *Increasing intensity of U.S. motorization, 1960–2000*

Year	Intensity	Decade-to-decade increment
1960	410 per 1,000	—
1970	531 per 1,000	121 per 1,000
1980	685 per 1,000	154 per 1,000
1990	755 per 1,000	70 per 1,000
2000	784 per 1,000	29 per 1,000

SOURCE: *Ward's Motor Vehicle Facts and Figures*, 2002, and *Statistical Abstract of the United States*, 2001, table 2, "Population: 1960 to 2000."

number of registered vehicles will continue to increase because of immigration and robust birthrates. If saturation occurs at a motorization level of 800 vehicles per 1,000 population, the U.S. motorization level could still approach 270 million vehicles in 2025, up from 249 million in 2000.[5] This increase in registrations would be fully consistent with current projections of U.S. population growth. Following the same logic, U.S. motor vehicle registrations could approach 325 million by 2050, given projected growth.

One implication of this crude forecast is that increasing demands will be made on a highway system that is not now being expanded at the pace necessary to accommodate them. A second population dynamic—the aging of the baby boom generation—will make this shortcoming doubly problematic. With the retirement of the boomer generation, highway safety will emerge as an increasingly critical national issue, just as crowded classrooms emerged as a critical national issue in 1951 and 1952 when the boomers first went to school. After 2015, increasing traffic and a bulge in the population of drivers older than 70 will impose a new and urgent array of traffic safety issues. And with increasing VMT, a growing population will continue to impose increasing demands on global oil supplies and the environment unless we can make significant improvements in both the fuel efficiency of the automobile and the efficiency and serviceability of mass transit. Still another implication is that it will be absolutely essential that U.S. automakers achieve cash flows sufficient to finance the development of a next generation of cars and trucks that are fuel-efficient, environmentally benign, and thoroughly crashworthy.

The Decreasing Momentum of U.S. Motorization after 1980

Table 7.4 shows the increase in freeway mileage, VMT, and vehicle registrations that the United States recorded from 1960 to 2000. We report these in two symmetric 20-year blocks because these time segments allow us to distinguish

Table 7.4 *Increase in miles of freeway, vehicle registrations, and VMT*

	1960–80	1980–2000	1960–2000
Increase in miles of freeway, both urban and rural	42,536	28,726	71,262
Increase in vehicle registrations (in millions)	81.9	65.8	147.7
Increase in VMT (in billions)	808	1,223	2,031
Increase in U.S. population (in millions)	42.7	54.6	101.8
Increase in VMT per capita	1,700	2,240	3,940
Increase in registrations per 1,000 population	275	100	375

SOURCE: FHWA, *Highway Statistics*, table HM-36, 1960, 1980 and 2000, table MV-200, 1900–1995, and 2000; *Ward's Motor Vehicle Facts and Figures*, 2002, "Annual Motor Vehicle Miles of Travel," 21.

between the increments and the activity levels of the "peak production" stage of the interstate program (1960–80) and the program's later "finishing up" stage (1980–2000).

Table 7.4 shows that 71,262 miles of freeway were built from 1960 to 2000; it also shows that vehicle registrations increased by 147.7 million during this same period, while the U.S. population increased by only 101.8 million. More telling, annual VMT increased by more than 3,900 miles per capita. The observations and conclusions that can be drawn by using table 7.4 in an incremental mode of analysis are even more interesting. One such observation is that the pace of U.S. motorization reached its peak during the period 1960–80 in terms of the number of motor vehicles added per 1,000 population. No earlier period and no later period produced as large an increment in motor vehicle ownership. So does the interstate explain the intensity of U.S. motorization? Or were other factors at work that would better explain the same outcome?

We know, of course, that there were many: the growth of GDP and GDP per capita; the already established American preference for home ownership and suburban residence; the many baby boomers who reached driving age in the 1970s; the increasing number of women entering the workforce in the 1980s and 1990s; the growth of suburban office employment—all contributed to the growing number of two- and three-vehicle households.

Table 7.5 uses index values to illuminate the decadal trend of these variables. Using the table as our point of reference, we can construct a narrative history that reveals the temporal interplay of these variables following World War II. It can be summarized as follows: The most explosive postwar increase in the level of U.S. motorization occurred between 1950 and 1980. With the economic recovery and return of economic confidence that followed World War II, the growth of motor vehicle ownership outpaced the growth of GDP from 1950 to 1960. After 1960, the pace of motorization roughly paced the growth of GDP

Table 7.5 *An index of cohorts of U.S. motorization, 1950–2000*

	1950	1960	1970	1980	1990	2000
Vehicle registrations	67	100	147	210	255	300
Vehicles per 1,000 pop.	79	100	130	167	185	191
Home ownership rate	97	100	113	114	119	123
GDP	71	100	151	207	283	388
GDP per capita	84	100	132	164	192	248
Population, age 15–24	91	100	148	173	151	159
Women in the workforce	79	100	136	192	245	322
Suburban share of office space	—	100	150	250	350	450
Households with 2 vehicles	—	100	260	271	341	402
Miles of urban freeway in service	14	100	470	900	1,167	1,433
Urban VMT	66	100	171	257	385	501

SOURCE: U.S. Bureau of the Census, Series Q 187–198 and FHWA, table MV-2000, 1900–1995 and 2000; *Ward's Motor Vehicle Facts and Figures*, 2002, "Vehicle Miles of Travel"; *Historical Statistics of the United States*, Series Q 243 and "Surfaced Mileage of State Primary (Highway) Systems," FHWA, *Highway Statistics*, summary to 1995, table SM-211, and continuation in *Ward's Motor Vehicle Facts and Figures*, 2003, 68; U.S. Dept. of Labor, "Employment Status of the Population, 1960-2000"; McGuckin and Srinivasan, *Journey-to-Work Trends in the United States and Its Major Metropolitan Areas, 1960-2000*, FHWA, Report no. EP-03-058, June 2003; Maddison, *World Economy: Historical Statistics*, 85–86, 88–89; author's extrapolation of the suburban share of metropolitan office space based on fragmentary data in Kotkin, *New Geography*, 37.

until 1980, then slowed as motor vehicle ownership began to approach saturation levels in the 1990s.

Urban freeway development lagged behind motorization in the 1950s, but accelerated dramatically in the 1960s and 1970s under the auspices of the interstate highway program, opening the metropolitan periphery for settlement and enabling developers to achieve economies of scale in housing construction. This same period saw a sharp increase in drivers ages 16 to 24. It also saw a significant increases in women's workforce participation, suburbanization, GDP per capita, suburban office space, and households with two or more vehicles. In turn, the resulting growth of suburban population and employment contributed significantly to the increase in two-car households and to explosive growth in VMT.

After 1980, continuing increases in women's workforce participation and related increases in household buying and borrowing power averted early saturation of the demand for automobile ownership. Simultaneously, the construction of metropolitan beltways provided the infrastructure to support the continuing development of suburban housing and growth of suburban population and employment. By 1980, suburb-to-suburb commuting was as common as a commute destined for the central city in most metropolitan areas. After

1980, increasing women's workforce participation and the increasing prevalence of suburban and sunbelt residence explain why the United States did not experience saturation in terms of motor vehicles per capita. And, taken together, these many dynamics explain the continuing growth of VMT that occurred between 1980 and 2000.

The present intensity of U.S. motorization is the cumulative by-product of a century of history. America's early leadership in the mass production of cars and trucks, its long-standing world leadership in per capita GDP, its pioneering roles in the development of credit financing for both home and motor vehicle ownership, its once abundant supply of domestic oil, cheap gasoline, and America's advantageous economic position in the years following World War I—all of these explain America's early leadership in motorization. These early developments were reinforced by the economic confidence, demographic trends, and postwar nesting instincts of the generation of young Americans who fought in World War II, leading to mass motorization by 1957. In turn, the interstate highway program accommodated continuing motorization and contributed to the ongoing spatial reorganization of U.S. metropolitan areas, creating suburban environments that are conducive to safer use of the automobile but increasingly dependent on the automobile for mass transportation.

Freeways and auto-oriented suburban design mitigated many of the safety problems and inconveniences that had been associated with the early years of motorization, but these same measures led to increasing automobile dependence in those suburbs and sunbelt cities that have experienced most of their growth and development since World War II. The expansion of trucking and innovations in distribution enabled counterpart adjustments in goods movement that supported the growth of suburban commerce and employment. Together, this multitude of supply and demand dynamics has produced a level of motor vehicle ownership and use that is nationally pervasive and globally unique. These same dynamics, both public and private, have compromised transit's ability to compete effectively with the automobile, public ownership and subsidy notwithstanding. Thus the interstate clearly contributed to the present intensity of U.S. motorization, but it was not a singularly decisive factor, nor did it precipitate transit's decline. That was already well under way in the 1920s.

The Present Status of Metropolitan Highway Programs

Metropolitan freeway construction continues today, but at a much slower pace than that of the 1960s and 1970s. Another generation of expressways, parkways, and tollways is being built in suburban settings, but virtually none will be built in the central cities or the radial corridors that serve them. This seems unavoidable, given the dislocation and conflict that was associated with building the urban routes of the interstate system and the cessation of right-of-way acquisition for new construction on new alignments, which has become the norm for most state highway programs.

Funding for continuing highway investment has been authorized, but no substantial future infusion of new funds for new construction on new alignments is likely because the interstate program itself has reached sunset and been replaced with a surface transportation program that is explicitly multimodal in character and also more project-oriented and regionalist in its approach to metropolitan investment. To date, Congress seems pleased with ISTEA and its multimodal orientation and with the emphasis on sponsored projects, the increased emphasis on local control, and the increased opportunity for members of Congress to "bring home the bacon."

There are two final reasons that future metropolitan freeway development will be limited: the increased difficulty of right-of-way acquisition and the increased volatility of gasoline prices and gas tax revenues, which will make it difficult to arrive at any legislative or congressional consensus favoring an increase in the fuel tax for highway construction purposes. Such reluctance was clearly evident after the 1973 and 1989 oil shocks, and more of the same seems likely following the current price shocks. Thus, like the U.S. automobile industry, the nation's highway program has been buffeted by the price shocks associated with the OPEC oil embargo, the Iranian revolution, and the second war in Iraq.

The state highway departments have weathered these fiscal shocks just as the automakers weathered the oil shocks, but not without significant damage to their construction programs. In the late 1970s and 1980s, the cash flow problems of state highway departments led to the virtual termination of right-of-way acquisition within metropolitan areas.[6] With metropolitan right-of-way acquisition curtailed, intervening growth and development have substantially diminished the ability of the states to assemble continuous rights-of-way for future freeway construction. State highway officials reluctantly agree that this largely unreported consequence of the oil shocks has and will constrain their ability to execute any substantial program of future freeway development in many metropolitan areas. This has significant implications for future congestion levels and for congestion-related emissions in metropolitan areas.

Oils Shocks and the Highway Program

Table 7.6 provides a framework for understanding the impact of the oil shocks on state and federal highway programs. The first column shows that capital outlays for highway construction increased steadily from 1960 to 2000 in current

Table 7.6 *Capital outlays for U.S. highway construction, 1960–2000*

Year	Capital outlays in billions of current $	Capital outlays in billions of constant 1987 $	Capital outlays as a % of GDP	Capital outlays in 1987 $ per million VMT
1960	6.3	27.3	2.2	38
1965	8.4	33.4	2.3	38
1970	11.6	33.2	2.3	30
1975	14.4	24.7	1.9	19
1980	20.3	23.2	1.6	21
1985	26.6	26.6	1.5	15
1990	35.2	32.4	1.5	15
1995	44.2	36.8	1.6	15
2000	61.3	44.3	1.8	16

SOURCE: Author's calculations based on FHWA, *Highway Statistics*, table HF202C, 1960–2000.

dollar terms. On first inspection, this would seem to indicate that the 1973 and 1979 oil shocks had only minimal impact on the nation's highway program. But a different picture emerges when we report capital outlays for highways in terms of their inflation-adjusted buying power and their relationship to the size of the nation's GDP. The second column shows that the real dollar buying power of state highway programs declined significantly during the period of price inflation that followed the OPEC embargo and the Iranian revolution. In fact, in real dollar terms, the nationwide highway program did not recover its pre-OPEC buying power until 1993 or 1994. The third column shows that capital outlays for highways have declined significantly as a percentage of GDP; it also shows that the highway program's recovery was belated and partial. Column 4 reveals the most important consequence of curtailed highway investment. It shows in real dollars terms the trend of highway investment per million vehicle miles traveled in the United States. This indicator shows how substantially the growth of traffic, as measured by VMT, has outpaced U.S. highway investment, especially since the OPEC oil embargo. And because highway funding has remained tight, rights-of-way have not been acquired for a next generation of suburban expressways. Thus excessive volumes of traffic are unavoidably being concentrated in existing freeway corridors. This has produced both increasing congestion and delay and the excess emissions and fuel consumption that are associated with stop-and-start driving. At the same time, suburban development has gradually preempted abandoned railroad rights-of-way and other continuous strips of land that highway planners had once hoped could provide future rights-of-way for a next generation of suburban expressways and beltways. The implication is that a commitment to renewed right-of-way acquisition must be made soon, if we want useful right-of-way to be available to meet future highway needs.

Clearly, table 7.6 has important implications for the future. One is that continuing concentration of traffic in existing corridors will result in continuing future increases in congestion, delay, congestion-related fuel consumption, and pollutant emissions, with a next generation of such increases especially likely in suburban settings. Another implication is that this congestion could be anticipated and ameliorated, at least in some metropolitan areas, if we were prepared to make a renewed commitment to suburban right-of-way acquisition and suburban parkway development. The third implication is that what is most needed is a funding source for right-of-way acquisition. In the spirit of ISTEA and TEA-21, it would be appropriate that federal funds for such purposes be flexible enough to permit investment in rights-of-way for light rail and parkways. We emphasize light rail and parkways rather than heavy rail and freeways because they scale more appropriately for successful integration in suburban environments and for effective integration with a multimodal approach to planning for both Smart Growth and congestion management.

Thus we would hope that both right-of-way acquisition and parkway construction could eventually gain traction in the context of T-21. Light rail has already gained momentum in the context of planning for Smart Growth and redevelopment in an increasing number of midsized cities. A comparable commitment to parkway development could reduce the excessive concentration of traffic in existing freeway corridors and the excess fuel consumption and pollutant emissions that are associated with the operation of freeways that are congested for many hours of the day.

The Post-Interstate Era

The Intermodal Surface Transportation Efficiency Act of 1991 (ISTEA) set an end date for interstate-specific appropriations, in effect taking the first step that led to eventual sun-setting of the interstate highway program. ISTEA, in combination with the later Transportation Equity Act of 1998, has produced a de facto dilution of the programming authority of the states and their highway departments in metropolitan areas while placing increased emphasis on multimodal and multijurisdictional planning for metropolitan transportation. Paired with this emphasis on multimodal planning are funding streams that offer increased modal flexibility and put greater emphasis on intermodal coordination. ISTEA has also resulted in increased efforts to coordinate planning for transportation and land use.

ISTEA was adopted in 1991 and reflects Washington's long-standing responsiveness to urban mayors and its increasing openness to environmental concerns. In turn, the first Bush administration's DOT emphasized to its client state and local agencies that ISTEA was a major break with the policies and priorities of the interstate era. With its passage, the administrators of the federal highway and transit programs told their institutional constituents that ISTEA

> recognizes that the Interstate Highway System is nearly complete, and that system preservation rather than construction needs to become the higher priority.
>
> Furthermore, ISTEA recognizes the changing development patterns, the economic and cultural diversity of metropolitan areas, and the need to provide metropolitan areas with more control over transportation in their own regions.
>
> It envisions achieving this through strengthening planning practices and coordination between States and metropolitan areas and between [the] private and public sector, and improving linkages and connections between different forms of transportation. . . .
>
> The ISTEA also reflects an understanding of the constraints imposed upon further expansion of the highway network, particularly in metropolitan areas, and that the maximization of system efficiency and system preservation need to become priorities.
>
> Finally, ISTEA includes unprecedented linkages to achievement of the air quality objectives embodied in the Clean Air Act Amendments of 1990 and in state air quality plans.[7]

As the items in this DOT memorandum suggest, ISTEA represented "a shift in Congressional attention to the local and regional dimensions of transportation policy."[8] It also reflects the increasing role that both Congress and demonstration projects have come to play in programming highway and transit funds on a project-by-project basis. In this sense, ISTEA also represented a shift away from the twin priorities of the interstate era—funding state freeway construction in metropolitan areas and sustaining the financial and administrative partnership that linked the Federal Highway Administration and the state highway departments. Clearly, the federal highway program remains a national priority but no longer such an overriding first priority.

Congress rebuffed criticism from highway departments and highway contractors and reaffirmed this policy shift in 1998 when it reauthorized ISTEA as TEA-21. Writing in 1999, Paul Lewis and Eric McGee concluded, "The days of highway-dominated federal policy are gone. A new coalition has awakened and matured and another "iron triangle" policymaking system has been perturbed. Suburban sprawl, "Smart Growth" and "livable" communities have become national political buzzwords. It is thus likely that federal transportation policy will continue to be viewed in large part from the perspective of how it affects local development and local environments."[9]

Some urbanists are inclined to view the sunset of the interstate highway program as a critical transition in the history of federal transportation policy. We concur that ISTEA and TEA-21 have engaged new players in programming federal highway and transit funds, but we do not view this administrative development as a hinge event. Instead, we expect that continuity will remain the norm for most aspects of transportation policy. The state highway departments will make continuing progress in the development of the national highway system, while the difficulty of urban right-of-way acquisition will continue to limit metropolitan freeway development. With revenues for highway investment likely to remain constrained, a next generation of metropolitan toll roads like those built in the suburbs of California and Washington, D.C., is likely to be built in similar growth centers elsewhere. The politics of the federal transit program will yield continuing emphasis on rail transit. Portland's experiment with Smart Growth will be replicated in many local variants, and in the older neighborhoods of distressed cities, planners will increasingly endorse the downsizing of redevelopment to neighborhood scale and recast it as transit-oriented development. Dial-a-ride systems are likely to remain the dynamic growth segment of the transit industry and will make a difference in the quality of transit service available to the transit dependent in suburban settings, but at a cost per rider much greater than taxi voucher programs.

We are living in a period in which experimentation is quite vigorous but not very far-reaching. Thus ISTEA is best interpreted as a codification of changes in policy and practice that were already in progress. But none of the experiments we have itemized are likely to change the course of U.S. motorization or substantially dampen the personal, educational, and commercial advantages that have favored the growth of suburban population and employment. Thus we interpret ISTEA, T-21, and the sunset of the interstate program as an event freighted with political symbolism, but not a hinge event in U.S. transportation history.

Consistent with this conclusion, we expect that single-family housing of moderate density will remain the dominant mode of suburban growth and that most Americans will continue to vote with their wheels, choosing home ownership over an urban lifestyle, especially during a family's child-rearing years. And with the continuing growth of the suburban population and suburban employment, the automobile will remain America's primary and largely unchallenged form of mass transportation.

In the context of these expectations, it seems likely that changes in the fuel and motive power of the automobile will prove the next hinge events in the future evolution of American motorization. If so, successful transition to a sustainable form of motorization will hinge on the financial stability of the domestic automobile industry and its ability to deliver a next generation of automobiles that embody a transformational change in motor vehicle motive power and motor vehicle fuels.[10]

Summing Up

1. The oil shocks of 1973 and 1979 had damaging long-term impacts on the financial health of the U.S. automobile industry but no lasting impact on the intensity of U.S. motorization. Because oil is a basic ingredient in asphalt, the oil price shocks also had significant impacts on the cost of highway construction and maintenance.

2. The oil shocks also produced circumstances conducive to the sale of the smaller, more fuel-efficient cars and passenger trucks manufactured by Japanese and European automakers. By 2003, imports accounted for 27.4 percent of U.S. passenger car sales, up from 15.3 percent in 1973.

3. Between 1973 and 2003, light trucks increased from 21.3 percent of U.S. motor vehicle sales to 55.7 percent. Thus there has been a significant bifurcation of the U.S. passenger vehicle market, with the sales of both import cars and domestically built light trucks both increasing substantially. The sales volumes of full-sized domestically manufactured cars has declined accordingly.

4. The profitability and borrowing power of the U.S. automobile industry has been damaged by the decline in domestic car sales and the volatility of truck sales, which, in turn, reflect the volatility of both gasoline prices and the geopolitics of oil.

5. The oils shocks notwithstanding, the intensity of U.S. motorization increased by 100 vehicles per 1,000 population from 1980 to 2000. This was substantially less than the increase from 1960 to 1980 and an indication that the U.S. market is beginning to approach saturation in terms of motor vehicles per 1,000 population.

6. VMT increased more on a per capita basis from 1980 to 2000 than it did from 1960 to 1980. This confirms that the suburbanization of population and employment that followed the construction of the interstate has had a significant impact on VMT.

7. Capital outlays for highway construction declined in real dollar terms following the oil shocks. Congress authorized catch-up expenditures in the late 1980s. But relative to the growth of GDP and VMT, highway expenditures remained substantially lower than they were during the peak years of interstate construction. Accounting for inflation and the growth of VMT, capital outlays for highways in 2000 were only 42 percent of what they were in 1960.

8. Since 1991, the legislation underpinning federal highway and transit investment has been revised to increase modal discretion and give

metropolitan areas a larger voice in determining metropolitan investment priorities. This same legislation provided a framework for Congress to reach consensus on catch-up expenditures for highways.

9. ISTEA and T-21 codified and accelerated changes in highway and
transit policy already under way before their adoption. Within the
beltway, ISTEA was perceived as a major reorientation of federal policy. Beyond the beltway, its most significant impact has been an increase in funding levels for both highways and transit and an increase
in "pork barrel" projects, developments unlikely to mark a hinge event
in the history of American motorization.

10. The future trajectory of U.S. motorization is likely to hinge on the
future evolution of motor vehicle technology. A key determinant will
be the degree of success achieved by the U.S. automakers and their
global rivals in developing a next generation of motor vehicles that is
substantially more fuel- and carbon-efficient than the present one. This
will be no small challenge, because two of the Big Three automakers
are experiencing serious financial difficulties.

EIGHT

The Competitive Difficulties
of the U.S. Automakers

In the wake of the gasoline price surge of 2004–2007, the American automobile industry has experienced financial difficulties strikingly similar to those experienced by street railways following World War I. The automakers' recent revenues have been insufficient to support the cost structures created during the golden days when they dominated the U.S. market and enjoyed much larger sales volumes. The proximate causes of the automakers' present financial difficulties are the oil shock associated with the war in Iraq, reduced demand for the full-sized passenger vehicles that were once the bread and butter of General Motors, Ford, and Chrysler, and the loss of sales and market share to import competition. Starting from a 15 percent market share in 1973, imports sales rose to a 26 percent share of domestic passenger car sales in 2003.[1] This trend has continued, resulting in credit downgrades for General Motors and Ford and a wave of plant closures and layoffs.

A handful of production statistics will illuminate the cause of U.S. automakers' competitive difficulties. Over the past 20 years, the number of passenger cars built by the U.S. automakers for sale in the United States has declined 53 percent. During this same period, domestic truck production increased 143 percent—a large increase, but on a relatively small base. The increase in domestic truck production was insufficient to offset the decline in domestic passenger vehicle production, with the result that total domestic vehicle production still declined almost 5 percent while the U.S. population was increasing 35 percent.[2] This long-term downtrend was amplified further by the impact of the Iraq war on oil import prices and the impact of Hurricane Katrina on Gulf Coast gasoline production and nationwide fuel prices. The result for October 2005 was a year-over-year sales decline of 24 percent for GM and 20 percent for Ford. Daimler-Chrysler reported a 4 percent sales gain, and Japanese automakers reported gains of 10–12 percent.[3] But GM sales were rebounding by 2007, and there were strong indications that the Mercedes-Chrysler marriage was not an easy one. In any case, what seems clear is that the long-term erosion of domestic passenger car sales has left the U.S. manufacturers with a sales mix that is heavily loaded with SUVs and pickup trucks. This is a commercial advantage in good times but a risky sales mix in a world that is prone to episodic spikes in the price of gasoline.

The Underlying Causes of the Automakers' Financial Distress

The international motor vehicle marketplace of the twenty-first century is brutally competitive. But the same cannot be said of the U.S. market in the 1950s and 1960s. The consensus of most economists is that market power was highly concentrated in the postwar automobile industry and that General Motors was the nation's overwhelmingly dominant automaker. It is also widely agreed that GM's competitors practiced follow-the-leader pricing, creating a domestic market characterized by oligopolistic competition.

This was possible because competition based on product innovation slowed dramatically after 1930. As David Mowery and Nathan Rosenberg have observed, "The fundamental architecture of the automobile was achieved by roughly 1925, an enclosed steel body mounted on a chassis, powered by an internal combustion engine. And by the end of the 1930s, as Raff and Trajtenberg show in their analysis of change in the performance and other attributes of automobiles, the rate of improvement in product characteristics had virtually ceased."[4]

Technological stagnation is not an accurate characterization of the automobile industry today, but economist Lawrence J. White argued that it was an accurate description of the industry between 1946 and 1970. Based on the industry's oligopolistic tendencies and its follow-the-leader pricing, White described the American auto industry of the late 1960s as a "technologically stagnant industry in terms of its product." He noted that "cars are not fundamentally different from what they were in 1946; very little new technology has been instigated by the industry. The product has been improved over the last twenty years, but these have been small improvements with no fundamental changes. The sources for these improvements have often been the components suppliers, rather than the auto companies themselves; and the auto companies have been slow to adopt these improvements."[5]

In defense of the automakers, we should note that they practiced an advanced form of role differentiation that entailed relying on their suppliers for technological improvement while focusing their attention on the productivity of their assembly lines. Nonetheless, we concur with the appraisal that technological innovation slowed substantially from 1946 until the OPEC embargo of 1973.

The Oil Shocks and the Import Invasion

The oil shocks of 1973 and 1979 and the arrival in U.S. showrooms of a second generation of imports introduced Americans to the superior fuel efficiency of imported cars and set in motion dynamics that have led to long-term declines in both the volume of domestic passenger car sales and the profitability of the domestic automakers. The first oil shock caught the U.S. auto industry with a production mix that was heavily loaded with eight-cylinder family-sized cars at a time when consumers, especially first-time buyers, had a powerful incentive— the price of gasoline—to buy fuel-efficient compact and midsized vehicles.[6] The persistent affinity of many baby boomers for import cars has haunted the U.S. automobile industry ever since.

We should emphasize that no decrease in the intensity of U.S. motorization accompanied the oil shocks. Auto ownership continued to increase and transit's commute share continued to decline after a one-year rebound. But there was a dramatic shift in car buying behavior as many U.S. buyers turned to smaller, more fuel-efficient imports in lieu of the larger, costlier, and more powerful vehicles that had long been the stock in trade of the domestic automakers. As a result, the market shares, production volumes, and profit margins of the domestic automakers declined, while the volume of imports and the fuel efficiency of the cars available for sale, both import and domestic, increased. What evolved over time was a diverse mix of cars and trucks, both domestic and imported, that was strongly influenced by the evolving preferences of the baby boomers and the increased buying power of working women and two-worker households.

During the next 30 years, the domestic market for passenger cars was dominated on both coasts by imports, while the domestic automakers drew an increasing share of their revenues from the sale of trucks and SUVs and the operations of their finance subsidiaries. The truck share of vehicles in operation increased from 19 percent in 1973 to 24 percent at the onset of the Iranian revolution, to 31 percent in 1990, and to 40 percent by 2000.[7] After 1990, many of these trucks were SUVs. During the same period, increasing American dependence on imported petroleum was committing the United States to an interventionist policy in the Middle East most clearly evidenced by two wars in Iraq. This was the cascade of aftershocks that has made the oil shocks of 1973 and 1979 hinge events in the history of American motorization. The oil shock associated with the second war in Iraq seems to be having a similarly significant impact. It led to a brief but steep decline in SUV sales, a profitless recovery driven by rebates, and the 2005 downgrade of General Motors corporate bonds to "junk" status by Standard and Poor's.[8]

Ford suffered a lesser but still damaging downgrade, and by 2007 Ford was reckoned the least stable of the U.S. automakers. On the other hand, that designation would apply to Chrysler if Mercedes resolved to dissolve their alliance.

Why Was the Auto Industry So Vulnerable to Import Competition?

Two factors were primary. One was the steadily downward trend of U.S. gasoline prices in the 1960s, which reinforced the tendency of U.S. car buyers to prefer heavy vehicles with V-6 and V-8 engines and high-end horsepower.[9] For most U.S. motorists, the temporary 60 percent increase in gasoline prices that came with the 1973 OPEC oil embargo struck like a bolt out of the blue.

The second factor that has made the U.S. auto industry vulnerable to import competition was the less than vigorous nature of the competition that characterized the U.S. auto industry before the import invasion. In a pre-embargo study of the structure, conduct, and performance of the U.S. auto industry, Lawrence White concluded that high barriers to entry had created circumstances conducive to oligopolistic competition in the American automobile industry after World War II. Following the war, White wrote, the domestic automakers were largely successful in avoiding price competition by "adhering to a pattern of price leadership by General Motors." The result of GM's market dominance, White concluded, was an industrywide tendency to develop similarly positioned product lines that were sized, styled, and priced to fit the buying power of middle- and upper-middle-income households, the dominant demographic segments of the postwar auto market. White emphasized that GM's marketing strategy relied on "styling and model change . . . rather than fundamental technological change to induce replacement."[10] In turn, follow-the-leader pricing allowed the U.S. manufacturers to avoid destructive competition while buying labor peace with generous wage and benefit programs. As long as sales volumes were increasing, wage increases could be largely offset by economies of scale and continuing efficiencies in assembly-line production, limiting the size of the cost increases that had to be passed on to consumers. This strategy for simultaneously maintaining labor peace and automaker profitability proved sustainable as long as international competition was minimal. But it literally "ran out of gas" after the OPEC oil embargo and the Iranian revolution.

As a Commerce Department study observed in 1985, "The U.S. manufacturers developed automobiles that were very large, very powerful, and fuel inefficient, but adapted to the peculiarities of the American markets of the 1960s."[11] These "peculiarities" included a still robust supply of domestic petroleum and fuel taxes that were much lower than those of France, Germany, Great Britain, Italy, Sweden, and Japan. Another uniqueness of the U.S. market was the economies of scale that its producers could achieve through mass production. Exploiting the opportunity created by a mass market, the U.S. auto manufacturers focused on investment in production technology, while leaving most innovation in vehicle technology to engine manufacturers and other suppliers. Thus much of the technological improvement in American cars was attributable to the suppliers of engines and component parts. The most significant of these postwar innovations were power steering and V-8 engines, both suited to the development of a large and roomy car that matched U.S. family size during the baby boom generation. For their part, the auto manufacturers focused on improvements in the technology and productivity of their assembly lines, which produced major gains in labor productivity and significant savings in production costs.[12]

European and Japanese manufacturers made engineering and product development decisions in a very different social context where postwar GDP was substantially lower on a per capita basis, oil was imported and heavily taxed, postwar optimism was restrained, family sizes were smaller, postwar buying power was severely limited, cities were denser, and transit was still vigorously competitive. The engineering and sizing choices made in postwar Europe and Japan gave much greater emphasis to economy and fuel efficiency. Germany and France introduced the fuel-injection engine and steel-belted radial tires, both relevant to fuel-efficient driving. Smaller size, lower curb weights, and superior aerodynamics also made European and Japanese cars more fuel-efficient than their American counterparts.[13] Thus after the oil shocks of 1973 and 1979, imports were widely embraced by U.S. consumers. European automakers also led in the introduction of such safety features as disc brakes, fully independent suspension, unit-body construction, and impact-absorbing design.

The essential validation of White's analysis of oligopolistic tendencies in the U.S. market was provided by the ease with which Japanese imports were able to underprice the domestic automakers in the small-car segment of the U.S. market after the second oil shock. As a result, Japan's share of world automobile production increased from 4 percent in 1965 to 25 percent by 1980. The eventual depth and breadth of the U.S. market for compact and midsized cars seems to confirm both the limits of competition in the U.S. market before the 1973 embargo and the relatively high break-even point for small and midsized cars that had been built into the domestic industry's cost structure by its pension obligations and wage rates. This dysfunctional legacy from the days of oligopolistic competition continues to haunt the U.S. automakers today.[14]

During the 1950s and 1960s, the U.S. automakers kept peace with labor by making generous concessions on both wages and benefits, concessions that were possible because price competition between the automakers was far from vigorous. General Motors typically announced its vehicles and prices first, leaving Ford and Chrysler to follow suit. Follow-the-leader pricing provided a temporarily effective strategy for avoiding price competition and buying labor peace. The strategy was sustainable as long as efficiencies in assembly-line production enabled the manufacturers to maintain gains in labor productivity.[15] But the decline in demand for domestic cars that followed the oil shocks undermined the industry's strategy for steadily improving assembly-line output and labor productivity. In the absence of increasing production and sales volumes, it has become more difficult for the domestic automakers to offset increasing labor costs by increasing the efficiency of production.

The domestic industry's financial difficulties were amplified by the Corporate Average Fuel Economy requirements mandated by Congress after the 1979 oil shock to meet a sales weighted fuel-efficiency standard. The only feasible way to do this was to increase small car sales. Rebates and other price incentives were needed to sell the small cars designed and built by the domestic manufacturers on this hurry-up basis. In turn, problems with the drivability of these cars damaged the reputation of the domestic automakers for quality and reliability, especially in comparison to the price and quality of the second generation of Japanese imports.[16] The cumulative long-term impact of these many dynamics was a 43 percent decline in the retail sales of passenger cars built by the domestic automakers from 1973 to 2003.

Vans, Pickups, and SUVs

Since the late 1980s, vans, pickup trucks, and SUVs have been the principal growth segment and profit center of the U.S. auto manufacturers. But because of their difficulty competing in the small car and Euro-style segments of the market, U.S. manufacturers have become dependent on trucks and SUVs, customers in the South, Midwest, and Southwest, and the borrowing power of the suburban population for their continuing profitability. In this sense, the U.S. auto manufacturers could face future economic difficulties not unlike those that the streetcar companies faced in the late 1920s, after losing their midday, evening, and weekend ridership. More specifically, the U.S. automakers' cost structure is incompatible with financial success in the small economy car segment of the domestic market, and its styling traditions are mismatched with the international styling preferences of many higher-end buyers in the coastal markets. This limits the domestic industry's ability to appeal to first-time buyers and buyers at the top end of the income distribution. It also explains the domestic automakers' focal emphasis on sales in the light truck/SUV segment of the market. This is where their reputation remains solid and where they have derived most of their profits since 1991. But dependence on this segment of the market entails high risk in a world where gasoline prices have become increasingly volatile.

U.S. Automakers since the Oil Shocks of 2004–2007

Industry observers are increasingly dubious that the Big Three automakers can all survive without substantial downsizing. Much more than styling and product mix are at issue because the global automobile industry has developed a serious overhang of excess production capacity. As the *Economist* reported early in 2005:

> There is [global] capacity in place to produce about 80 million cars and other light vehicles (pickups, SUVs, and so on). Yet production is running at barely 60 million a year, so the factories are only three quarters full in an industry where utilization rates need to top 80 percent to ensure decent profits. . . . Of course, much of this excess capacity is being installed in China and other parts of the Asia-Pacific region in anticipation of growth prospects that are awesome. . . . But too much of this excess capacity lies in North America and Europe where too many producers are producing too many cars and selling them at too little profit. Detroit keeps its factories at full tilt only by offering huge discounts and other sales incentives. . . . Hence the profitless prosperity offered by strong car sales in recent years. The same is increasingly true in Europe.[17]

On May 5, 2005, Standard and Poor's moved to downgrade GM's bonds to "junk status" and Ford's bonds to one notch above junk. In this context, commentary in the trade press became more explicit. The week following the downgrade, the *Economist* warned, "As America's two leading carmakers see their domestic market share shrink to dangerous levels, there is a growing realization that their strategies for dealing with chronic problems are failing."[18]

By 2007, the tone in the trade press had shifted significantly. Industry watchers were expressing confidence that General Motors' lineup of new looks and new nameplates would allow it to turn the corner and sustain industrial recovery. On the other hand, the trade press was expressing increasing concern that neither Ford nor Chrysler could return to profitability without major concessions from their unions or a resort to bankruptcy proceedings—in Chrysler's case, an explicit acknowledgment that its pairing with Mercedes seems likely to prove a failed marriage. In GM's case, a strike looks to be its most serious present risk. Historians have learned, from painful experience, not to hazard guesses about the future in such circumstances, and this historian will follow suit.

What we will note is that there is a mismatch between U.S. automakers' current sales volumes and their legacy costs. This mismatch has three dimensions. One is the continuing difficulty in achieving any satisfactory return on investment in the compact and subcompact segments of U.S. market. The second is the vulnerability of the profitable truck and SUV segments to oil shocks like those that perturbed the domestic market after the 1979 Iranian revolution and again during the war in Iraq. The third is the resulting loss of U.S. market share to import competition, which has deprived U.S. automakers of the economies of scale they need to support cost structures premised on the much higher production and sales volumes that they enjoyed in the past.

The underlying problem that makes a bankruptcy scenario remotely plausible for at least one of the U.S. automakers is that the domestic automakers' passenger car sales volumes are barely sufficient to support their cost structures. Most economists agree the problem is rooted in legacy costs, especially pension benefits that are owed to retired workers, which are outsized relative to sales volumes and revenue levels diminished by import competition. Stated another way, the present problem for the U.S. automakers is that the domestic marketplace has been so fragmented by international competition that the U.S. automakers can no longer be assured of sales volumes sufficient to realize the economies of scale that were the source of their envied productivity and profitability. European automakers are experiencing a less extreme version of the same cost-revenue squeeze.

Problems That Are Hard to Solve

The problems that the U.S. automakers face are not of recent origin. Passenger car production volumes were cyclic but downward trending for 1973–2001, while current production volumes suggest that a new low may have been reached in 2006. Thus the present downtrend is a protracted one longer than 30 years in duration. Not coincidentally, this downtrend began with the OPEC oil shock of 1973.

The economics can be stated simply: The U.S. automobile industry has a product lineup that sells well when gasoline prices are low but not when prices are volatile or rising sharply. And because its passenger car sales volumes have been cyclic but downward trending since 1973, its cost structure and its pension obligations no longer match its production levels, sales volumes, and earnings. U.S streetcar companies experienced closely analogous problems after World War I. As they lost off-peak and weekend ridership, they were no longer able to generate operating revenues sufficient to justify reinvestment or to finance the borrowing they would have needed to modernize plants and equipment. For exactly the same reason, the present financial difficulties of the U.S. automakers have to be considered a matter of serious national concern.

Shifting our perspective from the past to the near future, we can see four trends: continuing globalization of automobile ownership, related global increases in vehicle travel and CO_2 emissions, rapidly increasing global demand for oil, and substantial volatility in oil prices. In this context, the U.S. automakers simply must increase the fuel efficiency of the motor vehicles they sell while reducing their CO_2 emissions and production costs. It will be difficult to reduce fuel consumption and CO_2 emissions with any mix of strategies that does not include a transformational change in the technology of the automobile and an increase in fuel taxes. The recent financial difficulties of GM, the financial difficulties of Ford, and the now obvious cracks in the Mercedes-Chrysler alliance make that challenge even more difficult.

Summing Up

1. The oil shocks produced by the 1973 OPEC oil embargo, the Iranian revolution, and the war in Iraq have had significant long-term effects on the U.S. automobile industry and the U.S. economy. The most important have been an increase in auto imports and a sustained long-term decline in the demand for the passenger cars produced by the domestic automakers. Sales of passenger trucks and SUVs have partially filled this gap, but they now account for a dangerously large share of the revenues that the U.S. automakers generate.

2. With fuel-efficient imports capturing an increasing share of domestic automobile sales, the number of passenger cars built by the U.S. automakers declined 49 percent from 1973 to 2001. Thus the profit margins of the U.S. automakers now hinge primarily on the demand for light trucks and SUVs.

3. The U.S. automakers are experiencing financial difficulties because they no longer enjoy the sales volumes and revenue streams necessary to support their cost structures. In this regard, the automakers and mass

transit have much in common. Both are struggling with legacy costs and labor-management frictions that have been inherited from glory days long past.

4. The competitive difficulties of the domestic automakers have compromised their profitability, and the leading U.S. automaker has flip-flopped on the question of whether it can afford the development and launch costs associated with the rollout of two new technologies, gas-electric hybrid vehicles and hydrogen fuel cell vehicles, in the span of roughly two decades.

PART THREE

Evolving Challenges in an Evolved Environment

Since the 1973 OPEC oil embargo, the Soviet Union has collapsed, and the European Union has displaced NATO as the entity that speaks for many of Europe's shared concerns. The United States remains the world's wealthiest nation and is now its sole superpower, but it seems to be losing its standing as a good neighbor.

Today we are seen as the nation that produces the largest share of the world's CO_2 emissions and makes the greatest demands on the world's oil supply. The intensity of U.S. motorization, our minimal fuel taxes, and the "oil wars" that we have fought in the Middle East are the "bill of particulars" itemized by our critics.

In the pages that follow, we will examine both the circumstances that produced these perceptions almost overnight and the potential for mitigating the most problematic impacts of U.S. motorization.

NINE

The Changing Valance of
U.S. Motorization

For decades, global leadership in motor vehicle manufacturing, petroleum refining, automobile ownership, and highway improvement was a largely un-
alloyed advantage for the United States. The U.S. automobile industry was the
world leader in value added by manufacturing; U.S. oil companies dominated
global oil exploration and accounted for more than half of all oil production as
late as 1960. With the interstate, highway investment caught up with the growth
of U.S. motorization, and freeways opened new frontiers for suburban development. All contributed mightily to the growth of U.S. GDP. During these years,
world leadership in motor vehicle ownership was a matter of national pride, and
owning both a home and two cars became an indicator of a family household's
social and financial standing.

By 1970, three generations of middle-class Americans had become accustomed to automobile ownership. Metropolitan freeway development and postwar suburbanization were well under way, and the comfort, convenience, and
reliability of the automobile were widely taken for granted—that is, until the
OPEC oil embargo of 1973. Before the embargo, the most serious adverse side
effects of the automobile were traffic accidents, congestion, and air pollution.
These problems were susceptible to amelioration, and they were tackled ac-

cordingly. Freeways were built to accommodate urban traffic growth, and road-way networks were redesigned to reduce the frequency and severity of auto-mobile accidents and to discourage the intrusion of fast-moving traffic in the residential neighborhoods of new suburbs. Driver education was required as a prerequisite for obtaining a license, drunken drivers were prosecuted, and auto-mobiles were redesigned inside and out to mitigate the severity of accidents when they occurred. As automotive pollution emerged as a public health issue, emission controls were mandated under federal law and installed on new cars to reduce tailpipe emissions. Over time, ambient air quality standards were im-posed as more was learned about the impact of air pollution on sensitive cohorts of the population. In each case, significant amelioration was achieved at a reasonable cost and with overwhelming public support.

Differences between the Past and Present Externalities of Motorization

The unresolved externalities of motorization pose a challenge that is different from those that the United States and its automakers have successfully resolved in the past. These unresolved externalities include the following:

- The episodic gasoline price shocks associated with instability in the Mid-dle East.
- The uncomfortable alliances and serial interventions that the United States has pursued in order to sustain the flow of oil from the Middle East.
- The U.S. balance-of-payments deficits associated with an increasing vol-ume of imported oil and automobiles.[1]
- An increasing tonnage of motor vehicle CO_2 emissions that is at odds with the international consensus on the risks of global warming.[2]

The most important difference between these later externalities and those that were resolved earlier is their scale. The first resolved externalities of the automobile were of a domestic scale. They affected drivers, passengers, other motorists, pedestrians, and, in the case of air pollution, metropolitan areas and their residents. These were problems that could be substantially mitigated by education, regulation, investment, incremental changes in highway and vehicle design, and evolutionary changes in automotive technology. But as the intensity of motorization has increased over time, it has produced externalities of in-creasingly international scale. These second-generation externalities of motor-ization are problems that no one automaker or nation can resolve by acting alone.

Another difference is the evolved international context in which these problems have arisen as policy issues. In 1991, the collapse of the Soviet Union fractured the political alignments of the cold war era, leading to the eventual reunification of Germany, the emancipation of Eastern Europe, and the eastward expansion of the European Union. The collapse of the Soviet Union produced a new international balance of power, one in which the United States stands conspicuously alone as the world's sole military-industrial superpower. In this evolved international order, Germany and France no longer view the United States as such an indispensable ally, and they no longer muffle their criticism of the United States on issues such as CO_2 emissions and energy policy. At the same time, China is evolving into an economic and military superpower with the potential for eventually challenging U.S. influence in Asia. China may also eventually surpass the United States as the nation that accounts for the largest volume of CO_2 emissions. At present, the United States is the world "leader" in oil consumption and CO_2 emissions. In turn, global warming and the second war in Iraq have become subjects of unusually open and vigorous disagreement between the United States and many of its former cold war allies. These are fraternal disagreements, but pointed ones nonetheless. With tongue in cheek, *New York Times* columnist Thomas Friedman put it this way: "So, we're toast, right? I mean, that's pretty much the pervasive global assumption these days: The 19th century belonged to England, the 20th century belonged to the United States, and the 21st century will belong to China. Tell your children to study Mandarin."[3]

The international politics of global oil consumption, global warming, and the war in Iraq largely account for America's diminished international standing. This is most evident in the very different international reactions to the OPEC oil shock of 1973 and the oil shocks of 2004–2007. In the case of the OPEC oil embargo of 1973, the United States and its G-7 allies shared the role of aggrieved parties. In the case of the second war in Iraq, the United States is widely seen as an imprudent interventionist, and in the case of global warming, the United States is perceived as a reckless loner. This change in perception is a by-product of the United States' new status as the world's solitary superpower. It is also a by-product of the United States and Australia's present reluctance to embrace the Kyoto accord on global warming unless comparable demands are placed on China and India, which are expected to become the world's number one and number three emitters of CO_2 emissions by the year 2050.[4] The U.S. and Japan are, of course, the present numbers one and two.

The changing perception of America's international presence is also a by-product of the global diffusion of the environmentally pessimistic worldview first articulated by Donella Meadows et al. in *The Limits to Growth* and later popularized by population biologist Paul Ehrlich and such influential European Greens as Gro Harlem Brundtland.[5] Brundtland chaired the UN commission that gave the first broad public exposure to the concept of sustainability and the potential risks of global warming. The 1987 Brundtland report, entitled *Our Common Future*, declared:

> The ultimate limits to global development are perhaps determined by the availability of energy resources and by the biosphere's capacity to absorb the by-products of energy use. These energy limits may be approached far sooner than the limits imposed by other resources. First, there are the supply problems: the depletion of oil reserves, the high cost and environmental impact of coal mining, and the hazards of nuclear technology. Second, there are the emission problems, most notably acid pollution and carbon dioxide build-up leading to global warming. . . . Sustainability requires a clear focus on conserving and efficiently using energy. . . . The simple duplication in the developing world of industrial countries' energy use patterns is neither feasible nor desirable.[6]

By 1995, global warming had become a focal concern of the United Nations and the international environmental movement, and sustainability had become a watchword in the debate over national energy policy, automobile dependence, and the future of personal transportation by automobile.[7] In 1997, UN conferees reached consensus on the Kyoto accord on global warming, an international treaty that pledged the advanced industrial nations to adopt policies sufficiently aggressive to roll back their CO_2 emissions by an average of 5.2 percent by the year 2012. The United States was initially assigned a 7 percent reduction target because it was—and is—the nation that accounts for the largest share of the world's greenhouse gas emissions. These initial targets were significant in terms of their likely impact on the economic growth of the advanced industrial nations, but were known from the beginning to be insufficient to reverse global warming because the required rollback was small relative to the growth of global GDP and global emissions—and because no emissions mitigation was required of China, India, and other rapidly industrializing nations.[8] The Bush administration repudiated the accord because these rapidly industrializing nations were exempted. It was, nonetheless, approved by the United Nations in 2004, with Russia providing the decisive vote.

The United States as a Global Holdout

The U.S. contribution to global warming, its present opposition to the Kyoto accord, the intensity of U.S. motorization and petroleum use, and the size of the U.S. trade deficits that are associated with oil and auto imports have become increasingly contentious issues, both domestically and internationally. U.S. CO_2 emissions are seen as a critical matter because they account for 24 percent of the global total and are a matter of particular dissonance between the United States and the nations of the European Union, which collectively emit 2,026 kilograms of CO_2 per capita, compared with the United States at 5,202 kilograms per capita.[9]

French and German criticism of the United States in the post–cold war era is fueled by the additional fact that one out of every nine barrels of oil that the world produces is consumed on an American street or highway, a use pattern that many European and developing nations view as unconscionably wasteful.[10] This appraisal rests on the historical fact that oil has played an essential role in the early stages of industrial development in almost all of the world's advanced economies and is now playing a similarly important role in many emerging industrial nations. In this context, many of America's European and Third World critics view the use of the automobile for mass transportation as a wasteful preemption of an international resource that is vital for economic development.

Clearly, the international politics of oil, automobile dependence, and global warming have created tensions between the United States and many of its long-term European allies. A key factor underlying this tension is the sharply different approach that the United States takes to fuel taxation. In the United States, the primary use of fuel taxes has been to finance highway construction, repair, and maintenance. In other G-7 nations, substantially higher fuel taxes have been used for the purpose of suppressing oil import requirements, encouraging automotive fuel efficiency, and financing the general fund operations of state and provincial governments. These historical differences in fuel tax policy reflect historical differences in resource endowments. Until the 1980s, the United States was an oil-rich nation, while Europe was an oil-poor continent that had to import most of the oil it consumes. Since 1980, the United States has run up international trade deficits substantially proportional to its oil import requirements and to the dollar value of its motor vehicle imports. In the process, the United States has become the world's most indebted nation in terms of its balance-of-payments deficit, its federal deficit, and its international borrowing requirements.

Other G-7 nations have suppressed their oil import requirements by increasing fuel taxes. The United States has not. Taxes still account for only 23 percent of the cost of a gallon of gasoline in the United States. The tax share per gallon is notably higher in every other G-7 and Commonwealth nation:

United States	22.6%
Canada	42.2%
New Zealand	42.5%
Australia	54.3%
Japan	54.9%

Italy	66.1%
France	71.7%
Germany	72.0%
United Kingdom	74.4%[11]

In responding to energy issues, the United States is at a diplomatic disadvantage because its fuel tax rates are so clearly out of step with the conservation-minded rates adopted by every other nation in its international peer group.

As this discussion suggests, the United States continues to behave like the oil-surplus nation that it was in the 1960s rather than the oil-importing nation that it has been since 1974. In turn, the Bush administration's rejection of the Kyoto accord has combined with the second war in Iraq and the renewed volatility of world oil prices to further diminish America's standing in the court of world opinion.

U.S.-European differences on the subject of motorization and fuel taxation are, in part, predictable policy differences between an oil-producing nation and a constellation of longtime oil-importing nations. In the case of the war in Iraq, these differences were exacerbated by U.S. impatience with diplomacy and the urgency created by the difficulty of conducting military operations in the Iraqi desert during the heat of summer. But U.S.-European differences also stem from the inherent difficulties of America's post–cold war position as the world's sole economic and military superpower and Washington's reluctance to pursue energy conservation as aggressively as the European Union.

International Appraisals of U.S. Motorization

Two international research teams—Newman/Kenworthy and Pucher/Lefèvre—have framed the environmental problems associated with mass motorization in terms of "automobile dependence."[12] They argue that the accommodation of the automobile in U.S. metropolitan areas has produced settlement patterns inimical to transit use, walking, and bicycling, while other nations with older cities and higher densities have retained much higher levels of transit use and walkability. Newman and Kenworthy endorse the proposition that mass transit and nonmotorized transport are the appropriate remedies for automobile dependence.

Our analysis of U.S. motorization leads to a different conclusion—that U.S. motorization has been under way for so long and has become so deeply imbedded in the fabric of American life and the geography of daily travel that it is now the automobile and the road network that provide mass transportation for U.S. metropolitan areas. In turn, the task of rebuilding transit ridership under public ownership has proven far more costly and much less effective than Congress and most experts anticipated in the 1960s.

These findings lead to the conclusion that the United States will have to develop its own fitting response to the problems posed by global warming and the gradual depletion of global oil supplies. Transit can play a significant role in those financial centers that are the nation's prime transit markets. But many of our major industrial cities have experienced deindustrialization and population losses and now account for a substantially diminished share of the national population. They have been displaced in the pecking order of American cities by sunbelt cities with much lower population densities and far lower per capita rates of transit use. The unfortunate but unavoidable implication is that transit no longer has the nationwide leverage that would be needed to produce any large-scale reduction in U.S. CO_2 emissions or U.S. oil import requirements. The further implication is that, in the United States, the evolution of automotive technology and automotive fuels—combined with higher taxes on carbon-based fuels—will have to play this primary role if we hope to make a difference that is large enough to matter.

TEN

The Road to
Sustainable Motorization

The litany of complaints about the intensity of American motorization typically includes the automobile's contribution to global warming and metropolitan air pollution, its dependence on imported petroleum, and its adverse impact on America's international trade deficit—along with stubbornly high accident and fatality rates, metropolitan congestion, and suburban sprawl. More than half of these complaints center on the internal combustion engine: its seemingly stalled-out fuel efficiency, its combustion by-products, its requirements for petroleum-based fuels, and its thirst for imported oil. Only one of these complaints—the one about congestion—is a direct complaint about the automobile as transportation. In this sense, most of the problems associated with the automobile are externalities of the internal combustion engine: they inhere to the ICE and the carbon-based fuel it uses, rather than the automobile per se.

Both the advantages and the liabilities of the internal combustion engine are well known. On the positive side, the ICE is a known technology that is well supported by a robust network of manufacturers, dealers, after-market parts suppliers, mechanics, fuel refiners, fueling stations, and pipelines. Refinements in fuel composition and add-on technologies have substantially reduced tailpipe emissions, but problems remain in terms of meeting ambient air quality standards, especially in sunbelt cities where ozone concentrations are problematic. Energy efficiency has been improved by electronic fuel injection and by changes in nonmechanical aspects of automotive design including aerodynamics and the substitution of lighter weight materials. Dependence on imported oil has been reduced marginally by blending gasoline with corn-based ethanol, an accepted option in the Midwest where corn and ethanol production is concentrated. Incremental improvement in the automobile and its fuels is ongoing.[1] But it has been dwarfed by the magnitude of the challenges posed by global warming, oil depletion, and the recurrent price volatility of imported oil and domestic gasoline.

With motorization and industrialization both occurring on a global basis, there are increasing demands on the world's oil supplies and increasing use of the world's atmosphere as a sink for both CO_2 emissions and industrial pollution. China, for example, already accounts for 18 percent of global CO_2 emissions, and India is close to surpassing Japan, which accounts for 5 percent. Simultaneously, another tier of smaller Asian nations is approaching industrialization levels comparable to those Korea and Taiwan achieved 20 years ago. This is the context in which the United States has faced increasing global pressure to curb the CO_2 emissions associated with the use of hydrocarbon fuels, the internal combustion engine, and pervasive motorization. These pressures are particularly intense because the United States accounts for less than 5 percent of the world's population but fully 23 percent of world energy consumption and an estimated 35 percent of all CO_2 emissions associated with road transport. Another reason for pressure from other nations is that American fuel taxes are among the lowest in the world, even though the United States imports three times more petroleum than any other nation.[2]

Table 10.1 uses index values to show the relative price of gasoline in the United States and other G-7 nations on a tax-inclusive basis. It shows the price levels characteristic of 2001, a year of friction but not serious instability in the Middle East. It shows that U.S. motorists have paid far less for a gallon of gasoline than their counterparts in other G-7 nations in such periods of geopolitical stability. In 2004, the U.S. invasion of Iraq produced an interruption in oil supply from the Middle East and a third global oil shock, which had significant short-term impact on world oil prices. This prolonged new oil shock focused renewed attention on the U.S. share of global oil consumption and produced new calls for the United States to moderate its demands on the world's oil supply. Each oil shock has also focused short-term attention on the relative fuel inefficiency of the vehicles manufactured by U.S. automakers and global disparities in tax-inclusive gasoline prices. But each previous oil shock has also been followed by price normalization and new lows in crude oil prices. Thus oil and gasoline prices have not provided any consistent long-term incentives for

Table 10.1 *Tax-inclusive gasoline prices in G-7 nations in 2001*

	Gasoline	Vis-à-vis U.S.
United States	100	—
Canada	139	1.4x
Japan	238	2.4x
Germany	257	2.6x
France	273	2.7x
Italy	280	2.8x
United Kingdom	349	3.5x
Average excluding United States	256	2.6x

SOURCE: International Energy Agency, *Energy Policies of IEA Countries*, 2002.

U.S. automakers to produce fuel-efficient vehicles or for U.S. consumers to purchase them, hence the present sales volatility in the U.S. auto market and the financial problems of the U.S. automakers.

If we focus on three trends—increasing CO_2 emissions, increasing global demands on the world's finite oil supplies, and the episodic volatility of world oil prices—we can get to the crux of the matter. Automobile ownership and personal mobility remain a personal advantage for Americans as individuals, but the intensity of U.S. dependence on carbonaceous fuels and on oil from unstable parts of the world has become an industrial, economic, and diplomatic liability for the United States in its role as a member of the international community of nations.

Dependence on carbon-based fuels is also problematic for the global environment, and U.S. dependence on oil from unstable parts of the world poses a recurring risk of oil price shocks to the United States and global economies. If gasoline prices were consistently high, U.S. consumers and the U.S. automakers would adjust their motor vehicle purchasing and production decisions accordingly. But gasoline prices have not been consistently high. Quite the contrary: the 40-year trend of real dollar gasoline prices has been gradually downward but punctuated with violent upswings in price during the OPEC oil embargo, the Iranian revolution, and the war in Iraq. Thus the secular trend of world oil prices has sent mixed signals that have encouraged Americans to buy SUVs when gasoline prices are low and to buy imports when gasoline prices are high. In turn, the oil shocks and the volatility of consumer preferences have wreaked havoc with both the profitability and the reputations of the U.S. automakers.

This is the context in which the Bush administration committed the federal government to sharing the initial costs of developing hydrogen fuel cell vehicles and deploying the fueling infrastructure necessary to support their initial diffusion. The underlying premise of this initiative is that creating a sustainable form of motorization will hinge on reinventing the automobile in ways that enable successful diversification of automotive fuels, a substantial reduction in American use of carbonaceous fuels, and a mix of fuel supplies that makes imported oil an option rather than a necessity. To this we would add that creating a sustainable form of motorization will require compound changes in automotive technology and fuels and in the energy feedstocks and production processes that are used to produce fuel. In other words, it will require orchestrated changes in automotive technology, automotive fuels, and our fuel production processes.

Toward a Sustainable Form of Automobility

Most auto industry and academic technologists agree that effective mitigation of greenhouse gas emissions will eventually force compound changes in automotive engines and power trains, automotive fuels, and the energy feedstocks and production processes used to produce automotive fuels. Necessarily, this transformation will occur in half-steps rather than one great leap forward. Indeed, a next generation of motor vehicles that embody important half-steps in engine technology and fuels has already been brought to market. Hybrid gas-electric vehicles have proved to be effective fuel savers in congested urban settings where their technology is particularly well adapted to stop-and-start driving conditions. Likewise, a generation of vehicles with internal combustion engines modified to operate on a blended mix of gasoline and ethanol has gained significant acceptance in the Midwest, where ethanol distilled from corn is both widely available and affordable, thanks in part to state subsidies.

Looking to the future, there is an emerging consensus, though not a unanimous one, that fuel cell vehicles powered by hydrogen will emerge as the technology best equipped to reduce the nation's oil import requirements and U.S. dependence on oil from the volatile Middle East. As Joan Ogden has emphasized, its benefits for the environment and for energy-supply security are primary reasons for considering hydrogen as a future automotive fuel.[3] Depending on the feedstocks used to produce hydrogen and the cost of sequestering CO_2 emissions associated with some hydrogen production processes, fuel cell vehicles could also play a significant role in reducing CO_2 emissions. The most immediately salient environmental benefit of fuel cell vehicles would be the elimination of the tailpipe emissions associated with the internal combustion engine. These include carbon monoxide, nitrogen oxides, sulfur dioxide, and other precursors of photochemical smog. On the other hand, fuel cell vehicles are promising but not yet competitive in terms of such basics as affordability, fuel cell operating life, and vehicle range. Nor is fueling infrastructure in place to support commercialization on any significant scale.

Although fuel cell vehicles may prove the ultimate successor to the internal combustion engine, most scientists and engineers agree that they will not be ready for the road in commercially significant numbers for another 15–20 years. One of the reasons for such caution is that many of the expected benefits of fuel cell vehicles will accrue to the global environment and the world's population at large—benefits that will not make a fuel cell vehicle salesworthy unless it also satisfies more mundane car buying expectations such as affordability, longevity, and driving range. This explains the don't-expect-too-much-too-soon endorsement that hydrogen and hydrogen fuel cell vehicles received in a 2004 study by the National Research Council and the National Academy of Engineering: "The impacts on oil imports and CO_2 emissions are likely to be minor during the next 25 years. Thus hydrogen—though it could transform the energy system in the long run—does not represent a short-run solution for any of the nation's energy problems." But over the longer term, the same study concluded, a national transition to "a fleet of light-duty vehicles fueled entirely by hydrogen would dramatically reduce U.S. oil consumption and imports."[4]

Hydrogen Fuel Cell Vehicles

Hydrogen fuel cells are capable of generating electricity by combining liquid or gaseous hydrogen with oxygen from the air to produce an electrical current. Water is the sole by-product of this electrochemical reaction. A hydrogen fuel cell vehicle can be accurately described as an electric vehicle that requires refueling but not recharging. It uses a fuel—liquid or gaseous hydrogen—that is used in industrial applications and already available in quantities sufficient to support the initial diffusion of fuel cell vehicles.

The first modern application of hydrogen fuel cells was in producing on-board electricity for the Gemini and Apollo spacecraft. In their automotive application, stacked fuel cells are used to generate the electricity necessary to power an electric motor or motors that can deliver torque to the wheels of a motor vehicle. Power is generated by a chemical reaction rather than by combustion and is delivered as electricity to an electrical motor or motors. In an internal combustion engine, energy is created by spark ignition of a fuel, usually gasoline, and is delivered from piston to crankshaft and from crankshaft to wheels as rotational energy, with combustion by-products being released as exhaust gas. The process of energy conversion in a fuel cell vehicle is more efficient than in an internal combustion engine, and no pollutant or CO_2 emissions are directly generated by the workings of the fuel cell or the electric motors that the fuel cell powers.

These are the characteristics that recommend fuel cell vehicles as a potentially superior alternative to an automobile powered by gasoline and an internal combustion engine. We emphasize "potentially" because the overall energy efficiency and CO_2 emissions advantage of fuel cell vehicles are contingent rather than intrinsic. They depend on the feedstocks used to produce hydrogen and the energy efficiency of the hydrogen production process.[5] The most economical method of producing hydrogen—natural-gas reforming—produces a substantial volume of CO_2 emissions, but the sequestration of emissions is not expected to represent a make-or-break difference in the cost of hydrogen fuel over the long run.[6] Even allowing for carbon sequestration, a National Academy of Engineering study has concluded that hydrogen could be competitive with gasoline in terms of its cost and energy content if there were demand sufficient to support both industrial-scale production of hydrogen and pipeline distribution.[7] Getting to such sales volumes is the essence of the "chicken or egg" problem that confronts both hydrogen production and hydrogen fuel cell vehicles.

The present generation of research prototype fuel cell vehicles have the power and pickup necessary for success in the marketplace, and four automakers—GM, Daimler-Chrysler, Toyota, and Honda—have demonstrated prototype vehicles with sufficient range (300 miles between hydrogen fill-ups) for commercial viability.[8] Still needed for commercial success are significant reductions in fuel cell costs, the prospect of sales volumes sufficient to achieve economies of scale, and the resolution of a number of durability and manufacturability issues.

The National Academy of Engineering expects that technologically mature fuel cell vehicles will be some 2.4 times more energy efficient than the same vehicle powered by an internal combustion engine and 1.7 times more energy efficient than a hybrid gas-electric vehicle on a so-called tank-to-wheels basis.[9] This suggests that fuel cell vehicles will have significant appeal to a future generation of buyers because it will cost less to fuel and operate them on a per-mile basis than a conventional automobile or a hybrid gas-electric vehicle. It also suggests that they could have a significant future impact on U.S. oil import requirements. Whether they can produce correspondingly large benefits in terms of reducing CO_2 emissions will hinge on the feedstocks used to produce hydrogen and the sources of energy used to power the hydrogen production process. Maximum CO_2 reduction could be achieved through the use of off-peak hydroelectric power or nuclear energy to produce hydrogen fuels from natural gas.[10] During the early years of fuel cell vehicle diffusion, it is expected that hydrogen will be generated at evolved fueling stations that process natural gas on site without CO_2 capture or sequestration.[11] It is also expected that fuel cell vehicles will be more "expensive, have less range, and be more difficult to refuel" than the automobile as we now know it.[12]

Automakers are confident that fuel cell vehicles will mature into a technology that is superior to the automobile, as we now know it, on most dimensions of driving performance. They are confident, for example, that fuel cell vehicles will have better acceleration from 0 to 30 miles per hour than present gasoline- and diesel-powered vehicles, that they will generate no combustion by-products and thus no tailpipe emissions (except water), and that they will be much more energy efficient on a tank-to-wheels basis than hybrids, diesels, and cars powered by a conventional internal combustion engine. Fuel cell vehicles could also be more energy efficient on a well-to-wheels basis if the energy used to process their fuel is derived from off-peak hydroelectric, nuclear, or wind power. Diesels and conventional ICEs are likely to remain superior for on-demand acceleration at high speeds, but they will be unable to compete with fuel cell vehicles in terms of their acceleration from a standing stop, their potential for emissions reduc- tion, or their operating cost per mile.[13] Thus fuel cell vehicles have significant potential for public acceptance, especially in urban and suburban driving en- vironments. They will have less advantage for high-speed travel between cities.

Whether fuel cell vehicles can prove commercially viable will hinge on three key factors: the cost of producing them, the perception that their per- formance justifies their cost, and the perception that hydrogen fuel will be safe to use and readily available wherever you go. Fuel cell vehicles must meet these tests before they can be sold in volumes that justify mass production; conversely, mass production will be essential for achieving the economies of scale necessary to reduce production costs. These are the "chicken and egg" problems that must be resolved for the successful diffusion and commercializa- tion of fuel cell vehicles.

The Challenge of Commercialization

Toyota's Taiyo Kawai has itemized the advances in technology that must be achieved before mass production of fuel cell vehicles can begin:

> Improvements in hydrogen storage must be achieved before the vehicle can be commercially marketed. Safety is another major concern. Further testing must be performed to determine and reduce the risk associated with carrying hydro- gen and high voltage batteries. Finally, maintenance and storage issues must be addressed. Costs of servicing the vehicle during its use, as well as the environ- mental impact from recycling and disposal of the vehicle at its end of life, require further investigation. . . .
>
> [At present,] the Fuel Cell Hybrid Vehicle's limited driving range is one of the largest hurdles to its marketability. . . . [But the] most difficult issue for market introduction is the hydrogen infrastructure [necessary for fueling fuel cell vehicles]. Today, there is practically no hydrogen infrastructure [in place for fueling].[14]

The National Academy of Engineering has reached an equally cautious appraisal. Despite significant federal and private-sector investment, fuel cell prototype costs for light duty vehicles are still a factor of 10–20 times too expensive, and these fuel cells are short of required durability.[15]

Daniel Sperling and James Cannon agree that huge amounts of engineering are still needed to improve manufacturability, ensure long life and reliability, and withstand temperature extremes.[16] Of the many obstacles to diffusion, the National Academy of Engineering concluded that "success in overcoming the major stumbling block of on-board [fuel] storage is critical for the future transportation use of fuel cells."[17]

The NAE also noted that fuel cell vehicles "will excel in fuel economy and emissions reduction. On the negative side, for the foreseeable future they will likely be expensive, have less range, and be more difficult to refuel."[18]

On the other hand, Lawrence D. Burns, a respected GM executive, has told Congress, "We are targeting to design and validate an automotive-competitive fuel cell propulsion system by 2010. By 'automotive competitive' we mean a system that has the performance, durability, and cost (at scale volumes) of today's internal combustion engine systems. This aggressive timetable is a clear indication that fuel cell technology for automotive applications is industry driven and that this technology has matured to a point where such timing is indeed possible."[19]

Even if initial diffusion is possible on GM's timetable, it could be two or three decades before scale economies can be achieved and fuel cell vehicles can be made available in numbers large enough to have significant impact. This raises a serious issue: Will the world's automakers, governments, and companies such as Ballard Power Systems have the stamina to sustain fuel cell R&D and the investment levels associated with early production for the decades that may be required to reach scale volumes? Justice Department authorization for automaker alliances—GM and Nissan, for example, and Mercedes, Ford, and Ballard—is one reason to expect automaker persistence. Fear of being left behind is another motivator. And Sperling has articulated a third compelling reason for expecting the leading automakers to pursue the development of fuel cell vehicles through to a successful conclusion. Sperling's argument begins cautiously:

> Hydrogen is neither the easiest nor the cheapest way to gain large near and medium term societal benefits. Hybrid electric vehicles, cleaner combustion engines, and cleaner fuels will provide almost as much benefit on a per vehicle basis at a much lower cost. . . . The case for hydrogen is compelling only over the longer term, largely by creating a motor vehicle that is superior in performance to conventional vehicles, and also fundamentally different. . . . Importantly, hydrogen fuel cell vehicles provide special attractions to automakers. By

eliminating most mechanical and hydraulic subsystems, they provide greater design flexibility and the potential for using fewer vehicle platforms and therefore more efficient manufacturing approaches. As a result, the automotive industry, or at least an important slice of it, sees fuel cells as its inevitable and desired future.[20]

GM's Lawrence Burns confirms that the most significant attribute of fuel cell vehicles is the potential they create for "system simplification." As Burns testified to Congress in July 2005, "[GM has] made significant progress on cost reduction through technology improvements and system simplification. Our progress has convinced us that fuel cell vehicles have the potential to be fundamentally better automobiles on nearly all attributes important to our customers; a key to enabling high-volume sales. And with just one tenth as many moving propulsion parts as conventional systems, our [envisioned] design has the potential to meet our cost and durability targets."[21]

The line of reasoning advanced by Burns and Sperling suggests that it is "system simplification" and corresponding manufacturing efficiencies that will provide the pathway for successful commercialization of fuel cell vehicles. They will do so by creating a win/win/win opportunity for the automakers to meet their environmental obligations while restoring their production efficiencies and labor productivity. In other words, the commercialization of fuel cell vehicles would open the door for automakers to reengineer not only their products but also their production processes and their cost structures. The potential for this win/win/win outcome has created a powerful incentive for the automakers to persevere in the development of fuel cell vehicles. Just as important, it will create circumstances in which no competing automaker can afford to be left behind.

On the other hand, the expected cost of delivering hydrogen to its point of sale and its limited initial availability could prove a significant obstacle to the salability of fuel cell vehicles. Indeed, the purchase of fuel cell vehicles in numbers sufficient for the automakers to achieve economies of scale seems likely to hinge on the perception that hydrogen will be a safe fuel that is reasonably priced and conveniently available most places you go. But the perception that hydrogen is widely available is unlikely to jibe with reality in the early years of hydrogen vehicle diffusion, creating a significant risk of delayed or even failed diffusion. Failed diffusion, of course, has been the outcome of every previous fuel efficient vehicle program funded by the federal government. For this reason, the automakers have taken great pains to emphasize that the development of fuel cell vehicles is an industry-driven initiative and that Congress has authorized cooperative efforts between the auto and oil industries to ensure the availability of fuel when fuel cell vehicles are sufficiently mature for initial diffusion.[22]

The eventual success of the automaker's fuel cell vehicle rollout will hinge on vehicle costs, vehicle performance, fuel availability, fuel cost, and the feed-stocks used to produce hydrogen fuels. Economically successful rollout will hinge on effective coordination and collaboration between the auto and hydro-gen industries because industry surveys indicate that "the price of hydrogen has a very strong impact on the expected sales of fuel cell vehicles."[23] Research by Shell's hydrogen division illuminates the nature of the challenge. It shows that there is a tension between fuel availability and fuel cost: too many fueling stations equipped to sell hydrogen would drive up fuel costs, whereas too few would drive down the salability of fuel cell vehicles. Getting the balance right is essential for the initial diffusion of fuel cell vehicles and hydrogen fuels.

The success of any fuel cell vehicle rollout will also hinge on the staying power of the automakers in the early years of diffusion. And that in turn will hinge on successful collaboration between the automakers and the petrochemi-cal industry in rolling out fuel cell vehicles and high-quality hydrogen fuels on the same timetable. A cooperative research effort by GM and Shell has sketched the broad outlines of a strategic alliance designed to bring hydrogen fuel and hydrogen fuel cell vehicles to market on the same timeline. In the early years of fuel cell vehicle diffusion, GM would provide Shell with reformers that enable on-site reformation of natural gas into hydrogen at Shell fueling stations. Shell would truck natural gas to its filling stations for on-site processing.[24] Geographi-cally, both Shell and GM would focus their hydrogen and hydrogen-vehicle rollouts in prime urban markets such as the Northeast and California where there is sufficient buying power to support the initial rollout of fuel cell vehicles and a population base large enough and wealthy enough to make television advertising productive.

Even with Justice Department–approved cooperation of this sort, it is un-clear how quickly the automakers will be able to achieve economies of scale in hydrogen vehicle production. Nor is it clear how soon the demand for hydrogen fuel will be sufficient to justify pipeline delivery. These are critical questions because it is unlikely that hydrogen can be cost-competitive with gasoline as a motor vehicle fuel in the absence of high-volume production and pipeline distribution. In fact, the National Academy of Engineering concluded that governmental subsidies would be necessary, at least initially, to reduce the cost of hydrogen fuel to a level that is cost-competitive with the use of gasoline in hybrid vehicles.[25]

This discussion has three implications. The most obvious is that the eco-nomics of successful diffusion remain unsettled. Another is that the economics of high-volume production of hydrogen fuels may not pencil out if the se-questration of CO_2 emissions is required. Still another is that continuing anti-trust exemptions and initial governmental subsidies will be necessary to enable the automakers and the energy companies to reach sales volumes that make high-volume production of fuel cell vehicles and hydrogen fuel commercially viable. For all of these reasons, it should be clear that the diffusion of fuel cell vehicles does not offer a short-term strategy for substantially reducing CO_2 emissions, U.S. oil import requirements, or the U.S. balance-of-payments deficit. Fuel cell vehicles seem likely to make a vital future contribution, but the timeframe for significant impact looks to be 25–30 years.

Thus we are left with considerable uncertainty. Neither fuel cell vehicles nor the expansion of transit service seem likely to deliver any substantial short-term reduction in CO_2 emissions or oil import requirements. Nor does hydrogen fuel hydrolyzed from natural gas offer a credible pathway to the reduction of CO_2 emissions without CO_2 capture and sequestration. We also know that large-scale plants capable of producing hydrogen in volumes that scale compatibly with pipeline distribution of hydrogen are likely to be the most efficient means of producing hydrogen in the long run and thus the most promising pathway for the diffusion of fuel cell vehicles. But pipeline distribution looks to be at least 20 years in the future. So what is the most promising strategy for accelerating our national transition to hydrogen fuels? Our judgment is that the federal government should avoid long-term subsidies for hydrogen fuels, but share with industry the cost of sequestering CO_2 emissions and other environmental mitigations necessary to expedite the diffusion of hydrogen fuels and fuel cell vehicles. This conclusion reflects our judgment that the natural gas pathway for the diffusion of fuel cell vehicles is the most pragmatic option for near-term diffusion.

How Soon Can Fuel Cell Vehicles Be Ready for Initial Diffusion?

Based on the tank-to-wheels energy efficiencies reported by the National Academy of Engineering, the U.S. Department of Energy has scripted a plausibly optimistic scenario for the future diffusion of both hybrid and fuel cell vehicles. This consciously optimistic timeline sees the initial production of hydrogen fuel cell vehicles beginning in 2015. Vehicles powered by an ICE would still account for 80 percent of new vehicle sales in 2015, and most of the rest would be hybrids. In this "optimistic diffusion scenario," fuel cell vehicles are expected to capture a 15 percent share by 2020, reach sales parity with hybrids by 2030, and dominate the market thereafter.[26] In our judgment, market dominance by 2040 would be a safer bet, given the recent resiliency of cars powered by an internal combustion engine, the sluggish sales of hybrids, and the remaining uncertainties about fuel cell costs and hydrogen fuel availability.

Most experts expect that the initial diffusion of fuel cell vehicles will have to depend on regionalized production and distribution of hydrogen, because no nationwide network of pipelines suitable for the transportation of hydrogen is presently available.[27] Unavoidably, initial diffusion of fuel cell vehicles would be concentrated where hydrogen production is presently concentrated and in additional locations where production and distribution by truck proves economical. The economics of hydrogen distribution by truck would be market restrictive and could encourage automakers to make loss-minimizing decisions about fuel cell vehicle production and rollout. This response would reduce the automakers' initial losses, but could also block the path to economies of scale.

This was the context in which General Motors initially broached the idea that the states and the federal government play a significant role in the deployment of fueling infrastructure.[28] More recently, the automakers have emphasized alliances with energy companies and plans for initial distribution of hydrogen by tanker trucks and target marketing in prime urban markets defined by both the nation's largest agglomerations of population in the Northeast and West and by proximity to existing hydrogen processing facilities. In this scenario, pipeline development would be deferred until the marketing of fuel cell vehicles is well under way.

Successful diffusion of fuel cell vehicles will most likely hinge on five preconditions:

1. Successful development of fuel cell technology to the point that commercialization is feasible because the product is both cost-competitive with hybrid vehicles and more energy efficient on a tank-to-wheels basis.
2. The development of alliances between automakers and energy companies to facilitate coordinated installation of fueling infrastructure and the implementation of regionalized marketing strategies targeted in likely high-volume markets for fuel cell vehicles.
3. Distributed processing of natural gas into hydrogen by reformation at fueling stations after delivery by tanker trucks.
4. Federal involvement in both financing and establishing standards for the sequestration of CO_2 emissions associated with production of fuel.
5. Increasing confidence on the part of the driving public that hydrogen is a safe and affordable fuel that will be reliably available most places you go.

Over time, region-by-region diffusion of fuel cell vehicles would contribute to a nationwide reduction in metropolitan air pollution, U.S. oil import requirements, and automotive CO_2 emissions, but the size of the reduction in CO_2 emissions would be small at first and contingent on the fuel stocks and energy used to produce hydrogen. Capture and sequestration of the CO_2 emissions generated during the hydrogen fuel production process will be necessary to realize the fuel cell vehicles' full potential for reducing greenhouse gas emissions. This will not be possible in the early stages of diffusion during which natural gas reformation will be occurring on-site at fueling stations.

In this author's judgment, the barrier most likely to stymie the successful

commercialization of fuel cell vehicles is the "chicken or egg" problem associated with the mass production of fuel cell vehicles and the availability of hydrogen fuel sufficient to support mass production. General Motors anticipates that
this can be resolved with a regional strategy for fuel cell vehicle diffusion initially focused in the nation's largest population agglomerations and media markets: California, New York, and its northward and southward extensions to
Boston and Washington, D.C. This, it should be emphasized, is a market-driven
strategy for the diffusion of fuel cell vehicles and hydrogen fuels.

At this point in our discussion, what should be clear is that it will take both
corporate conviction and patience for a market-driven strategy to succeed. It
should also be clear that a market-driven strategy for diffusion is not likely to
match up with current international timetables for CO_2 emissions reduction
under the Kyoto accord, which, of course, the United States had still not signed
as of late 2007.

That leaves us with two "iffy" conclusions: If the commercial field tests of
fuel cell vehicles marketability prove successful, it may be realistic to expect that
fuel cell vehicles could dominate new car sales by 2035 or 2040. But if they
cannot, it might take until 2060 or beyond to achieve the technological displacement of automobiles fueled by gasoline and powered by an internal combustion
engine. This would render U.S. compliance with the Kyoto accord essentially
impossible. It would also deprive the United States of one of its most promising
strategies for reducing U.S. demands on the world's oil supply, our petroleum
import requirements, and our CO_2 emissions.

These risks and uncertainties suggest that it is imperative that we Americans have a serious national discussion about petroleum conservation and the
role of fuel taxes in achieving it.

ELEVEN

Motorization and Sustainability:
History and Prospect

This book began with the observation that the United States relies on cars and trucks for mass transportation. In the pages that followed, we have shown how and why the United States became the world's most pervasively motorized nation and how and why mass transit has been marginalized in U.S. metropolitan areas.

Many planners and urbanists believe that the marginalization of mass transit was primarily attributable to the interstate highway program, metropolitan freeway development, and the continuing suburban population growth that accompanied it. A different picture emerges from tracing transit's history from the late nineteenth century to the present. This longer history situates the onset of transit's financial difficulties at the beginning of the twentieth century when the U.S. economy evolved from a deflationary bias to an inflationary bias. Franchise agreements that mandated a fixed fare combined with inflation to deprive street railways of the profitability they needed to attract continuing private investment. After 1907, the history of street railways is a history of gradual financial attrition and corresponding difficulty in securing the capital necessary for modernization, service extension, or grade separation. During World War I, inflation and federally mandated wage increases for transit workers further diminished the transit industry's earnings, destroying the borrowing power that streetcar companies would have needed to finance postwar reinvestment and modernization. Street railways never recovered, and of the nation's primary transit markets, only New York City made any substantial further investment in rapid transit during the 1920s.

The same era produced the first hinge event in the history of global motorization: Henry Ford's pathbreaking 1908 experiment with assembly-line production of the Model T. Thereafter, the trajectory of U.S. motorization was steadily upward and gross investment in transit was steadily downward. Net disinvestment became the transit industry's nationwide norm in 1916 and persisted until the 1960s when Congress finally authorized the federal funding necessary for public acquisition of public transportation and subsequent reinvestment and ridership recovery.

Given this chronology, the decline of transit and its ridership cannot be attributed to the interstate or unbalanced public policy. U.S. transit use had already declined from its peacetime peak of 147 rides per capita in 1926 to 70 rides per capita in 1955. Much of the intervening decline was attributable to increasing automobile ownership.

Mass motorization, the interstate, and suburbanization have stymied transit's efforts to rebuild market share under public ownership. Clearly, the interstate enhanced the value of automobile ownership and contributed to the accessibility of outlying acreage susceptible to development as affordable housing for would-be homeowners. It also contributed to the increase in vehicle miles of travel in U.S. metropolitan areas and to the reconceptualization of suburban street layouts. The tiered hierarchy of roads that resulted was designed to shelter the residential neighborhoods of suburban communities from the intrusion of fast-moving traffic. The unintended side effect was to make walking and transit use more difficult. This did not trigger arterial transit's competitive decline, but it has made the eventual expansion of transit service under public ownership more costly and much less productive than planners anticipated.

During the interstate era, transit rides per capita of the national population slipped from 70 in the year 1955 to 33 in the year 2000. Thus freeway development and suburbanization clearly contributed to the continuing marginalization of mass transit. But a substantial portion of transit's decline was also attributable to the loss of smokestack industries in the industrial cities of the northeastern and north central states and the consequent drop in central city population and employment in major transit markets. During this same period, national leadership in population and employment growth shifted from frostbelt cities to the suburbs and the sunbelt where urban densities and transit use rates are much lower. Public ownership and public subsidy have stabilized aggregate transit ridership in the range of 33–35 rides per capita, but have not prevented continuing decline in transit's commute share.

Public ownership, subsidized operation, the expansion of suburban service, and stable fares have enabled transit to attract significant numbers of new riders, especially in the suburbs and the sunbelt and during off-peak hours. Transit has continued to experience losses in both commuter ridership and central city ridership in the industrial states of the frostbelt, primarily due to deindustrialization and the loss of jobs. Demographically, transit's largest gains in ridership since public ownership are attributable to non-work trips being made by students, shoppers, elderly and handicapped persons, and suburban residents. Geographically, transit's most significant recent gains in ridership have been realized in sunbelt states that have experienced significant Hispanic migration—Arizona, California, Florida, and Texas.

Until 1990, in terms of raw numbers, the commuter ridership lost in the northeast and north central states was greater than the commuter ridership added in the rest of the nation. According to the 2000 census, between 1990 and 2000, transit broke even in terms of commuter usage. It neither gained nor lost riders, but continued to lose commute share.

The 2010 census should tell us whether transit has successfully rebased and begun to rebuild commute share. That issue is still unresolved because the 2000 census contained both good and not-so-good news for public transportation. The not-so-good news was that transit lost commute share among working residents in all six of its most important central-city markets: New York, Chicago, San Francisco, Washington, D.C., Boston, and Philadelphia. The decline in transit's commute share seems to reflect the gentrification occurring in these major financial centers. On the other hand, transit achieved gains in commute share in select sunbelt cities. All told, transit ridership—as opposed to transit's commute share—increased 5 percent from 1990 to 2000, due primarily to gains in off-peak noncommuter ridership.

Accommodating Motorization

From 1960 to 2000, the U.S. population increased 57 percent, GDP increased 147 percent in real dollar terms, motor vehicle ownership increased 148 percent, motor vehicle fuel consumption increased almost 200 percent, and VMT increased 282 percent. These growth rates underline the strong link between U.S. GDP, motorization, and the intensity of American vehicle use. They also reveal the scale of the extraordinary challenges that automakers, highway departments, oil companies, air quality management agencies, and energy regulators faced in the process of keeping pace with U.S. motorization and suburbanization.

What stands out is that—despite prodigious increases in auto ownership, VMT, and motor vehicle fuel requirements—the United States has been successful in accommodating continuing motorization without excessive increases in congestion, travel times, or pollutant emissions. Much greater difficulty has been encountered in avoiding disruptions in the nation's oil and gasoline supplies. Nor can progress be made overnight in the development of fuel cell vehicles, which will eventually enable significant reductions in oil imports and CO_2 emissions. The U.S. track record since 1960 can be summarized as follows:

- Freeway development has kept increases in urban congestion and delay at an acceptable level despite continuing motorization.
- Los Angeles and San Francisco are the principal metropolitan areas in which congestion and delay can accurately be described as chronic and excessive.
- Taken together, freeway development and the increasing location of both households and workplaces in suburban settings have been largely successful in keeping the lid on journey-to-work travel times in most other U.S. cities.
- Tailpipe emission controls have been largely successful in restoring healthful air quality. The exceptions are found in those sunbelt metropolitan areas where difficult meteorological conditions, exceptionally high rates of motorization, poorly maintained older cars, and intense congestion have combined to produce hard-to-manage air quality problems.
- The domestic and international automakers have made slow but steady progress in improving automotive fuel efficiency.
- The petroleum industry has been largely successful in locating new reservoirs of oil sufficient to replace oil fields experiencing depletion.
- U.S. oil prices declined steadily from 1934 through 1972.
- Since the OPEC oil embargo of 1973, U.S. oil prices have become increasingly volatile, but they reached their all-time low in 1998.[1]
- Since the 1980s, finding new reservoirs of oil sufficient to keep pace with increasing global demand for oil has entailed drilling in settings that are increasingly difficult for reasons environmental, political, and economic. This is problematic because U.S. domestic oil production now accounts for only 12 percent of global petroleum output, down from 72 percent in 1923.[2]
- Conflict and unrest in the Middle East and aggressive pricing by some Middle Eastern and South American oil producers have produced a series of price shocks and an unusually prolonged increase in crude oil and gasoline prices since 1998.
- There is no expert consensus on the price trend of crude oil that will prevail when political stability is eventually restored in the Middle East.
- Given the complications posed by CO_2 emissions and global warming, there is little expert consensus on how long the world can continue to rely

on carbonaceous fuels to power motor vehicles. But there is widespread agreement that the diffusion of fuel cell vehicles can be well under way before oil availability per se poses a significant constraint on automobile ownership in the United States.

As this itemization suggests, lawmakers, highway departments, and the auto and oil industries have worked together to accommodate motorization and mitigate many of its adverse impacts. On the other hand, outcomes in Los Angeles and San Francisco show that there are practical limits to the ability of large but still fast-growing metropolitan areas to accommodate traffic growth by means of freeway development and paired efforts to improve transit service. More problematic, the four oil shocks since 1973 indicate that there is an increasingly delicate balance between supply and demand in the global oil market that has conferred increasing market power on producer nations.

The reasons for the increased volatility of U.S. gasoline prices since 2004 include the war in Iraq, gamesmanship on the part of some oil-producing nations, the breakdown in negotiations over Palestinian sovereignty, increasing demand for oil from China, India, and other industrializing nations, America's own increasing demand for oil, its increasing dependence on oil imports, and the capping—for future use—of oil wells in older domestic fields that long produced a significant volume at low cost. These dynamics do not indicate that the world's oil supply is about to run out, but they do suggest that we have entered a new era in which it will no longer be realistic to expect that the discovery of productive new reservoirs of oil will reliably enable American refiners to produce gasoline in large volumes at a price that is steadily declining in real dollar terms.

The View from Abroad

The opinion of U.S. motorization held by other nations is far more critical than the portrait we have just constructed. In part, this is attributable to America's envied position as the world's sole economic and military superpower. But it can also be attributed to America's reluctance to moderate its own demands on the world's oil supply and join other nations in a determined effort to reduce the CO_2 emissions associated with global warming. This critical view is further reinforced by the fact that the United States accounts for only 5 percent of the world's population but fully 35 percent of the CO_2 emissions attributable to road transport.[3]

As a result, even our staunchest allies are increasingly critical of U.S. fuel taxes, which are much lower than those in any other G-7 nation—$.46 per gallon compared with $3.14 on average for the other six G-7 nations.[4] Even

Canada's fuel taxes are 107 percent higher than those in the United States. Based on economic rather than political or geopolitical considerations, most American economists agree that our nation's fuel taxes should be pegged closer to Canadian levels to encourage both conservation and improvements in automotive fuel efficiency. At the same time, most U.S. economists agree that we need not and should not impose fuel taxes of European heft.[5]

Looking to the Future

A near-global consensus has emerged that motorization of U.S. intensity generates an excessive volume of CO_2 emissions and makes excessive demands on the world's oil supply. Nonetheless, the United States has been reluctant to implement measures such as gasoline surtaxes or an explicit carbon tax assigned to mitigate CO_2 emissions. However, the U.S. auto and energy industries are vigorously exploring fuel and motive power alternatives to the internal combustion engine.

Many scientists, engineers, and automakers view fuel cell vehicles powered by hydrogen as the automotive technology most likely to displace the internal combustion engine and reduce the world's dependence on petroleum. But from the vantage point of 2007, it appears that 10–15 years of continuing developmental effort will be necessary to produce a fuel cell vehicle that is both affordable and suited for everyday use.[6] And even at that point, the availability of high-quality hydrogen fuel could remain an obstacle to nationwide diffusion.[7]

In anticipation of eventual high-volume production of hydrogen fuels, automakers are forging alliances with oil companies to supply hydrogen at major-brand gas stations. For example, the joint strategy developed by GM and Shell calls for distributed processing of natural gas into hydrogen using small-scale reformers located at Shell service stations. Natural gas would be trucked to stations for on-site reformation. The initial campaign to market hydrogen fuel cell vehicles and hydrogen fuel will most likely be targeted in the nation's largest metropolitan areas and primary media markets—those in the northeastern and north central states and in California.[8] At maturity, hydrogen fuel would flow to market through a nationwide network of hydrogen pipelines.

Significant diffusion is expected to be under way within 15 years. But as Martin Wachs emphasizes, "Every reasonable projection of technological change [indicates] that gasoline and diesel fuel will dominate the market for surface transportation for at least two decades and probably three."[9]

In the interim, hybrid gas-electric vehicles and flexible-fuel vehicles that run on blended gasoline-ethanol fuels are the technologies competing for buyers focused on fuel economy and energy efficiency. Hybrids can nominally reduce CO_2 emissions and the motor vehicles' demand for oil, but nowhere near enough to offset the increase in petroleum demand and CO_2 emissions that will be associated with the continuing growth of the U.S. population. Flex-fuel vehicles have also enjoyed rapid diffusion in the Midwest, where the production of ethanol made from corn is widely subsidized by producer states and the U.S. Department of Agriculture. Ethanol blends are less widely available elsewhere, and the diffusion of flex-fuel vehicles has been correspondingly limited. In other words, the United States has in its technology pipeline no ready-for-commercialization automotive technology that would enable our nation to accommodate expected population growth without increased CO_2 emissions and increased oil import requirements.

What Are Our Options?

Many environmentalist believe that the national policy response that would be most effective in encouraging fuel conservation and reducing CO_2 emissions would be an additional tax on the price of gasoline and its carbon content. The case for such a tax rests on the cascade of incentives it would produce—for increased transit use and carpooling, for energy-conscious driving behavior, and for energy- and carbon-conscious vehicle purchasing and production decisions. But several caveats are in order. Recent research suggests that Americans seem to have developed considerable "immunity" to the kind of oil and gasoline price shocks that have accompanied the war in Iraq.[10] The partial U.S. shift to smaller, more fuel-efficient vehicles has buffered the impact of price shocks for at least some households, and the household income gains of the past decade have kept gasoline prices affordable despite the significant oil price shock associated with the war in Iraq. But the primary reason may be that most Americans now live and work in metropolitan suburbs where the only transportation alternative to cars is grin and bear it.

In any event, securing a congressional majority in favor of a surtax on the price of gasoline is no small matter, even though the political fallout from a higher fuel or carbon tax could be fully mitigated with an offsetting reduction in other taxes.

This creates a social, political, and environmental quandary. The political viability of fuel surtaxes has yet to be proven; fuel cell vehicles are not yet ready for market, and even if U.S. vehicle registrations were to remain stable at their 2000 level of 784 vehicles per 1,000 population, U.S. population growth alone would be sufficient to increase registrations from the 217 million vehicles recorded in 2000 to over 300 million by 2050, an increase of 38 percent.[11] Ceteris paribus, this paired growth in population and vehicles would produce an increase in VMT and CO_2 emissions that has to be considered unacceptably risky, given the uncertainties that remain about the future cost and performance of fuel cell vehicles and environmental risks associated with global warming.

In this context, America will have little choice but to experiment with urban and suburban in-fill and other forms of higher-density housing development, which have the potential for reducing sprawl, automobile use, and VMT while encouraging transit use and increasing the walkability of American cities.[12] But we should do so with caution and a fully realistic understanding that higher-density development can produce both an increase in transit use and an increase in congestion and congestion-related fuel consumption, and if higher density development results in substantially greater congestion and a relatively small increase in transit use, its net environmental benefits would be marginal at best and negative at worst.

The American Conundrum

The discussion above illuminates the challenge facing the United States. Settlements of European density and fuel taxes of Canadian heft would be necessary to motivate any substantially higher level of U.S. transit use and carpooling. At the same time, the history of motorization and suburbanization and the present geography of commuting suggest that the ownership of two cars and a conventional single-family home will remain the overwhelmingly dominant aspiration of the American middle class. We can also expect that suburban employment growth will continue to fuel suburban population growth and that families will continue to seek safe neighborhoods with good schools, stable property values, and room for children to play. These characteristically American expectations have inclined middle-income families to seek home ownership in the suburbs since the early twentieth century. We see little evidence that these dynamics are spent. Instead, the declining population of America's older industrial cities, the increasing predominance of suburban employment, the growth of the sunbelt and suburban populations, and the increasing share of two- and three-car households all signal that cars and trucks will remain America's overwhelmingly dominant form of mass transportation. Indeed, gentrification and parking perks are already at work, increasing the level of motor vehicle ownership in those wealthiest U.S. central cities that are the nation's bedrock transit markets.

In any event, continuing population growth will increase the number of cars and trucks that Americans own in the aggregate. That number could exceed 300 million by the year 2050 due solely to population growth. This prospect is, of course, precisely what leads environmentalists to the conclusion that the trajectory of U.S. motorization is unsustainable. It also leads to the question: How can the United States reduce its contribution to global warming and to the instability of global energy prices? More specifically, what can we expect of transit? What should we expect of the U.S. automakers and the vehicles they manufacture? And what should we expect of public policy?

It will be difficult for transit to capture market share from the automobile unless an effective remedy can be found for the problem of "peaking," which produces crush loads during peak commute hours and near-empty coaches during the rest of the day. Adding coaches and drivers to serve the peak is an extraordinarily costly way to build ridership because of the incremental cost of equipment and labor that has no productive use during the rest of the day. Resolving this problem would require fundamental changes in transit's way of doing business—for example, cross-training drivers to perform maintenance during off-peak hours or contracting out with taxi companies to provide taxi-van service on heavily patronized transit routes during peak commute hours. That would require transit management and transit unions to reach joint agreement on issues that have been notorious flashpoints for labor-management disagreement. But, absent such measures, transit can only generate modest gains in ridership given its present level of operating subsidy and the constraints imposed by its contract agreements and work rules.

The implication is that transit may be unable to deliver truly significant gains in ridership unless Congress is prepared to restore federal operating subsidies or muster the courage to increase U.S. fuel taxes.[13] Based on Canadian experience, we know that higher fuel taxes would produce a substantial increase in transit ridership, but we also know that previous proposals to increase U.S. fuel taxes have been characterized as "the electric third rail" of surface transportation politics. Thus transit's potential for significant contributions could be stalemated if Congress remains reluctant to restore federal operating subsidies and if transit labor and management are unable to reach a constructive compromise on work rules and productivity improvement.

What Can We Expect from Fuel Cell Vehicles?

At the present rate of technological maturation, fuel cell vehicles will not dominate the U.S. market for another 30–35 years. Accelerated to respond to the challenge of global warming, this timetable might be moved up, but achieving market dominance within 25 years is widely conceded to be unrealistic. And even then, accelerated commercialization of hydrogen fuel cell vehicles will require an unprecedented level of cooperation between the federal government and the automobile and energy industries.

In the early stages of this transition, we expect that the federal government's most strategically useful contribution would entail short-term subsidies that enable hydrogen fuels to be marketed at a price roughly equivalent to the future price that will prevail once economies of scale have been achieved. This policy judgment reflects recent consumer research at Shell Oil, which indicates that the demand for fuel cell vehicles will be highly sensitive to the price of hydrogen fuel.[14] As scale economies are achieved, it would be appropriate for these subsidies to be phased out and those federal funds redirected to enable hydrogen producers to capture and sequester CO_2 emissions. We believe these subsidies should also be withdrawn as energy companies master the art of capturing and sequestering CO_2 emissions and after sound protocols for effective carbon sequestration have been developed. Then, as the demand for hydrogen fuel increases, it would be appropriate for the emphasis and focus of federal funding to shift again—this time to stimulate the development of a national network of dedicated hydrogen pipelines with a rate structure explicitly favorable to the future transportation of hydrogen derived from renewables. This is essential for reducing CO_2 emissions.

In the scenario we have just constructed, the diffusion of fuel cell vehicles would engage both industry and government in an enormously complex process of technological transition. It is our judgment that government can play its role in this process most effectively if all parties understand from the beginning that federal funding will be available to match initial private investment but not to provide continuing subsidy. The partnerships that we have proposed emphasize those activities we judge to be most essential for jump-starting the initial diffusion of fuel cell vehicles. But ultimately it will be up to the automakers to develop evolved vehicles that match the buying power and the performance expectations of their customers, and it will be up to an evolved energy industry to produce and market hydrogen and sequester the CO_2 emissions that will initially be generated by the hydrogen production process.

If the internal combustion engine's advantages of incumbency can be overcome, the diffusion of fuel cell vehicles could substantially reduce metropolitan air pollution, U.S. oil import requirements, and the automobile's direct contribution to CO_2 emissions. More ambiguous is their total impact on CO_2 emissions. That will hinge on the sequestration of the CO_2 emissions associated with the current industrial practice of producing hydrogen fuel from natural gas and a successful effort to increase the share of hydrogen fuel generated from renewable feedstocks.

Getting More from Transit

With a wait of 20–25 years for fuel cell vehicles to produce meaningful reductions in the automobile's CO_2 emissions, policymakers may have to turn to transit for a second contribution to CO_2 emissions reduction. In this second pass, a dual focus would be essential—on the ridership increase necessary to reduce automobile use and on the productivity gains necessary to increase ridership without producing an outsized increase in operating costs per rider. To achieve these results, transit's work rules will have to evolve and transit's latitude to contract out will have to increase.

The potential for simultaneously increasing transit's commute share and its labor productivity is best indicated by the results that transit achieved in Las Vegas by contracting out. The result there was a stunning 1.7 percentage point gain in transit's commute share—from 2.4 percent to 4.1 percent—between 1990 and 2000. This was the largest gain in transit commute share of any city with a population of a million or more. Extrapolated to the nation as a whole, a comparably large percentage point gain could increase transit's nationwide commute share from its present 4.7 percent to 6.4 percent—a 36 percent increase.[15] Such gains are clearly worth pursuing, but would not come close to producing a net reduction in either automotive travel or oil import requirements if VMT continue to increase by the 13 percent that they did last decade. This discouraging observation reflects the limited leverage that transit can exert on its own initiative, given its present market share and the low fuel taxes presently levied in the United States. This suggests that over the next 20 years it is the nation's fuel-tax policies that will determine whether the United States can respond effectively to the challenges of global warming, petroleum depletion, and gasoline price volatility. This may not be welcome news, but we believe it is a fully accurate appraisal.

The Case for Fuel Surtaxes

With world oil prices exhibiting more frequent volatility and the emergence of a scientific consensus on the likely risks of global warming, we can and should expect Washington to be more aggressive in encouraging fuel conservation and regulating CO_2 emissions. In the context of the Supreme Court's 2007 ruling on the regulation of greenhouse gas emissions, we can envision Congress giving its first serious consideration to the merits of a carbon surtax on the price of gasoline that would be large enough to provide a meaningful incentive for Americans to conserve fuel, purchase motor vehicles that are carbon-efficient, and use public transportation in larger numbers.

But what level of fuel tax would be appropriate? The present average state fuel tax in the United States is $.46. The Canadian average is $.95 and the present average for the G-7 nations, including the United States, is $2.75.[16] Without the United States, the six-nation G-6 average would be $3.14. Most U.S. economists agree that present European fuel taxes are much higher than is necessary to pay for road construction and maintenance and to "put a price" on the social and environmental costs associated with automobile accidents and the automobile's adverse effects on the environment. Parry and Small estimate that an "optimal" fuel tax for the United States—one based on the cost of providing highways, policing them, and pricing the full social and environmental costs of automobile use—would closely approximate the fuel tax now levied in Canada.[17] In round numbers, that tax would be $1.00 per gallon of fuel consumed.

A conservation surtax that increases the total U.S. tax on gasoline to $1.00 would reduce both the number of trips Americans make by automobile and the miles they drive, especially for discretionary purposes. Secondary impacts would include increased demand for fuel-efficient vehicles, increased carpooling and transit use, and driving behavior that is more fuel-conscious. And if this tax were imposed on the carbon content of automotive fuels, fuel taxes could also accelerate the transition to hydrogen as a primary automotive fuel. In other words, higher fuel taxes would produce a cascade of responses, each of which would produce a modest reduction in oil imports, fuel consumption, air pollution, and CO_2 emissions. Singularly, each impact would be modest, but cumulatively the impact would be substantial if we include the impacts on vehicle purchase decisions and the mix of vehicles produced over the long term.

On the other hand, a $.50 per gallon surtax would add to the financial strain already experienced by low- to moderate-income households. In our judgment, this strain makes it absolutely essential to pair any increase in fuel taxes with offsetting tax rebates, either universal or targeted for lower-income households, trucking companies, and workers whose use of a car or truck is an occupational necessity. Combined with such adjustments, this author believes that fuel surtaxes would produce a desirable and long overdue response to the most serious externalities associated with pervasive motorization.

Not an Easy Sale

Many Americans would vigorously disagree with our endorsement of higher fuel taxes, perhaps anticipating a return to stability in the Middle East or a next generation of oil discoveries. Our expectation is less optimistic. We see a global oil market characterized by increasing demand, cartel-restrained supply, and higher production costs associated with continuing geopolitical volatility in the Middle East and South America and near-term exhaustion of oil reserves in the North Sea and Mexico. We also see eventual exhaustion of those oil fields that were least costly to exploit. Thus the twenty-first century seems likely to produce oil price volatility substantially greater than that which prevailed from 1920 to

1998, unless prolonged stability can be achieved in the Middle East and the petroleum industry can successfully devise new production methods that can extend the productive life of those oil wells that have been capped since the 1990s, when oil prices reached their all-time low in real dollar terms.[18]

A handful of statistics will illustrate how dramatically the picture has changed since the 1920s when the United States led the world in domestic oil production. In 1926, the United States accounted for 70 percent of the world's oil production, but by 2000, U.S. domestic production had fallen to 12 percent of the world total, and domestic consumption exceeded domestic production by a ratio of 2.2 to 1.[19]

Today, the economics and international politics of global warming, the increasing volatility of global oil prices, and the present competitive difficulties of the American automobile industry are all signaling the need for an orderly transition in automobile engines and automotive fuels. A fuel surtax of $.50 that increases the total tax on gasoline to $1.00 would be the surest way to accelerate this transition. Even with this increase, U.S. gasoline taxes would remain less than one-third of those imposed by the European nations in our G-7 peer group.[20]

We suspect many Americans would shake their heads and say, "On top of all our other energy problems, would you like to see a higher tax on gasoline?" Our answer is yes, a conservation surtax based on the carbon content of automotive fuels would provide the essential push that a market economy needs to conserve fuel, produce more fuel-efficient vehicles, and diversify the mix of fuels that our automobiles are designed to use. That makes a fuel surtax the surest way to reduce fuel price volatility in the short term and to stimulate technological substitution, fuel substitution, and mode shift in the long term. But we would also fully agree with our fellow Americans that any increase in fuel taxes should be offset by a compensatory reduction in sales or income taxes.

Closure

The automobile and motorization have had a profound impact on the development of American cities and their travel and settlement patterns since World War I. For this reason, public ownership and subsidy of mass transit have provided insufficient lift for transit to rebuild its share of commuter trips or substantially increase its national use rate, which has stalled at 33–35 rides per capita, down from 147 in 1926. For the same reason, it will be difficult for transit to achieve a major increase in its future market share in the absence of higher fuel taxes.

Transit's limited rebound under public ownership indicates that our nation's future success in mitigating the environmental impacts of motorization will likely hinge on the price of gasoline and the future evolution of automotive technology. A fuel cell vehicle powered by hydrogen that can be processed without atmospheric release of CO_2 emissions seems to be the most promising automotive technology for the future. But fuel cell vehicles are not yet ready for mass production and may not be fully ready for diffusion for another 15 years. Thus market dominance looks to be 25 years away at best. Nor is it likely that the first generation of hydrogen fuels can be brought to market and priced competitively without using production processes that generate CO_2 emissions.

Such is the American conundrum: we can continue to earn global resentment by deferring instrumental action on oil imports and automotive CO_2 emissions, or we can follow Canada's constructive example and impose a surtax on motor vehicle fuels that is sufficient to create a meaningful incentive for fuel conservation.

Raising U.S. fuel taxes by $.50 would trigger a cascade of small, individually appropriate adjustments that would reduce America's collective demand for oil imports and the automobile's contribution to CO_2 emissions.[21] In urban settings, these personal choices would entail increased transit use. In suburban settings, carpooling would be more prevalent. Among solo drivers, the most common adjustment might involve sharing a ride once or twice a week. In family neighborhoods, more parents would consider sharing carpool duty instead of driving their children individually to school or sports practice. Over the longer term, more Americans—both urban and suburban—would trade their gas-guzzlers for a more fuel-efficient vehicle. We know to expect this mix of adjustments because these are precisely the adjustments that Americans have made during each of the oil price shocks that have jolted the economy since 1973.

For the same reason, we can be confident that fuel surtaxes would motivate car buyers to pay more attention to fuel efficiency. And with this shift in consumer focus, no automaker could risk delay in bringing fuel cell vehicles to market.

Any plan for higher fuel taxes would be met, at least initially, with resistance from American motorists and fierce opposition from major segments of the oil, automobile, and trucking industries, just as the 1956 legislation to finance construction of the interstate system with higher fuel taxes was initially opposed by U.S. automakers, truckers, oil companies, and auto clubs. Based on this history, it would be politically perilous for Congress to enact legislation increasing fuel taxes without an offsetting reduction in other taxes.

The most effective way to secure public acceptance of higher fuel taxes would be a simultaneous reduction in the excise or income taxes paid by households, an approach that would create a desirable incentive for fuel conservation without impairing household buying power.[22] If a durable congressional consensus on this kind of tax swap can be achieved, American motorists would finally have a meaningful incentive to conserve fuel, use transit, and share rides on a sustained basis. By the same token, the U.S. automakers would have greater incentive to focus on fuel efficiency and better reason for confidence in the salability of fuel-efficient vehicles.

A 50-cent increase in U.S. fuel taxes would send an unambiguous signal to the American people that fuel conservation and the reduction of CO_2 emissions are a national priority. It would also reassure our allies that the United States understands its global environmental obligations and the responsibility it must shoulder as the world's wealthiest, most powerful, and most thoroughly motorized nation. A fuel tax increase would provide the incentive necessary to encourage fuel conservation and prime the automotive marketplace for the diffusion of hydrogen fuel cell vehicles, and those would be important first steps on the road to sustainable motorization.

GLOSSARY

Commute share. The percentage of trips made by each mode of transportation for the purpose of getting to work.

Initial motorization. The early years of the motorization process, which resulted in an automobile and truck ownership rate of 150 vehicles per 1,000 population.

Mass motorization. A later stage in the process of motorization that entails extensive ownership of cars and trucks for moving both people and goods. It is defined here as 400 motor vehicles per 1,000 population. By 2000, 23 of the world's wealthier nations qualified. The United States did so in 1958.

Mass transit. Public transportation by bus or rail.

Motorization. The long-term process that leads to extensive ownership of cars and trucks for both personal and commercial purposes.

Pervasive motorization. Less than 10 percent of the workforce walks to work or commutes by public transportation. Only the United States and New Zealand had attained this level by 2000. The United States did so in 1980 when its combined auto and truck ownership rate reached 685 motor vehicles per 1,000 population.

NOTES

1. Motorization in the United States and Other Industrial Nations

1. See Jeffrey R. Kenworthy and Felix B. Laube, *An International Sourcebook of Automobile Dependence in Cities, 1960–1990* (Boulder: University Press of Colorado, 1999).

2. George M. Smerk, "Public Transportation and the City," in *Public Transportation*, 2d ed., ed. George Gray and Lester Hoel (Englewood Cliffs, N.J.: Prentice-Hall, 1992), 8–15.

3. Bureau of the Census, *Street and Electric Railways, 1902* (Washington, D.C.: Government Printing Office, 1902).

4. Angus Maddison, *The World Economy: Historical Statistics* (Paris: OECD, 2003), 49, 84.

5. T. K. Derry and T. I. Williams, *A Short History of Technology* (Oxford: Clarendon Press, 1960), 370ff.

6. David Mowery and Nathan Rosenberg, "Twentieth-Century Technological Change," in *The Cambridge Economic History of the United States*, ed. Engerman and Gallman, 3:803ff.

7. See "The Elevator," in *"Scientific American" Inventions and Discoveries*, by Rodney Carlisle (Hoboken, N.J.: John Wiley, 2004), 260ff.

8. John P. McKay, "Comparative Perspectives on Transit in Western Europe and the United States, 1850–1914," in *Technology and the Rise of the Networked City in Europe and America*, ed. Joel A. Tarr and Gabriel Dupuy (Philadelphia: Temple University Press, 1988), 3–21.

9. Bureau of the Census, *Street and Electric Railways, 1902*. The electrification of street railways was slowed by municipal regulators in Europe, largely for aesthetic reasons, but "shot through the American street railway industry like current through a copper wire." This marvelous simile is thanks to McKay, "Comparative Perspectives."

10. David W. Jones, *Urban Transit Policy* (Englewood Cliffs, N.J.; Prentice Hall, 1985), 30–36.

11. Ibid., 47–48.

12. Leonard Fanning, *Foreign Oil and the Free World* (New York: McGraw-Hill, 1954), 326.

13. Author's calculations based on Maddison, *World Economy: Historical Statistics*.

14. Motor Vehicle Manufacturers Association, *Motor Vehicle Facts and Figures*, 1926 and 1952.

15. David Jones, 1978 and 1990 interviews with Richard M. Zettel, economic consultant for the California State Senate Committee on Streets and Highways; Federal Highway Administration (FHWA), *America's Highways, 1776–1976* (Washington, D.C.: Government Printing Office, 1976).

16. FHWA, *America's Highways*; Zettel interview.

17. Kenworthy and Laube report population densities for their sample of U.S. cities that are roughly half that of their sample of Canadian cities. Canadian cities are, in turn, roughly half as dense as their European counterparts. See Kenworthy and Laube, *International Sourcebook*, 548, table 5.5.

18. After World War II, European traffic engineers viewed parking as the critical constraint on urban motorization in Germany, France, the United Kingdom, and Italy. It can similarly be described as posing a significant constraint on automobile use in Montreal, Quebec, New York, Boston, and Chicago, but few other North American cities. Conversely, the free parking available in most American suburbs and sunbelt growth centers virtually ensures that the automobile will remain America's primary form of mass transportation.

19. George Charlesworth has cogently observed that London's outer-ring road has been completed, but most of the radial routes of the nationwide motorway network proposed for London have not been built. In effect, he concludes, "parking control" has emerged as the de facto means of traffic management in London. See George Charlesworth, *A History of British Motorways* (London: Thomas Telford, 1984). See also the city map of London in the *Atlas of the World* (New York: Oxford University Press, 2001). Little has changed since Charlesworth's history of British motorways was published in 1984.

20. Peter Hall, *Cities in Civilization* (New York: Pantheon Books, 1998), chapter 24, "Paris: The City of Perpetual Public Works," 745. See also *Atlas of the World*, 23.

21. Otto Sill, director of City Engineering, Homburg Germany, "The Role of Automobiles in Cities," Institute of Traffic Engineers, 1965 *Proceedings*, 59–65. Sill concluded that "the use of the automobile for going to work no longer seems practicable" in German cities.

22. Ibid., 62.

23. American Public Transportation Association (APTA), passenger trips by mode, 1907–2003.

24. Bert Bolin et al., *The Greenhouse Effect, Climatic Change, and Ecosystems* (New York: John Wiley, 1986), xxv–xxxi. See also William D. Nordhaus, "Economic Approaches to Greenhouse Warming," in *Global Warming: Economic Policy Responses*, ed. Rudiger Dornbusch and James M. Poterba (Cambridge: MIT Press, 1992), 33–69.

25. Donella H. Meadows et al., *The Limits to Growth* (New York: Universe Books, 1972), 24; U.S. Bureau of Economic Analysis, *Business Statistics, 1963–91* (Washington, D.C.: Government Printing Office, 1992), 81.

26. Maddison, *World Economy: Historical Statistics*, table 2b, p. 86.

27. Motor Vehicle Manufacturers Association, *Motor Vehicle Facts and Trends*, 1976.

28. U.S. Bureau of Economic Analysis, *Business Statistics*, 1963–91, 76–79.

29. *Ward's Motor Vehicle Facts and Figures*, 2002.

30. Albert Rose, *Governing Metropolitan Toronto: A Social and Political Analysis*, 1953–1971 (Berkeley: University of California Press, 1972), 129–32, 134–39. See also Kenworthy and Laube, *International Sourcebook*, 610, table 6.4.

31. IEA, *Energy Policies of IEA Countries, United States, 2002 Review* (Paris: OECD/IEA, 2002), 103.

32. Canadian estimate from John Pucher and Christian Lefèvre, *The Urban Transport Crisis in Europe and North America* (Basingstoke: Macmillan, 1996), 163. American estimate based on 1992 passenger trips reported by the APTA and U.S. Census estimates of the U.S. population for 1992.

33. Kenworthy and Laube, *International Sourcebook*, 529, table 5.1.

34. Author's calculations based on *Ward's Motor Vehicle Facts and Figures*, 2002, and population estimates from Maddison, *World Economy: Historical Statistics*.

2. Transit's American History, 1880–1929

1. Jones, *Urban Transit Policy*, 28–37. See also Smerk, "Public Transportation and the City," 12–14, and Edward J. Mason, *The Street Railway in Massachusetts* (Cambridge: Harvard University Press, 1932).

2. Bureau of the Census, *Street and Electric Railways*, 1902, 7–13, and APTA, *Transit Fact Book*, 1948, 16. The APTA was a membership organization that reported the ridership for its affiliated streetcar, bus, and rapid transit companies. The 1926 ridership reports understate transit ridership relative to contemporary reports because commuter rail ridership was not reported and many smaller operators were not APTA affiliated in 1926.

3. Wholesale prices were consistently downward trending from the end of the Civil War to 1886, somewhat volatile in the 1890s, and upward biased after 1896. See U.S. Bureau of the Census, *Historical Statistics of the United States: Colonial Times to 1970*, Series E 52–63 and E 40–51, 200–201.

4. See Kevin Phillips, *Wealth and Democracy* (New York: Broadway Books, 2002), 51. According to Phillips, streetcar magnates accounted for 3 of the 30 wealthiest Americans of the first decade of the twentieth century.

5. The early days of speculative investment produced a legacy of ill will toward street railways. As the American Electric Railway Association conceded in 1932, "The average man's mind is filled with the suspicion and prejudice that are the outgrowth of evils associated with the promotional stage of street railways of 25 or 30 years ago when they were in a boom period and no provision for their regulation . . . had been made." See AERA, "The Urban Transportation Problem" (New York: AERA, 1932).

6. Bureau of the Census, *Historical Statistics*, Series E 40–51, 200.

7. Melville Jack Ulmer, *Capital in Transportation* (Princeton: Princeton University Press, 1960), appendix F, 405–6, table F-1; U.S. Bureau of Census, *Historical Statistics*, Series Q 264–273, "Electric Railways, Summary: 1890–1937," 727.

8. Jones, *Urban Transit Policy*, 39–43.

9. Leo Wolman, *Ebb and Flow in Trade Unionism* (New York: National Bureau of Economic Research, 118.

10. Jones, *Urban Transit Policy*, 40; Bureau of the Census, *Historical Statistics*, Series 135–166, "Consumer Prices Indexes," 210, and Series Q 264–273, "Electric Railways, Summary: 1890–1937," 727.

11. Emerson P. Schmidt, *Industrial Relations in Urban Transportation* (Minneapolis: University of Minnesota Press, 1937), 161.

12. APTA, *Transit Fact Book, 1948*, 16, table 5, "Urban Population, Total Rides and Rides per Capita."

13. AERA, *Urban Transportation Problem*, table 1, "Income Statement of the Electric Railway Industry, 1917–1931," 6.

14. Brian Cudahy, *Cash, Tokens, and Transfers: A History of Urban Mass Transit in North America* (New York: Fordham University Press, 1990), 151.

15. The Sixteenth Amendment to the U.S. Constitution authorizing the federal income tax took force in 1913. The same year, Congress authorized the so-called Tariff Act of 1913, which authorized taxpayers to itemize and take tax deductions for property taxes paid to local governments and interest paid on home mortgages. See Michael S. Carliner, "Development of Federal Home Ownership Policy," Fannie Mae Foundation *Housing Policy* 9, no. 2 (1998).

16. Following World War I, state legislatures intervened to exempt street railways from municipal regulation and subject them to price and service regulation by state public utility or public service commissions. This new venue enabled transit properties to obtain legal authorization for fare increases or service reductions. Regulation prolonged transit's ability to operate under private ownership but did not produce industrial recovery and renewal. Instead, it short-circuited the process of bankruptcy and reorganization, which might actually have provided a more salutary framework for wholesale reorganization.

17. AERA, *Urban Transportation Problem*, 28.

18. R. H. Pinkley, "How the Industry Is Progressing," AERA *Proceedings* (New York: American Electric Railway Association, 1927), 127–29.

19. Joseph R. Stranskey, "Superhighway Development in the Milwaukee Metropolitan Area," *Roads and Streets*, August 1929, 271.

20. Cudahy, *Cash, Tokens, and Transfers*, 133–35.

21. Jones, *Urban Transit Policy*, 29. See also Peter O. Muller, "Transportation and Urban Form: Stages in the Spatial Evolution of the American Metropolis," in *The Geography of Urban Transportation*, ed. Susan Hanson (New York: Guilford Press, 1995), 29–47; George M. Smerk, "Public Transportation and the City," 12–15.

22. Bureau of the Census, *Historical Statistics*, Series 238–245, "Occupied Housing Units and Tenure of Homes, 1890–1970," and *Statistical Abstract of the United States*, 2002, table 931, "Total Housing Inventory for the United States, 1980–2001."

23. Jones, *Urban Transit Policy*, 30–43.

24. For a critical but influential analysis of the state of traction industry prior to this regulatory transformation, see Delos F. Wilcox, *Analysis of the Electric Railway Problem* (New York: privately published, 1921). See especially chapters 23 and 40 and his summary. Wilcox was an early advocate of public ownership and municipal operation of street railways. His advocacy was based on the financially conservative pattern of street railway investment that he observed in Great Britain. His view was widely discussed, but largely

dismissed because few Americans were inclined to widen the financial responsibilities of America's roistering big-city politicians of the 1920s.

25. James J. Flink, *The Car Culture* (Cambridge: MIT Press, 1975), 18.

26. John B. Rae, *American Automobile Manufacturers: The First Forty Years* (Philadelphia: Chilton, 1959), 109.

27. Automotive Manufacturers Association, *A Chronicle of the Automotive Industry in America, 1893–1952* (Detroit: AMA, 1953).

28. Thomas K. McCraw and Richard S. Tedlow, "Henry Ford, Alfred Sloan, and the Three Phases of Marketing," in *Creating Modern Capitalism*, ed. McCraw (Cambridge: Harvard University Press, 1997), 273–74, 282–83, 290.

29. Ibid., 299.

30. Automobile Manufacturers Association, *Automobile Facts and Trends*, 1921, 17.

31. Ibid., 16.

32. AERA, *Urban Transportation Problem*, 28.

33. James Dalton, "What Will Ford Do Next?" *Motor*, May 1926.

34. National Automobile Chamber of Commerce, *Facts and Figures of the Automobile Industry*, 1928, 11.

35. Robert S. Lynd and Helen N. Lynd, *Middletown* (New York: Harcourt, Brace, 1929), 253–54.

36. See F. W. Doolittle, *Studies in the Cost of Urban Transportation Service* (New York: AERA, 1916), 271.

37. Ibid., 247.

38. Jones, *Urban Transit Policy*, 51–52.

39. Arthur Saltzman, "Public Transportation in the Twentieth Century," in *Public Transportation*, 2d ed., ed. Gray and Hoel (Englewood Cliffs, N.J.: Prentice Hall, 1992), 38.

40. Cudahy, *Cash, Tokens, and Transfers*, 190.

3. The Great Depression and the New Deal

1. Peter Temin, "The Great Depression," in Stanley Engerman and Robert Gallman, *The Cambridge Economic History of the United States*, vol. 3, *The Twentieth Century* (Cambridge: Cambridge University Press, 2000), 301.

2. Ibid., 302–3, 305–10.

3. Ibid., 304.

4. David W. Jones, *California's Freeway Era in Historical Perspective* (Berkeley: Institute of Transportation Studies, University of California, 1989), 208.

5. Temin, "The Great Depression," 301.

6. Robert J. Samuelson, "The Great Depression," in *The Fortune Encyclopedia of Economics*, ed. David R. Henderson (New York: Warner Books, 1993), 196.

7. Cudahy, *Cash, Tokens, and Transfers*, 176.

8. FHWA, *America's Highways*, 246–48.

9. Bureau of the Census, *Historical Statistics of the United States: Colonial Times to 1970*, Series D 1–10, 126, and Series Q 235–250, 721.

10. AERA, *Urban Transportation Problem*, 11–12.

11. Jones, *Urban Transit Policy*, 87–88.

12. AERA, *Urban Transportation Problem*, 11.

13. Only in the largest cities would current ridership and the ability of streetcars to accommodate standees have justified reinvestment in streetcars.

14. This proved a technical violation of U.S. antitrust law, which resulted in eventual antitrust action against National City Lines and General Motors. Most of the transit properties involved in the complaint brought by the Justice Department were small operations in relatively small towns. Many were properties that had previously been affiliated with electric utilities, but had suffered forced divestiture under a previous Justice Department action against utility holding companies. In both instances, the actions brought by the Justice Department seem to represent overzealous prosecution of technical violations of antitrust law that seem unlikely to have caused any significant damage to rival suppliers of transportation or electricity or motor vehicles. For further discussion, see Saltzman, "Public Transportation," 37–39

15. Saltzman, "Public Transportation," 38.

16. Bradford C. Snell, *American Ground Transport: A Proposal for Restructuring the Automobile, Truck, Bus, and Rail Industries* (Washington, D.C.: Government Printing Office, 1974), 28–29.

17. Ibid., 31.

18. George W. Hilton and John F. Due, *The Electric Interurban Railways in America* (Stanford: Stanford University Press, 1960), 409. See also Seymour Adler, "The Political Economy of Transit in the San Francisco Bay Area, 1945–63," Institute of Urban and Regional Development, University of California, Berkeley, 1980.

19. Jones, *California's Freeway Era*, 119, 132; California Railroad Commission, *Report on Engineering Survey of the Pacific Electric Railway Company* (Sacramento: California Railroad Commission, 1939), 61, 109.

20. See, e.g., "Mass Rapid Transit for Los Angeles," *SC Engineer*, March 1955, 15.

21. California Railroad Commission, *Report*, 135 ff.

22. FHWA, *America's Highways*, 125.

23. Ibid., 80–83.

24. Ibid., 86–87.

25. Ibid., 108–9.

26. Ibid., 80–83, 86–87, 108–9. David Jones, oral history interview with Richard M. Zettel, principal consultant, Senate Highway and Public Works Committee, California Legislature, Spring 1978. See also Jonathan Gifford, "An Analysis of the Federal Role in the Planning, Design, and Deployment of Rural Highways, Toll Roads, and Urban Freeways," PhD diss., University of California at Berkeley, 1983.

27. The first federal fuel tax was imposed in 1932. A temporary Depression era measure, it was a not reserved for highway purposes as federal fuel taxes were after 1956. See Mary E. Forsberg, "Perspective on the Gas Tax and Car Registration Fees," New Jersey Policy Perspective, Trenton, New Jersey, 31 July 2005.

28. FHWA, *America's Highways*, 125.

29. Ibid., 124–25, 156, 247.

30. American Petroleum Institute, "Historical Trends in Motor Gasoline Taxes, 1918–2006," table 1, API, 6 September 2006.

31. Other state highway departments looked to New York and California as models for how to finance their state highway programs, according to Richard M. Zettel.

32. The Arroyo Seco Parkway that connected Pasadena with downtown Los An-

geles was the first "freeway" in the West, but its design was inspired by parkways that were built in suburban New York during the 1920s and 1930s. See Jones, *California's Freeway Era*, 174–82.

33. James Drake, *Motorways* (London: Faber and Faber, 1969), 27–30.

34. FHWA, *America's Highways*, 125.

35. Drake, *Motorways*, 27–30; Thomas MacDonald, "The Roads We Should Have," *Proceedings of the American Automobile Association*, 1936.

36. See MacDonald, "Roads We Should Have," 69; U.S. Bureau of Public Roads, *Toll Roads and Free Roads* (Washington, D.C.: Government Printing Office, 1939), 4, 89–98.

37. U.S. Bureau of Public Roads, *Toll Roads and Free Roads*, 95. See also *Interregional Highways*, House Document no. 379, 78th Cong., 2d sess. (Washington, D.C.: Government Printing Office, 1944), 1–7.

38. Charles Noble, "Modern Turnpike History Revisited," *Civil Engineering*, February 1979, 74. See also Gifford, "An Analysis of the Federal Role in the Planning, Design, and Deployment of Rural Highways."

39. U.S. Bureau of Public Roads, *Toll Roads and Free Roads*, 4–7, 95.

40. Ibid., 6–7.

41. *Interregional Highways*, 82n.

42. MacDonald, "Roads We Should Have," 69ff.

43. U.S. Bureau of Public Roads, *Toll Roads and Free Roads*, 108.

44. Ibid., 95.

45. *Interregional Highways*, 66–70, 82,150.

46. This new push was quite evident in ibid., 66–70, 82, 150.

47. Ibid., iv, 70.

48. FHWA, *America's Highways*, 93–95.

49. U.S. Bureau of Public Roads, *Toll Roads and Free Roads*, 102, plates 54 and 56, 109, plate 57, 109–11. See also *Interregional Highways*.

50. Highway and Transportation Committee, American Society of Planning Officials, "Highways and Transportation in Relation to Each Other and to Other Planned Development," National Conference on Planning, July 1940.

51. Joint Committee on Street and Highway Traffic Engineering Functions and Administration, *Traffic Engineering Functions and Administration* (Chicago: Public Administration Service, 1948), 99.

52. Ibid., 20ff., 99ff.

53. Harland Bartholomew, *The Present and Ultimate Effect of Decentralization upon American Cities* (Chicago: Urban Land Institute, 1940).

54. Ibid., 90–91

55. John F. Long, *Population Deconcentration in the United States*, U.S. Bureau of the Census, Special Demographic Analyses, CDS 81–1, issued August 1981, 18. By the year 2000, the share of the U.S. population that lives in cities of more than a million had increased to 13.2 percent due to the addition of three cities to the peer group of cities with a central city population greater than one million. These cities were Phoenix, San Diego and San Antonio—largely horizontal cities that have grown up with the automobile and a wide array of suburban employment opportunities. San Antonio was the largest of the three in 1930, with a central city population of 161,000. By the year 2000, San Antonio's central city population exceeded 1.1 million and its metropolitan population was 1.6 million.

56. *Interregional Highways* singled out New York, Los Angeles, Cleveland, St Louis, Newark, and Jersey City as cities with the lead in the development of a first generation of divided highways. But only five states (New York, California, New Jersey, Illinois, and Michigan) had built more than fifty miles of urban divided highway by 1946: Bureau of Public Roads, *Highway Statistics 1946*, table SM-13.

57. Cudahy, *Cash, Tokens, and Transfers*, 176–77.

58. *Interregional Highways*, 70–71.

59. FHWA, *Highway Statistics, Summary to 1985*, table SM-211.

60. Author's calculation based on *Historical Statistics of the United States*, Series Q 148–162, "Motor Vehicle Factory Sales and Registrations," 716.

4. World War II and Its Immediate Aftermath

1. Between 1945 and 1955, street railway ridership declined by 12 billion passengers, or 68 percent, while the mileage of railway track declined 65 percent. Much of the decline in ridership was part of an expected postwar correction. But the decline in trackage represented the beginning of the permanent abandonment of streetcar service in many cities. See *Historical Statistics of the United States*, Series Q 235–250, "Public Transit Mileage, Equipment and Passengers," 721.

2. "Postwar normalization" is the way transit operators representing the American Transit Association described the loss of ridership that occurred from 1945 to 1948 in their testimony before Congress.

3. *Historical Statistics*, Series Q 235–250, 721.

4. Reinvestment was essential for the streetcar companies because the industry's net capital expenditures had been negative each and every year from 1916 to 1950. In its absence, abandonment followed. See Ulmer, *Capital in Transportation*, 405–6, table F-1.

5. Cudahy, *Cash, Tokens, and Transfers*, 190.

6. Lyle C. Fitch and Associates, *Urban Transportation and Public Policy* (San Francisco: Chandler, 1964), 37.

7. At the 1962 congressional hearings that led eventually to federal aid for public transportation, BART was hailed as a prime example of what could be accomplished in other cities through the combination of public ownership, federal aid, and reinvestment. At the time, BART had not yet opened for service. Thus the plaudits were a bit premature.

8. *Interregional Highways*, iii–iv. The plan recommended an annual expenditure of $750 million to build 34,000 miles of interregional highways and provide stimulus for the U.S. economy "during the postwar adjustment period." Congress authorized expenditures on the interstate in the 1944 Highway Act, but no funds were specifically allocated to the Interstate; Congress expected interstate projects to compete on their merits with other primary highways already programmed for state funding.

9. Zettel interview.

10. FHWA, *America's Highways*, 166–69.

11. Bureau of Public Roads, *Highway Statistics 1956*, table FM-11.

12. American Association of State Highway and Transportation Officials, *The States and the Interstates* (Washington, D.C.: AASHTO, 1991), 20–24.

5. The Interstate and Pervasive Motorization, 1956–80

1. FHWA, *Highway Statistics, Summary to 1985*, table HM-255.

2. AASHTO, *The States and the Interstates*, 24–29, and FHWA, *America's Highways*, 171–74. For a more detailed chronology of events leading up to the passage of the 1956 Highway Acts, see David W. Jones, "Urban Highway Investment and the Political Economy of Fiscal Retrenchment," in *Current Issues in Transportation Policy*, ed. Alan Altschuler (Lexington, Mass.: Lexington Books, 1979), 75–77.

3. *Interregional Highways*, iii, 14; *Ward's Motor Vehicle Facts and Figures*, 2002, 71.

4. Author's calculation based on Ulmer, *Capital in Transportation*, 405.

5. FHWA, *Highway Statistics 2000*, table HM-36.

6. *Interregional Highways*, 4.

7. Flink, *Car Culture*, 213.

8. *Ward's Motor Vehicle Facts and Figures*, 2002, 71.

9. Bureau of the Census, *Historical Statistics of the United States*, Series N 241–245, 646, and *Statistical Abstract of the United States*, 2002, 595, table 931.

10. FHWA, *Journey-to-Work Trends in the United States and Its Major Metropolitan Areas, 1960–1990* (Washington, D.C.: Department of Transportation, Federal Highway Administration, Office of Planning, 1993), 2-2.

11. Kenneth L. Hess, "The Growth of Automotive Transportation," 1996, *www.klhess.com*, accessed 7 November 2007.

12. *Historical Statistics*, Series D 29–41, 131–32, and *Statistical Abstract of the United States*, 2001, 372, table 575.

13. *Journey-to-Work Trends, 1960–1990*, 2-2.

14. Maddison, *World Economy: Historical Statistics*, 86, 89; FHWA, *Highway Statistics, Summary to 1995*, "Motor Vehicle Registrations by Years, 1900–1995."

15. *Ward's Motor Vehicle Facts and Figures*, 2002, 71.

16. Middle-class housing of the 1920s was defined by the suburban bungalow. Most bungalow-style homes were built by a general contractor and a crew of four or five men. Typical builder volume was five or six houses a year. See Robert Sobel, *The Great Boom* (New York: St. Martin's Press, 2000), 89.

17. Carliner, "Development of Federal Home Ownership Policy."

18. Sobel, *The Great Boom*, 70.

19. Mark I. Gelfand, *A Nation of Cities: The Federal Government and Urban America, 1933–1965* (New York: Oxford University Press, 1975), 216–17.

20. For visual evidence of the state of the art in California and New York freeway and expressway development before the 1956 Interstate Act was passed, see the Association of State Highway Officials, "A Policy on Arterial Highways in Urban Areas" (Washington, D.C.: AASHTO, 1957), 333, 375, 376–79. As these illustrations suggest, California established the "gold standard" for building freeways in the early 1950s.

21. Carol E. Heim, "Structural Changes: Regional and Urban," in *Cambridge Economic History of the United States*, ed. Engerman and Gallman (Cambridge: Cambridge University Press, 2000), 3:149–51. See also Martin Mayer, *The Builders: Houses, People, Neighborhoods, Governments, Money* (New York: Norton, 1978), 368–71.

22. Sobel, *The Great Boom*, 89–91.

23. McCraw and Tedlow, "Henry Ford, Alfred Sloan, and the Three Phases of Marketing," 274–77.

24. *Interregional Highways* acknowledged the safety problems that could occur if freeways were not protected from encroaching development, but the Bureau's plan made no reference to the growth of outlying population and employment centers that could eventually rival the downtowns of a midsized city.

25. See Wilbur Smith and Associates, *Transportation and Parking for Tomorrow's Cities* (New Haven: Wilbur Smith and Associates, 1966), 42, fig. 22, Changing Patterns of Traffic Flow. See also 190.

26. Many of these oral history interviews were conducted on behalf of the American Association of State Highway and Transportation Officials for the Chicago Historical Society's *The States and the Interstates* (Washington, D.C.: AASHTO, 1991).

27. For critiques of this school of traffic engineering and suburban development, see Real Estate Research Corporation, *The Costs of Sprawl* (Washington, D.C.: Government Printing Office, April 1974). For a more contemporary, transit-focused view, see Robert Dunphy et al., *Developing around Transit: Strategies and Solutions That Work* (Washington, D.C.: Urban Land Institute, 2004).

28. Traffic engineers of the 1950s and 1960s made frequent reference to the functional differentiation of roadspace. For their part, land use planners spoke of "the cantonment of residential areas" and "keeping through traffic out of residential neighborhoods."

29. Harold Marks, "Geometrics of Local and Collector Streets," a paper presented to the Institute of Traffic Engineers, 1961 Proceedings, 107.

30. John Nolan and H. V. Hubbard, *Parkways and Land Values* (Cambridge: Harvard University Press, 1937), xi.

31. See Muller, "Transportation and Urban Form," 37–40. Muller argues that the tracked city of 1920 "truly worked." He also maintains that it was in this era that "intrametropolitan transportation achieved its greatest level of efficiency." Muller attributes this efficiency to the streetcar. Perhaps it would be more appropriate to attribute it to the match between streetcars and the then prevailing organization and density of U.S. metropolitan areas, then prevailing household income levels, and the still limited intensity of U.S. motorization.

32. See David W. Jones, "Mass Transit: Essential Service, Public Enterprise and Distressed Industry," a paper presented at the UCLA conference "Redefining, Reevaluating and Reinventing Transit," Lake Arrowhead, February 2002.

33. Automobile Club of Southern California, "Traffic Survey of Los Angeles Metropolitan Area," Los Angeles, 1936.

34. This somewhat counterintuitive finding deserves further investigation. The issues involved are precisely those that European engineers grappled with in determining how actively to accommodate urban motorization after World War II. Kenworthy and Laube have raised similar issues in *International Sourcebook*. This author concurs that Europe's postwar answer was an apt response given the then prevailing density of European cities and the delayed diffusion of the automobile due to World Wars I and II. But we judge it unlikely that a policy-driven effort to ratchet up transit ridership by increasing the density of settlement through redevelopment could, after the fact, produce comparably advantageous commuting outcomes in, say, Los Angeles. More likely, it would lead to more congestion, longer delays, and thus increased fuel consumption and pollutant emissions due to increased hours of travel and the increased incidence of stop-and-start driving in heavy traffic.

35. For population densities, see Kenworthy and Laube, *International Sourcebook*, 44.

36. Nancy McGuckin and Nanda Srinivasan, *Journey-to-Work Trends in the United States and Its Major Metropolitan Areas, 1960–2000* (Washington, D.C.: Department of Transportation, Federal Highway Administration, Office of Planning, 2003), exhibit 3.5, "Mean Travel Time to Work, 1990–2000."

37. For a contrary view, see Muller, "Transportation and Urban Form," 43–44.

38. James O. Wheeler et al., *Economic Geography* (New York: Wiley, 1998), 185–93.

39. McGuckin and Srinivasan, *Journey-to-Work Trends*, exhibit 3.6, "Percent Distribution of Workers by Travel Time to Work, 1980–2000."

40. David W. Jones, "The Bay Area's Transportation System: More and More Congested, but Still Surprisingly Access-Efficient," a paper presented at the Alameda County Symposium on Transportation and Land Use, Oakland, 1997. At this symposium, the author introduced the concept of a polyopolis, a polycentric metropolis in which suburban employment exceeds central city employment, the majority of work trips entail travel from one suburb to another, and average commute travel time remains less than 30 minutes thanks to increasing collocation of homes and workplaces in suburban settings. The 2000 census confirmed that this description now fits most U.S. metropolitan areas that grew up in the automobile era.

41. Wheeler et al., *Economic Geography*, 193.

42. McGuckin and Srinivasan, *Journey-to-Work Trends*, exhibit 3.5.

43. Wheeler et al., *Economic Geography*, 193.

6. Transit's Conversion to Public Ownership

1. Physical obsolescence was the most obvious form of obsolescence that dogged transit companies. Many companies had depleted their capital accounts to pay current expenses, and their rolling stock was in an advanced state of dilapidation. Less obvious but more difficult to ameliorate was the seemingly permanent loss of off-peak ridership and the revenues it had once generated. See Jones, *Urban Transit Policy*, 26 and table 2.8. See also Lyle Fitch and Associates, *Urban Transportation and Public Policy*, 38.

2. APTA, *Transit Fact Book*, 1997, 67–68, table 32.

3. U.S. Bureau of the Census, *Historical Statistics of the United States: Colonial Times to 1970*, Series Q 241–244, 721.

4. *Statistical Abstract of the United States*, 1962, 22–24, table 22.

5. Heim, "Structural Changes," 114.

6. Michael N. Danielson, *Federal-Metropolitan Politics and the Commuter Crisis* (New York: Columbia University Press, 1965), 26–35.

7. Ibid., 110–13.

8. Jones, *Urban Transit Policy*, 117.

9. Danielson, *Federal-Metropolitan Politics*, 138–39.

10. Fitch and Associates, *Urban Transportation and Public Policy*, 12–13, 18–19. See American Municipal Association, *The Collapse of Commuter Service: A Survey of Mass Transportation in Five Major Cities* (Washington, D.C.: AMA, 1960).

11. Fitch and Associates, *Urban Transportation and Public Policy*, 19.

12. Ibid., xii.

13. Ibid., 5–6.

14. As reported here, transit's long-term gains in ridership are somewhat inflated by

the exclusion of commuter rail ridership prior to 1980 and by the exclusion of dial-a-ride service before 1984. Their inclusion after 1984 increased transit's reported ridership by 3.9 percent. This, of course, was a bookkeeping change and not an actual increase in 1984 ridership.

15. McGuckin and Srinivason, *Journey-to-Work Trends, 1960–2000*, exhibit 4.13. For further interpretation, see also *Journey-to-Work Trends, 1960–1990* (Washington, D.C.: Department of Transportation, Federal Highway Administration, Office of Planning, 1993), and for the gold standard interpretation of the 1990 data, see Alan Pisarski, *Commuting in America* (Westport, Conn.: Eno Foundation, 1996).

16. APTA, *Transit Fact Book*, 1997, and APTA, "Transit Ridership Report, 1996–2004," at *www.apta.com/research/stats*, accessed 7 November 2007.

17. Many of the cities that have implemented light rail transit have made a simultaneous commitment to downtown redevelopment, creating a sense of time and place that distinguishes downtown from any other business and shopping center. In this author's judgment, this is a role for which light rail is uniquely suited and the intangible value added justifies the increment in cost associated with light rail vis-à-vis arterial bus service. Salt Lake City is a prime example of a redevelopment program and light rail installation that has been well coordinated and executed.

18. McGuckin and Srinivason, *Journey-to-Work Trends, 1960–2000*, exhibit 4.13.

19. *Statistical Abstract of the United States, 2002*, and Donald J. Bogue, "Population Growth in Standard Metropolitan Areas, 1900–1950" (Washington, D.C.: Housing and Home Finance Finance Agency, 1954), 61–71.

20. Roberto Suro and Audrey Singer, *Latino Growth in Metropolitan America* (Washington, D.C.: Brookings Institution Press, July 2002). See also Mary M. Kent and Mark Mather, "What Drives U.S. Population Growth?" *Population Bulletin*, University of Iowa Population Reference Bureau, December 2002, 35, table 6.

21. Edward L. Glaeser and Jesse M. Shapiro, "City Growth: Which Places Grew and Why," in *Redefining Urban and Suburban America*, ed. Bruce Katz and Robert E. Lang (Washington, D.C.: Brookings Institution Press, 2003), 1:28.

22. Author's calculations based on tables 1389 and 1390 in *Statistical Abstract of the United States, 2002*, 875.

23. This case study is based on McGuckin and Srinivason, *Journey-to-Work Trends, 1960–2000*, and complementary data from the 2000 census of population.

24. Joel Garreau, *Edge City: Life on the New Frontier* (New York: Doubleday, 1991), 428.

25. Wheeler et al., *Economic Geography*, 181.

26. See Jennifer Dill, "Smart Growth Transportation Planning in the Portland Region," a paper presented at the Annual Conference of the National Association of Environmental Professionals," Portland, Oregon, April 2004.

27. McGuckin and Srinivason, *Journey-to-Work Trends, 1960–2000*, exhibit 4.13.

28. Dill, "Smart Growth." See also James W. Hanks Jr. amd Timothy Lomax, "Roadway Congestion Estimates and Trends," Texas A&M University, 1991 and 2001.

29. McGuckin and Srinivason, *Journey-to-Work Trends*, exhibit 4.13. See also Parsons Engineering, "Las Vegas Valley Transit System Development Plan," 2002, 1–2; Wendell Cox, "Competition, Not Monopolies, Can Improve Public Transit," Heritage Foundation, appendix, 3; E. S. Savas and E. J. McMahon, Manhattan Institute for Policy Research, *Civic Report*, November 2002.

30. David W. Jones, "The Bay Area's Transportation Conundrum," a working paper prepared for the Alameda County Congestion Management Agency, Oakland, Calif., 1987.

31. Hanks and Lomax, "Roadway Congestion Estimates and Trends."

32. David W. Jones and Edward C. Sullivan, "TSM: Tinkering Superficially at the Margin?" *Transportation Engineering Journal*, ASCE, 104, no. 6 (November 1978).

33. APTA, "Transit Ridership Report," Las Vegas, 1993 and 2004.

34. Jones, *Urban Transit Policy*, 17, 114–23. See also *Hearings on S345*, Senate Banking and Currency Committee, Subcommittee on Housing (Washington, D.C.: Government Printing Office, 1961), 372.

35. APTA, *Transit Ridership Reports*, 4th quarter, 1993 and 2005.

36. APTA, "New Rail Starts," *www.apta.com/research/stats*, accessed March 2007.

37. *Historical Statistics of the United States, Colonial Times to 1970*, Series Q 241–244, 721, and *Statistical Abstract of the United States*, 2002.

38. APTA, "Light Rail Transit System Links," *www.apta.com/research/stats*, accessed 12 March 2007. Many of the cities presently in line for "new rail starts" are southern or sunbelt cities.

39. Author's calculations based on the American Public Transportation Association (APTA) *Public Transportation Fact Book* and the APTA *Transit Ridership Report*, 1996–2004, available online at www.apta.com/research/stats.

7. U.S. Motorization since the OPEC Embargo

1. U.S. Bureau of the Census, Foreign Trade Division, "U.S. Imports of Crude Oil: 1973–2005," http://www.census.gov/foreign-trade/statistics/historical/petr.pdf (accessed 15 February 2008). The annual figures reported by the Foreign Trade Division have been adjusted to reflect real prices in 1982 dollars.

2. Energy Information Agency, "Real Gasoline Pump Price: Annual Average, 1919–2005" (Washington, D.C.: EIA, March 2005).

3. "U.S. Retail Sales of Cars and Trucks," *Ward's Motor Vehicle Facts and Figures*, 2003.

4. "Motor Vehicles in Operation by Year," *Ward's Motor Vehicle Facts and Figures*, 2002, 46.

5. FHWA, *Highway Statistics*, 1994, table MV-9, and 2000, table MV-9.

6. For a discussion of the economics and politics of retrenchment, especially in right-of-way acquisition, see Jones, *California's Freeway Era*, 313–30.

7. Rodney E. Slater and Gordon J. Linton, "A Guide to Metropolitan Planning under ISTEA," letter of transmittal, U.S. Department of Transportation, 1991, 4.

8. Paul Lewis and Eric McGee, "A Puzzle of Policy Change: Federal Transportation Policy in the 1990s," Working Paper no. 99-09, Public Policy Institute of California, San Francisco, 1999, 22.

9. Ibid., 25.

10. "Ford and Chrysler Show Dark Outlook for U.S. Car Makers," *Wall Street Journal*, weekend edition, 16–17 January 2006. A bit of context for reading this headline is that two years previously, the headline in most U.S. business publications would have emphasized the "dark outlook" for GM and Ford.

8. The Competitive Difficulties of the U.S. Automakers

1. "U.S. Production and Factory Sales of Passenger Cars; Trucks, and Buses," *Ward's Motor Vehicle Facts and Figures,* 2004, 3.

2. "U.S. Retail Sales of Cars and Trucks," *Ward's Motor Vehicle Facts and Figures,* 2004, 15.

3. Sholnn Freeman, "SUV Sales Stall," *Washington Post,* national weekly edition, 10–16 December 2005, 19.

4. Mowery and Rosenberg, "Twentieth-Century Technological Change," 836–37.

5. Lawrence J. White, *The Automobile Industry since 1945* (Cambridge: Harvard University Press, 1971), 258.

6. U.S. Commerce Department Office of Business Analysis, *U.S. Motor Vehicle and Equipment Industry since 1958* (Washington, D.C.: Government Printing Office, 1985), 3–5.

7. *Historical Statistics of the United States,* Series Q 148–162, "Motor Vehicle Factory Sales and Registrations," 716, and FHWA, *Highway Statistics 2000,* table MV-9.

8. Jamie Butters and Jeffrey McCracken, "GM, Ford Credit Rated Junk," *Detroit Free Press,* 6 May 2005.

9. Commerce Department, *U.S. Motor Vehicle and Equipment Industry since 1958,* xii.

10. White, *Automobile Industry,* 273.

11. Commerce Department, *U.S. Motor Vehicle and Equipment Industry since 1958,* xii.

12. White, *Automobile Industry,* 211–14, 274.

13. Commerce Department, *U.S. Motor Vehicle and Equipment Industry since 1958,* 3–5.

14. See, e.g., "At GM There's Health Pay," *Fortune,* 7 February 2005, 22, and "GM Plans to Cut Salaried Staff; Overhaul Looms," *Wall Street Journal,* 31 March 2000, which reported: "This company needs restructuring. . . . [It] is sized for [a market share of] 35 percent and it's got 28."

15. White, *Automobile Industry,* 273.

16. Commerce Department, *U.S. Motor Vehicle and Equipment Industry,* 14–17.

17. "Car Industry: The Quick and the Dead," *Economist,* 29 January 2005, 10.

18. A primary dimension of the automakers' dilemma is that they cannot shrink their product lines and labor costs without generating insufficient revenues to meet their pension and health care obligations to retired workers. In GM's case there are two retirees for each worker currently employed in GM's automotive units. See "Extinction of the Car Giants," *Economist,* 14 June 2003, 11, 59–61. But GM's finance subsidiary is a robustly profitable business.

9. The Changing Valance of U.S. Motorization

1. U.S. Bureau of Economic Analysis, "Foreign Trade of the United States," 81.

2. International Energy Agency, "CO_2 Emissions: Sectoral Approach," in CO_2 *Emission from Fuel Consumption, 1971–2000* (Paris: OECD/IEA, 2002), II.4–II.5.

3. Thomas Friedman, "A Million Manhattan Projects," *Oakland Tribune,* 25 May 2006.

4. Robert Collier, "The Good Life Means More Greenhouse Gas," *San Francisco Chronicle*, 6 July 2005.

5. Meadows et al., *Limits to Growth*, 23–24; Paul Erhlich, *The Population Bomb* (New York: Ballantine Books, 1968).

6. World Commission on Environment and Development, *Our Common Future* (New York: Oxford University Press, 1987), 43.

7. See the Intergovernmental Panel on Climate Change, *Climate Change 2001: Mitigation* (Cambridge: Cambridge University Press, 2001), 73ff., 84ff.

8. "How Al Gore Lost His Balance in Kyoto," *Washington Post*, national weekly edition, 22–29 December 1997, 22–23.

9. International Energy Agency, CO_2 *Emissions from Fuel Combustion* (Paris: OECD/IEA, 2002), II.82.

10. Daniel Yergin, in testimony before the Senate Committee on Energy and Natural Resources, 30 April 1980. Cited in John M. DeCicco, "The 'Chicken or Egg' Problem Writ Large: Why a Hydrogen Fuel Cell Focus Is Premature," in *The Hydrogen Energy Transition*, ed. Sperling and Cannon (Boston: Elsevier Press, 2004), 221.

11. International Energy Agency, *Energy Policies of IEA Countries: United States, 2002 Review* (Paris: OECD/IEA, 2002), 103.

12. See Peter Newman and Jeffrey Kenworthy, *Sustainability and Cities: Overcoming Automobile Dependence* (Washington, D.C.: Island Press, 1999), and Pucher and Lefèvre., *Urban Transport Crisis*. See also Robert Cervero, *The Transit Metropolis* (Washington, D.C.: Island Press, 1998), and Dunphy et al, *Developing around Transit*.

10. The Road to Sustainable Motorization

1. New materials are enabling more complete combustion at higher temperatures and producing greater torque more efficiently. Such innovations are making it more difficult to write off the internal combustion engine, according to William L. Garrison, retired director of the Institute of Transportation Studies, University of California at Berkeley, in a personal communication with the author.

2. IEA, CO_2 *Emissions from Fuel Combustion, 1971–2000*, II.101, II.141, II.253, II.395.

3. Joan Ogden and Princeton Environmental Institute, "Prospects for Large-Scale Use of Hydrogen in Our Future Energy System," in testimony to the Committee on Science, U.S. House of Representatives, 3 March 2003, 5.

4. National Research Council and National Academy of Engineering, *The Hydrogen Economy: Opportunities, Costs, Barriers, and R&D Needs*, finding 6-2 and finding 6-11 (Washington, D.C.: National Academies Press, 2004), 83.

5. Ibid., 83, 118.

6. Ogden, "Prospects for Large-Scale Use of Hydrogen," fig. 7. See also Michael Wang and D. He, "Well-to-Tank Energy Use and Greenhouse Gas Emissions of Transportation Fuels," Center for Transportation Research, Argonne National Laboratory, June 2001, 1–17, I-22.

7. NRC/NAE, *Hydrogen Economy*, 63.

8. Joan Ogden, "Where Will the Hydrogen Come From? System Considerations and Hydrogen Supply," in *Hydrogen Energy Transition*, ed. Sperling and Cannon (Boston: Elsevier Press, 2004), 80–81.

9. Automaker Web sites are one way to track which automakers are "on track" and which seem to be lagging in the development of fuel cell technology.

10. NRC/NAE, *Hydrogen Economy*, 26.

11. As Ogden has emphasized, both the energy use and CO_2 emissions associated with the production of hydrogen fuel can be minimized by using off-peak power derived from base-load energy sources such as hydro, nuclear, and wind power. Ogden, "Where Will the Hydrogen Come From?" 79.

12. See NRC/NAE, *Hydrogen Economy*, 27.

13. Britta Gross, General Motors Research Labs, June 2006, personal communication with this author.

14. Taiyo Kawai, "Fuel Cell Hybrid Vehicles: The Challenge for the Future," in *The Hydrogen Energy Transition*, ed. Sperling and Cannon (Boston: Elsevier Press, 2004), 64–65.

15. NRC/NAE, *Hydrogen Economy*, 35

16. Daniel Sperling and James Cannon, "Hydrogen Hope or Hype," in *Hydrogen Energy Transition*, ed. Sperling and Cannon (Boston: Elsevier Press, 2004), 236.

17. NRC/NAE, *Hydrogen Economy*, 43.

18. Ibid., 27.

19. Lawrence D. Burns, General Motors senior vice president for research and development, in testimony before the House Subcommittee on Energy and Resources, Washington, D.C., 27 July 2005.

20. Sperling and Cannon, "Hydrogen Hope or Hype," 236.

21. Burns testimony. See also Steven Ashley, "On the Road to Fuel Cell Vehicles," *Scientific American*, March 2005.

22. Burns testimony.

23. Duncan Macleod, Shell Hydrogen, "Dynamics of Vehicle and Infrastructure Rollout," a joint study of Shell Hydrogen and General Motors, National Hydrogen Association Conference, exhibit 10, March 2006, 2.

24. Ibid., 3.

25. NRC/NAE, *Hydrogen Economy*, 38.

26. Ibid., 67.

27. Ibid., 40–41

28. Burns testimony, 3. See also Ashley, "On the Road to Fuel Cell Cars," 69.

11. Motorization and Sustainability

1. Most Americans perceive gasoline prices as steadily rising. This perception is accurate in terms of the nominal price that we have paid at the pump since the 1973 OPEC oil embargo. But in real-dollar terms, the long-term secular trend of gasoline prices has been more or less steadily downward since 1932. The exceptions to this trend are the price shocks associated with the OPEC embargo, the Iranian revolution, and the second war in Iraq. The sustained downward trend of real gasoline prices is one reason that Americans were buying SUVs in the 1990s: gasoline prices were reaching all-time lows. See U.S. Energy Information Agency, "Real Petroleum Prices, 1919–2003," at www .eia.doe.gov, accessed 7 November 2007.

2. Fanning, *Foreign Oil and the Free World*, 350, and George L. Perry, "The War

on Terrorism, the World Oil Market, and the U.S. Economy," Brookings Institute, analysis paper #7, October 2001, table A.

3. International Energy Agency, *CO₂ Emissions from Fuel Combustion: 1971–2000*, II.101, II.395.4.

4. Sonya Hoo and Robert Ebel, "An International Perspective on Gasoline Taxes," *Tax Notes* 108 (26 September 2005): 1565.

5. Ian Parry and Kenneth Small, "Does Britain or the United States Have the Right Gasoline Tax?" Energy Institute, University of California at Berkeley, July 2002.

6. See Martin Wachs's assessment of fuel cell vehicle prospects in "A Dozen Reasons for Raising Gasoline Taxes," Institute of Transportation Studies, University of California at Berkeley, research report UCB-ITS-RR-2003-1, 6–8.

7. NRC/NAE, *Hydrogen Economy*, 28–29.

8. Macleod and Shell Hydrogen, "Dynamics of Vehicle and Infrastructure Rollout," 2.

9. Wachs, "A Dozen Reasons," 10.

10. Jonathan Hughes, Christopher Knittel, and Daniel Sperling, "Evidence of a Shift in the Short-Run Price Elasticity of Gasoline Demand," research report UCD-ITS-RR-06-16, Institute of Transportation Studies, University of California at Davis, 2006.

11. U.S. Bureau of the Census, *Statistical Abstract of the United States*, 2002, "Resident Population Projections, 2002–2100."

12. See, e.g., Kenworthy and Laube, *International Sourcebook*, chapter 5. See also European Conference of Ministers of Transport, *Urban Travel and Sustainable Development* (Paris: ECMT/OECD, 1995).

13. Wachs, "A Dozen Reasons, " 1ff.

14. Macleod and Shell Hydrogen, "Dynamics of Vehicle and Infrastructure Rollout."

15. McGuckin and Srinivasan, *Journey-to-Work Trends, 1960–2000*, exhibit 4.13. By way of comparison, Smart Growth in Portland produced only a 21 percent increase in transit's commute share from 1990 to 2000.

16. See Hoo and Ebel, "International Perspective."

17. Parry and Small, "Right Gasoline Tax?" 11.

18. See Hoo and Ebel, "International Perspective." See also Parry and Small, "Right Gasoline Tax?" 2ff.

19. Fanning, *Foreign Oil and the Free World*, 350, and Perry, "The War on Terrorism," table A.

20. Higher fuel taxes are a primary reason that European vehicles are, on average, twice as fuel-efficient as those that Americans drive. See Federal Highway Administration, OHPI, "Motor Fuel Tax Rates for Selected Countries," February 2006.

21. Parry and Small, "Right Gasoline Tax?" 11.

22. With a 50-cent-per-gallon surtax on the price of gasoline, the average automobile owner would pay an additional $215 per year for gasoline, assuming a 20 percent reduction in fuel consumption. Any substantially lower surtax would produce only a modest incentive to conserve fuel and buy fuel-efficient vehicles.

BIBLIOGRAPHY

Adler, Seymour. "The Political Economy of Transit in the San Francisco Bay Area, 1945–63." Institute of Urban and Regional Development, University of California, Berkeley, 1980.

American Association of State Highway Officials. "A Policy on Arterial Highways in Urban Areas." Washington, D.C.: AASHO, 1957.

American Association of State Highway and Transportation Officials (AASHTO). *The States and the Interstates*. Washington, D.C.: AASHTO, 1991.

American Electric Railway Association. *The Urban Transportation Problem*. New York: AERA, 1932.

American Municipal Association. *The Collapse of Commuter Service: A Survey of Mass Transportation in Five Major Cities*. Washington, D.C.: AMA, 1960.

American Petroleum Institute. "Historical Trends in Motor Gasoline Taxes, 1918–2006." 6 September 2006.

American Public Transit Association (APTA). *Transit Fact Book*. 1943–.

——. *History and Provisions of the Federal Transit Act and Other Major Laws Affecting Public Transportation, 1961–2007*. Washington, D.C.: APTA, 2007 (*www.apta.com/research/stats/fedlaw/fta.cfm*, accessed 7 November 2007).

——. Various reports and publications available at *www.apta.com/research/stats*, accessed 7 November 2007.

Ashley, Steven. "On the Road to Fuel-Cell Vehicles." *Scientific American*, March 2005.

"At GM There's Health Pay." *Fortune*, 7 February 2005, 22.

Atlas of the World. 9th ed. New York: Oxford University Press, 2001.

Automobile Club of Southern California. "Traffic Survey of Los Angeles Metropolitan Area." 1936.

Automobile Manufacturers Association. *Automobile Facts and Trends*. Detroit: AMA, 1921.

——. *A Chronicle of the Automobile Industry in America, 1893–1952*. Detroit: AMA, 1953.

Bairoch, Paul. "International Industrialization Levels from 1750 to 1980." *Journal of European Economic History* 11, nos. 1/2 (Fall 1982).

Bartholomew, Harland. *The Present and Ultimate Effect of Decentralization upon American Cities*. Chicago: Urban Land Institute, 1940.

Bogue, Donald J. *Population Growth in Standard Metropolitan Areas, 1900–1950.* Washington, D.C.: Housing and Home Finance Agency, 1954.

Bolin, Bert, Bo Doos, Jill Jager, and Richard A. Warrick. *The Greenhouse Effect, Climatic Change, and Ecosystems.* New York: Published by John Wiley on behalf of the Scientific Committee on the Problems of the Environment of the International Council of Scientific Unions, 1986.

Butters, Jamie, and Jeffrey McCracken. "GM, Ford Credit Rated Junk." *Detroit Free Press,* 6 May 2005.

California Railroad Commission. *Report on Engineering Survey of the Pacific Electric Railway Company.* Sacramento: California Railroad Commission, 1939.

"Car Industry: The Quick and the Dead." *Economist,* 29 January 2005, 10.

Carliner, Michael S. "Development of Federal Home Ownership Policy." Fannie Mae Foundation *Housing Policy* 9, no. 2 (1998).

Carlisle, Rodney. *"Scientific American" Inventions and Discoveries.* Hoboken, N.J.: John Wiley, 2004.

Cervero, Robert. *The Transit Metropolis: A Global Inquiry.* Washington, D.C.: Island Press, 1998.

Charlesworth, George. *A History of British Motorways.* London: Thomas Telford, 1984.

Collier, Robert. "The Good Life Means More Greenhouse Gas." *San Francisco Chronicle,* 6 July 2005.

Cox, Wendell. "Competition, Not Monopolies, Can Improve Public Transit." Heritage Foundation at *http://www.heritage.org/Research/UrbanIssues/BG1389es.cfm,* accessed 7 November 2007.

Cudahy, Brian. *Cash, Tokens, and Transfers: A History of Urban Mass Transit in North America.* New York: Fordham University Press, 1990.

Dalton, James. "What Will Ford Do Next?" *Motor,* May 1926.

Danielson, Michael N. *Federal-Metropolitan Politics and the Commuter Crisis.* New York: Columbia University Press, 1965.

DeCicco, John M. "The 'Chicken or Egg' Problem Writ Large: Why a Hydrogen Fuel Cell Focus Is Premature." In *Hydrogen Energy Transition,* ed. Sperling and Cannon. Boston: Elsevier Press, 2004.

Derry, T. K., and Trevor I. Williams. *A Short History of Technology.* Oxford: Clarendon Press, 1960.

Dill, Jennifer. "Smart Growth Transportation Planning in the Portland Region." Paper presented at the Annual Conference of the National Association of Environmental Professionals," Portland, Oregon, April 2004.

Doolittle, F. W. *Studies in the Cost of Urban Transportation Service.* New York: American Electric Railway Association, 1916.

Drake, James. *Motorways.* London: Faber and Faber, 1969.

Dunphy, Robert T., et al. *Developing around Transit: Strategies and Solutions That Work.* Washington, D.C.: Urban Land Institute, 2004.

Energy Information Agency. "Real Gasoline Pump Price: Annual Average, 1919–2005." Washington, D.C.: EIA, March 2005.

Engerman, Stanley L., and Robert E. Gallman. *The Cambridge Economic History of the United States,* vol. 3, *The Twentieth Century.* Cambridge: Cambridge University Press, 2000.

Erhlich, Paul. *The Population Bomb.* New York: Ballantine Books, 1968.

European Conference of Ministers of Transport. *Urban Travel and Sustainable Development*. Paris: ECMT/OECD, 1995.

"Extinction of the Car Giants." *Economist*, 14 June 2003, 11, 59–61.

Fanning, Leonard M. *Foreign Oil and the Free World*. New York: McGraw-Hill, 1954.

Federal Highway Administration (FHWA). *America's Highways, 1776–1976*. Washington, D.C.: Government Printing Office, 1976.

Flink, James J. *The Car Culture*. Cambridge: MIT Press, 1975.

"Ford and Chrysler Show Dark Outlook for U.S. Car Makers." *Wall Street Journal*, weekend edition, January 16–17, 2006.

Forsberg, Mary E. "Perspective on the Gas Tax and Car Registration Fees." *New Jersey Policy Perspective Reports*, March 2002.

Freeman, Sholnn. "SUV Sales Stall." *Washington Post*, national weekly edition, 10–16 December 2005, 19.

Friedman, Thomas. "A Million Manhattan Projects." *Oakland Tribune*, 25 May 2006.

Garreau, Joel. *Edge City: Life on the New Frontier*. New York: Doubleday, 1991.

Gelfand, Mark I. *A Nation of Cities: The Federal Government and Urban America, 1933–1965*. New York: Oxford University Press, 1975.

Gifford, Jonathan. "An Analysis of the Federal Role in the Planning, Design, and Deployment of Rural Highways, Toll Roads, and Urban Freeways." PhD diss., University of California Berkeley, 1983.

Glaeser, Edward L., and Jesse M. Shapiro, "City Growth: Which Places Grew and Why." In *Redefining Urban and Suburban America*, vol. 1, ed. Bruce Katz and Robert E. Lang. Washington, D.C.: Brookings Institution Press, 2003.

"GM Plans to Cut Salaried Staff; Overhaul Looms." *Wall Street Journal*, 31 March 2000.

Gray, George E., and Lester A. Hoel, eds. *Public Transportation*. 2d ed. Englewood Cliffs, N.J.: Prentice Hall, 1992.

Hall, Peter. *Cities in Civilization*. New York: Pantheon Books, 1998.

Hanks, James W., Jr., and Timothy Lomax. *Roadway Congestion Estimates and Trends*. College Station: Texas Transportation Institute, 2002.

Heim, Carol E. "Structural Changes: Regional and Urban." In *Cambridge Economic History of the United States*, vol. 3, ed. Engerman and Gallman. Cambridge: Cambridge University Press, 2000.

Hess, Kenneth L. "The Growth of Automotive Transportation." 1996, *www.klhess.com*, accessed 7 November 2007.

Highway and Transportation Committee, American Society of Planning Officials. "Highways and Transportation in Relation to Each Other and to Other Planned Development." Typescript. National Conference on Planning, July 1940.

Hilton, George W., and John F. Due. *The Electric Interurban Railways in America*. Stanford: Stanford University Press, 1960.

Hoo, Sonya, and Robert Ebel. "An International Perspective on Gasoline Taxes." *Tax Notes* 108 (26 September 2005): 1565.

"How Al Gore Lost His Balance in Kyoto." *Washington Post*, national weekly edition, 22–29 December 1997, 22.

Hughes, Jonathan E., Christopher R. Knittel, and Daniel Sperling. "Evidence of a Shift in the Short-Run Price Elasticity of Gasoline Demand." Research report UCD-ITS-RR-06-16. Institute of Transportation Studies, University of California at Davis, 2006.

Intergovernmental Panel on Climate Change. *Climate Change 2001: Mitigation.* Cambridge: Cambridge University Press, 2001.

International Energy Agency. *CO₂ Emissions from Fuel Combustion: 1971–2000.* Paris: OECD/IEA, 2002.

———. *Energy Policies of IEA Countries, United States, 2002 Review.* Paris: OECD/IEA, 2002.

Joint Committee on Street and Highway Traffic Engineering Functions and Administration. *Traffic Engineering Functions and Administration.* Chicago: Public Administration Service, 1948.

Jones, David W. "The Bay Area's Transportation Conundrum." Working paper prepared for the Alameda County Congestion Management Agency, Oakland, 1987.

———. "The Bay Area's Transportation System: More and More Congested, but Still Surprisingly Access-Efficient." Paper presented at the Alameda County Symposium on Transportation and Land-Use, Oakland, 1997.

———. *California's Freeway Era in Historical Perspective.* Berkeley: Institute of Transportation Studies, University of California, 1989.

———. "Mass Transit: Essential Service, Public Enterprise, and Distressed Industry." Paper presented at the UCLA conference "Redefining, Reevaluating and Reinventing Transit," Lake Arrowhead, February 2002.

———. "Urban Highway Investment and the Political Economy of Fiscal Retrenchment." In *Current Issues in Transportation Policy,* ed. Alan Altschuler. Lexington, Mass.: Lexington Books, 1979.

———. *Urban Transit Policy: An Economic and Political History.* Englewood Cliffs, N.J.: Prentice Hall, 1985.

Jones, David W., and Edward C. Sullivan. "TSM: Tinkering Superficially at the Margin?" *Transportation Engineering Journal,* ASCE, 104, no. 6 (November 1978).

Kawai, Taiyo. "Fuel Cell Hybrid Vehicles: The Challenge for the Future." In *The Hydrogen Transition,* ed. Sperling and Cannon. Boston: Elsevier Press, 2004.

Kent, Mary M., and Mark Mather. "What Drives U.S. Population Growth?" *Population Bulletin,* University of Iowa Population Reference Bureau, December 2002.

Kenworthy, Jeffrey R., and Felix B. Laube. *An International Sourcebook of Automobile Dependence in Cities, 1960–1990.* Boulder: University Press of Colorado, 1999.

Kotkin, Joel. *The New Geography: How the Digital Revolution Is Reshaping the American Landscape.* New York: Random House, 2000.

Lewis, Paul, and Eric McGee. "A Puzzle of Policy Change: Federal Transportation Policy in the 1990s." Working paper no. 99-09, Public Policy Institute of California, San Francisco, 1999.

Long, John F. *Population Deconcentration in the United States.* Washington, D.C.: Census Bureau, Special Demographic Analyses, CDS 81-1, August 1981.

Lyle C. Fitch and Associates. *Urban Transportation and Public Policy.* San Francisco: Chandler, 1964.

Lynd, Robert S., and Helen N. Lynd. *Middletown.* New York: Harcourt, Brace, 1929.

MacDonald, Thomas. "The Roads We Should Have." In *Proceedings of the American Automobile Association,* 1936.

Macleod, Duncan, and Shell Hydrogen. "Dynamics of Vehicle and Infrastructure Rollout." Joint study of Shell Hydrogen and General Motors, National Hydrogen Association Conference, exhibit 10, March 2006.

Maddison, Angus. *World Economy: Historical Statistics*. Paris: OECD, 2003.

Marks, Howard. "Geometrics of Local and Collector Streets." A paper presented to the Institute of Traffic Engineers, 1961 Proceedings..

Mason, Edward J. *The Street Railway in Massachusetts*. Cambridge: Harvard University Press, 1932.

"Mass Rapid Transit for Los Angeles." *SC Engineer*, March 1955, 15.

Mayer, Martin. *The Builders: Houses, People, Neighborhoods, Governments, Money*. New York: Norton, 1978.

McCraw, Thomas K., and Richard S. Tedlow. "Henry Ford, Alfred Sloan, and the Three Phases of Marketing." In *Creating Modern Capitalism: How Entrepreneurs, Companies, and Countries Triumphed in Three Industrial Revolutions*, ed. Thomas K. McCraw. Cambridge: Harvard University Press, 1995.

McGuckin, Nancy, and Nanda Srinivasan. *Journey-to-Work Trends in the United States and Its Major Metropolitan Areas, 1960–2000*. Washington, D.C.: Department of Transportation, Federal Highway Administration, Office of Planning, 2003.

McKay, John P. "Comparative Perspectives on Transit in Western Europe and the United States, 1850–1914." In *Technology and the Rise of the Networked City in Europe and America*, ed. Joel A. Tarr and Gabriel Dupuy, 3–21. Philadelphia: Temple University Press, 1988.

Meadows, Donella H., et al. *The Limits to Growth*. New York: Universe Books, 1972.

Moody's Investors Service. *Moody's Transportation Manual*, 1954–2000.

Motor Vehicle Manufacturers Association. *Motor Vehicle Facts and Figures*. Published under various titles since 1933.

Mowery, David, and Nathan Rosenberg. "Twentieth-Century Technological Change." In *The Cambridge Economic History of the United States*, vol. 3., ed. Engerman and Gallman. Cambridge: Cambridge University Press, 2000.

Muller, Peter O. "Transportation and Urban Form: Stages in the Spatial Evolution of the American Metropolis." In *The Geography of Urban Transportation*, ed. Susan Hanson, 29–47. New York: Guilford Press, 1995.

National Automobile Chamber of Commerce. *Facts and Figures of the Automobile Industry*. 1928.

National Research Council and National Academy of Engineering. *The Hydrogen Economy: Opportunities, Costs, Barriers, and R&D Needs*. Washington, D.C.: National Academies Press, 2004.

Newman, Peter, and Jeffrey Kenworthy. *Sustainability and Cities: Overcoming Automobile Dependence*. Washington, D.C.: Island Press, 1999.

Noble, Charles. "Modern Turnpike History Revisited." *Civil Engineering*, February 1979.

Nolan, John, and H. V. Hubbard. *Parkways and Land Values*. Cambridge: Harvard University Press, 1937.

Nordhaus, William D. "Economic Approaches to Greenhouse Warming." In *Global Warming: Economic Policy Responses*, ed. Rudiger Dornbusch and James M. Poterba, 33–69. Cambridge: MIT Press, 1992.

Ogden, Joan. "Where Will the Hydrogen Come From? System Considerations and Hydrogen Supply." In *Hydrogen Energy Transition*, ed. Sperling and Cannon, 80–81. Boston: Elsevier Press, 2004.

Ogden, Joan, and the Princeton Environmental Institute. "Prospects for Large-Scale Use of Hydrogen in Our Future Energy System." In testimony to the Committee on Science, U.S. House of Representatives, 3 March 2003.

Parry, Ian W. H., and Kenneth A. Small. "Does Britain or the United States Have the Right Gasoline Tax?" University of California Energy Institute, Berkeley, March 2002.

Parsons Engineering. "Las Vegas Valley Transit System Development Plan." 2002.

Perry, George L. "The War on Terrorism, the World Oil Market, and the U.S. Economy." Analysis paper #7, Brookings Institution, October 24, 2001.

Phillips, Kevin. Wealth and Democracy: A Political History of the American Rich. New York: Broadway Books, 2002.

Pinkley, R. H. "How the Industry Is Progressing." AERA Proceedings. New York: American Electric Railway Association, 1927.

Pisarski, Alan. Commuting in America. Westport, Conn.: Eno Foundation, 1996.

Pucher, John, and Christian Lefèvre. The Urban Transport Crisis in Europe and North America. Basingstoke: Macmillan, 1996.

Rae, John B. American Automobile Manufacturers: The First Forty Years. Philadelphia: Chilton, 1959.

Real Estate Research Corporation. The Costs of Sprawl. Washington, D.C.: Government Printing Office, April 1974.

Regional Plan Association of New York. Traffic and Parking Study: A Plan for Improvement of Conditions in the Central Business Areas of New York City. New York: Regional Plan Association, 1942.

Rose, Albert. Governing Metropolitan Toronto: A Social and Political Analysis, 1953–1971. Berkeley: University of California Press, 1972.

Saltzman, Arthur. "Public Transportation in the Twentieth Century." In Public Transportation, 2d ed., ed. Gray and Hoel, 24–45. Englewood Cliffs, N.J.: Prentice Hall, 1992.

Samuelson, Robert J. "The Great Depression." In The Fortune Encyclopedia of Economics, ed. David R. Henderson. New York: Warner Books, 1993.

Savas, E. S., and E. J. McMahon. Civic Report. Manhattan Institute for Policy Research, November 2002.

Schmidt, Emerson P. Industrial Relations in Urban Transportation. Minneapolis: University of Minnesota Press, 1937.

Schrank, David, and Tim Lomax. 2002 Urban Mobility Study. College Station: Texas Transportation Institute, Texas A&M University System, June 2002 (http://mobility .tamu.edu).

Sill, Otto. "The Role of Automobiles in Cities." In Proceedings, Institute of Traffic Engineers, 1965, 59–65.

Slater, Rodney E., and Gordon J. Linton. "A Guide to Metropolitan Planning under ISTEA." Letter of transmittal, U.S. Department of Transportation, 1991.

Smerk, George M. "Public Transportation and the City." In Public Transportation, 2d ed., ed. Gray and Hoel. Englewood Cliffs, N.J.: Prentice Hall, 1992.

Snell, Bradford C. American Ground Transport: A Proposal for Restructuring the Automobile, Truck, Bus, and Rail Industries. Report prepared for the Subcommittee on Antitrust and Monopoly of the Senate Judiciary Committee. Washington, D.C.: Government Printing Office, 1974.

Sobel, Robert. The Great Boom. New York: St. Martin's Press, 2000.

Sperling, Daniel, and James Cannon, eds. *The Hydrogen Energy Transition: Moving toward the Post Petroleum Age in Transportation*. Boston: Elsevier Press, 2004.

Sperling, Daniel, and Eileen Claussen. "Motorizing the Developing World." *Access*, Spring 2004, 10–15.

Stranskey, Joseph R. "Superhighway Development in the Milwaukee Metropolitan Area." *Roads and Streets*, August 1929, 271.

Suro, Roberto, and Audrey Singer. *Latino Growth in Metropolitan America*. Washington, D.C.: Brookings Institution Press, July 2002.

Temin, Peter. "The Great Depression." In *The Cambridge Economic History of the United States*, vol. 3, ed. Engerman and Gallman, 301–28. Cambridge: Cambridge University Press, 2000.

Ulmer, Melville Jack. *Capital in Transportation, Communications, and Public Utilities*. Princeton: Princeton University Press, 1960,

U.S. Bureau of Economic Analysis. *Business Statistics, 1963–91*. Washington, D.C.: Government Printing Office, 1992.

U.S. Bureau of Public Roads. *Highway Statistics, 1945–.*

——. *Toll Roads and Free Roads*. Washington, D.C.: Government Printing Office, 1939.

U.S. Census Bureau. *Historical Statistics of the United States: Colonial Times to 1970*. 2 vols. Washington, D.C.: Government Printing Office, 1975.

——. *Street and Electric Railways*. Washington, D.C.: Government Printing Office, 1902, 1917.

U.S. Department of Commerce, Office of Business Analysis. *U.S. Motor Vehicle and Equipment Industry since 1958*. Washington, D.C.: Government Printing Office, 1985.

U.S. Department of Transportation. *Highway Statistics*. 1945–.

——. *Highway Statistics, Summary to 1985*. Washington, D.C.: Department of Transportation, 1986.

——. *Journey-to-Work Trends in the United States and Its Major Metropolitan Areas, 1960–1990*. Washington, D.C.: Department of Transportation, Federal Highway Administration, Office of Planning, 1993.

U.S. Energy Information Agency. "Real Petroleum Prices, 1919–2003" at www.eia.doe .gov, accessed 7 November 2007.

Wachs, Martin F. "A Dozen Reasons for Raising Gasoline Taxes." Institute of Transportation Studies, University of California, Berkeley Research Report UCB-ITS-RR-2003-1, 6–8.

Wang, Michael, and D. He. "Well-to-Tank Energy Use and Greenhouse Gas Emissions of Transportation Fuels." Center for Transportation Research, Argonne National Laboratory, June 2001.

Ward's Motor Vehicle Facts and Figures. Southfield, Mich.: Ward's Communications, 1999–.

Webster, F. V. "Urban Travel and Sustainable Development." OECD/ECMT Project Group on Urban Travel and Sustainable Development, May 1994.

Wheeler, James O., et al. *Economic Geography*. 3d ed. New York: Wiley, 1998.

White, Lawrence J. *The Automobile Industry since 1945*. Cambridge: Harvard University Press, 1971.

Wilbur Smith and Associates. *Transportation and Parking for Tomorrow's Cities*. New Haven: Wilbur Smith and Associates, 1966.

Wilcox, Delos F. *Analysis of the Electric Railway Problem.* New York: privately published, 1921.

Wolman, Leo. *Ebb and Flow in Trade Unionism.* New York: National Bureau of Economic Research, 1936.

World Commission on Environment and Development. *Our Common Future.* New York: Oxford University Press, 1987.

Zettel, Richard M. Interviews with David Jones, 1978 and 1990.

INDEX

David W. Jones is a historian and policy analyst who has taught at Stanford and the University of California at Berkeley. After earning his B.A. in history from Yale and his Ph.D. in communication from Stanford, Jones joined the research staff of the Institute for Transportation Studies at Berkeley, where he taught transportation policy, planning, and management. Since retiring from the university, Jones has served as a staff consultant for regional transportation planning agencies in the San Francisco Bay Area and for the Chicago Historical Society's oral history of the interstate highway program.